From the library of
Dean Robert J. Trebar

Much loved, sorely missed

"I Have Found My Voice"

Currents in Comparative Romance Languages and Literatures

Tamara Alvarez-Detrell and Michael G. Paulson
General Editors

Vol. 71

PETER LANG
New York • Washington, D.C./Baltimore • Boston • Bern
Frankfurt am Main • Berlin • Brussels • Vienna • Canterbury

Mary Frances Pipino

"I HAVE FOUND MY VOICE"

The Italian-American Woman Writer

PETER LANG
New York • Washington, D.C./Baltimore • Boston • Bern
Frankfurt am Main • Berlin • Brussels • Vienna • Canterbury

Library of Congress Cataloging-in-Publication Data

Pipino, Mary Frances.
"I have found my voice":
the Italian-American woman writer / Mary Frances Pipino.
p. cm. — (Currents in comparative Romance languages and literatures; vol. 71)
Includes bibliographical references and index.
1. American fiction—Italian American authors—History and criticism. 2. American fiction—Women authors—History and criticism.
3. American fiction—20th century—History and criticism. 4. Italian American women—Intellectual life. 5. Women and literature—United States.
6. Italian-Americans in literature. I. Title. II. Series.
PS153.I8P57   813'.5099287'08951—dc21   97-49386
ISBN 0-8204-3965-7
ISSN 0893-5963

Die Deutsche Bibliothek-CIP-Einheitsaufnahme

Pipino, Mary Frances:
"I have found my voice":
the Italian-American woman writer / Mary Frances Pipino.
–New York; Washington, D.C./Baltimore; Boston; Bern;
Frankfurt am Main; Berlin; Brussels; Vienna; Canterbury: Lang.
(Currents in comparative Romance languages and literatures; Vol. 71)
ISBN 0-8204-3965-7

The paper in this book meets the guidelines for permanence and durability
of the Committee on Production Guidelines for Book Longevity
of the Council of Library Resources.

© 2000 Peter Lang Publishing, Inc., New York

All rights reserved.
Reprint or reproduction, even partially, in all forms such as microfilm,
xerography, microfiche, microcard, and offset strictly prohibited.

Printed in the United States of America

Acknowledgments

There are several people I would like to thank for their parts in making this project a success: Kevin Walzer and Lori Jareo for their invaluable technical and editorial assistance; Amy Elder, Lisa Hogeland, and Fred Gardaphé for their unwavering support at all stages of this project; my family, especially my parents, James and Patricia Pipino, for 37 years of love, faith, and encouragement; and finally, my husband, Jerry Jaspers, for sticking with this (and me) over the years. *Ti amo.*

Acknowledgment is also made to the following to reprint material:

Excerpts from *Rosa: The Life of an Italian Immigrant* by Marie Hall Ets are reprinted by permission of the University of Minnesota Press. Copyright © Marie Hall Ets, 1970.

Quotations from Mari Tomasi's *Like Lesser Gods* are from the edition published in 1988 by the New England Press, Inc., Shelburne, VT.

Excerpts from *No Steady job for Papa* are reprinted with the permission of Frank Benasutti. Copyright © 1966 by Marion Benasutti. Originally published by Vanguard in 1966.

Excerpts from *Ella Price's Journal*, a novel by Dorothy Bryant, are reprinted by permission of The Feminist Press at The City University of New York. Copyright © 1972 by Dorothy Bryant. Originally published by Lippincott in 1972, The Feminist Press reissued the work, with an afterword by Barbara Horn, in 1997.

Excerpts from *Miss Giardino*, a novel by Dorothy Bryant, are reprinted with permission of The Feminist Press at the City University of New York. Copyright © 1978 by Dorothy Bryant. Originally published by Ata in 1978. The Feminist Press reissued the work, with an afterword by Janet Zandy, in 1997.

Excerpts from *Umbertina,* a novel by Helen Barolini, are reprinted by permission of the author and The Feminist Press at the City University of New York. Copyright © 1979 by Helen Barolini. Originally published by Seaview in 1979, The Feminist Press reissued the work, with an afterword by Edvidge Giunta, in 1999.

Excerpts from *Love in the Middle Ages* are reprinted with the permission of Helen Barolini. Copyright © 1986 by Helen Barolini. Originally published by William Morrow in 1986.

Excerpts from *Holidays* reprinted with the permission of New Rivers Press. Copyright © 1987 by Lisa Ruffolo.

Excerpts from "My Grandfather's Suit" are reprinted with the permission of the Purdue University Press. Copyright © 1991 by Lisa Ruffolo.

Reprinted with the permission of Scribner, a Division of Simon & Schuster from *The Star Café and Other Stories* by Mary Caponegro. Copyright © 1990 by Mary Caponegro.

Open market rights for *The Star Café and Other Stories* by Mary Caponegro. Copyright © 1990 by Mary Caponegro. Reprinted by permission of Georges Borchardt, Inc. for the author.

Excerpts from *Ghost Dance*, copyright © 1986, 1995 by Carole Maso (Hopewell: The Ecco Press 1986, 1995) reprinted by permission of Georges Borchardt, Inc. for the author.

Excerpts from *Claiming a Tradition: Italian American Women Writers* reprinted with permission of Mary Jo Bona. Copyright © 1989.

Portions of Chapter Two were first published as "Ella Price's Journal: The Subm/Version of Ethnic and Sexual Identity" in *Voices in Italian Americana* 7.1 (Fall 1996): 35–54.

Table of Contents

Introduction
1

Chapter One
Making America, Making Fiction: The Autobiographical Roots of Italian-American Fiction
13

Chapter Two
The Right of Passage: The Ethnic Narratives of Mari Tomasi and Marion Benasutti
37

Chapter Three
Dorothy Calvetti Bryant: The Subm/Version of Ethnic Identity
67

Chapter Four
Creating a Context: The Fiction and Criticism of Helen Barolini
97

Chapter Five
"Solving the Mystery": The Third-Generation Narratives of Lisa Ruffolo, Mary Caponegro, and Carole Maso
125

Conclusion
165

Bibliography
171

Glossary
177

Notes
179

Index
187

Introduction

> I am proud of my mother,
> dressed all in black,
> proud of my father,
> with his broken tongue,
> proud of the laughter
> and noise of our house.
>
> Remember me, ladies,
> the silent one?
> I have found my voice
> and my rage will blow
> your house down.
>
> —from "Public School No.18:
> Paterson, New Jersey" by
> Maria Mazziotti Gillan

This study examines a segment of the "literature of the margin," the margin in which, according to Mary Dearborn in *Pocahontas' Daughters*, "the factors of gender and ethnicity bring together the concept of 'otherness' as it exists in our culture" (6). I expand this analysis by considering the ways in which the notion of "otherness" in American culture, created in part by Anglo-Puritan thought, is complicated, intensified, and sometimes complemented by oppression based on gender within the ethnic group, in this case, Italian-American. I analyze the voices of Italian-American women writers—how they speak about their culture(s) and their histories as women and as members of an ethnic community.[1]

Listening to these voices is no easy feat, if only for the fact that they are difficult to locate. Critics have noted repeatedly that there is little evidence of a genuine Italian-American literary tradition. There is no single answer to the question of why this is so; indeed, scholars of Italian-American culture have set forth a multitude of explanations for this silence. In her introduction to *The Dream Book: An Anthology of Writings by Italian American Women* (1985), Helen Barolini explores what she calls the external and internal blocks to Italian-American artistry. The former includes factors such as the economics of publication and the difficulties of securing critical attention; the Catch-22 of publication for Italian-American writers (as it has been for many ethnic writers) is that the writing must look "ethnic" in order to garner any interest, yet is frequently dismissed as narrow, parochial, not really "American" literature if it adheres to that guideline. In "The Re-Visioning of New York's Little Italies: From Howells to Puzo," Lawrence J. Oliver notes that "Among the 'swarthy' Italians on display at the East Side 'Louvre,' the curious Anglo-American bourgeois could encounter new versions of Otherness to augment those objectified by the Black, the Asian, the Hebrew" (6).

Internal blocks to Italian-American writing, Barolini explains, include inhibiting forces such as the pull of the family, a mistrust of education and the written word, and the cultural stricture of *omertà* (silence), which forbids the revelation of self, of family, of community (and in Italian culture, these are all one and the same). The Italian-American novelist Gay Talese has pointed out that these forces inhibit the writing of Italian-American men and women alike; however, Barolini points to the limitations based on gender that inhibit women as they do not inhibit men.

All of this is not to say that Italian-American literature does not exist, that it has not been studied, or that attempts to articulate an Italian-American tradition have not been made. Rose Basile Green's *The Italian-American Novel: A Document of the Interaction of Two Cultures* (1974) examines the work of more than sixty authors of Italian-American heritage in light of the interaction of Italian and American culture and literary traditions. *From the Margin: Writings in Italian Americana* (1991) is an anthology of creative and critical writings by men and women of Italian-American heritage. Helen Barolini's *Dream Book* anthology is significant both for her extensive critical introduction, and for its uncovering of more than fifty Italian-American women writers, many of whom are out of print for lack of popular and/or critical attention. Despite these valuable efforts, Italian-American novelist Gay Talese could still ask in a 1993 issue of the *New York Times Book Review*, "Where Are the Italian-American Novelists?"

In this study, I show where some of these writers are, and where they have come from. It is important to realize that many of the factors that would inhibit, and indeed have inhibited, the voices of these writers have also served as catalysts for speaking out. This is not to suggest that Italian-American writers are the only ones to be marginalized by imposed silence (whether internal or external). Rather, I am suggesting, as Barolini does, that Italian-American women writers feel kinship with other groups of women writers, such as African Americans and Native Americans, based on this notion of "breaking the silence," whether that silence is imposed by external prejudice or from within the ethnic group by its values and traditions.

The concept of *omertà* is conventionally associated with the popular stereotype of the Italian American as *mafioso*, that rigidly enforced "code of silence" that protects the criminal "family" members from exposure to punishment. However, *omertà* has much further-reaching implications for Italian culture. It does not merely encompass the concept of discretion; rather, it is very similar to the African and Native American concepts of the sacred silent—the idea that some stories are not meant to be told or shared with certain people, particularly with "outsiders."

Omertà shares the religious underpinnings of the sacred silent—not in any institutionalized sense (i.e. of Roman Catholicism), but in the sense of a deep spiritual and moral imperative. Thus, the dilemma faced by Italian-American women is much the same as that of women belonging to other ethnic groups: making one's voice heard often risks betrayal (or, at least, perceived betrayal) of one's ethnic group, culture, and religious assumptions. Clearly, this risk is one that many ethnic women, Italian-American women among them, have needed to take.[2]

The most important theme for any Italian-American writer is the strength of family, stereotypically associated with the Italian American in popular culture, and it is this theme that unites (and in many ways dictated the choice of) the novels and short stories discussed in this study. Overwhelmingly, the authors explored here make explicit reference both in their fiction and in interviews to the pervasive and complex influence that the cultural institution of the family has had upon their work. In many ways, the family, rather than an individual character, is the true protagonist of Italian-American fiction. One contemporary writer, Lisa Ruffolo, in fact asserts that she felt her fiction found its truest expression when she decided to put "family first" as her subject. Few Italian-American writers would dispute the centrality of family to their experiences and identities. However, they seek to reclaim and redefine this image, which has been distorted, romanticized, and misunderstood. The strong and sometimes stifling force of family loyalty finds its roots in Italian history. Italy did not enjoy national unification until the mid-nineteenth century, and its people, particularly the poor *contadini* (peasants), suffered a long history of economic and political abuse at the hands of various rulers, including the Roman Catholic Church. Thus, the family came to be be seen as the only source of real security and strength, institutionalized as the focus of one's unswerving loyalty. Such a focus became problematic for Italian immigrants when confronted with the American ideal of "rugged individualism."

This conflict between family and independence was particularly pronounced for Italian women, who could turn only to their fathers, brothers, and later, husbands and sons, for security and protection. In Italian culture, to be a woman alone was to be a person without an identity or place in the world; such a woman was the object of pity or scorn. In return for such protection, a woman was to be the repository for all cultural values; while the men bore the responsibility for the family's physical survival, to the women fell the responsibility for spiritual and emotional survival (of course, in practical terms, women bore much of the responsibility for the family's physical survival as well). As Helen Barolini notes, this central role of women within the family was reinforced by the image of the Madonna, "the Holy Mother who prefigured all other mothers and symbolized them" (*Dream Book* 9). While this image of woman as mother and as center of the family is a powerful one, the mistake that many Italian-American writers have made (particularly men) is to assume "that this ideal of *serietà* [seriousness] was the be-all and end-all of a woman's life" (10). The paradox of American individualism for Italian immigrant women and their female descendants, then, is that the opportunity for a new life in America applied only to men. The constancy of women's traditional roles and identities within the family were taken for granted, despite the "New World" emphasis on freedom and individual achievement. Many of the writers in this study, as well as the characters they create, struggle to balance their need for individual identity in a culture that values individuality (though primarily for men) with the desire to maintain ethnic and communal ties.

It is crucial to understand the particular way in which the Catholic Church's influence was (and is) felt for most Italians and Italian Americans. Particularly for those who lived in the poorer, southern regions of Italy, the Church as an institution carried little weight in their everyday lives (although expressions of spirituality and religious faith were integral). Indeed, the Church and its representatives were viewed as just another variation of the grasping, greedy kings and landowners who exploited the peasants and appropriated the fruits of their labor in the form of exorbitant taxes and tributes. *Contadini* religion was a pastiche of Roman Catholic dogma and folk beliefs and practices. For the *contadini*, whose world view was largely fatalistic, the role of the saints as intercessors became of utmost importance. Each village had its own patron saint, as well as a spot sacred to that saint. Likewise, the Madonna gained importance for her role as intermediary between humans and God. However, the priest's role as God's representative was largely derided or ignored, because to the *contadini* he was complicit with the forces of political and economic oppression—the village priest often had the finest dwelling and the choicest food. However, the freedom to deride or ignore the priest was largely a male prerogative; women, because of their responsibility for maintaining the spiritual health of the family/community, interacted with the priest on an almost daily basis and accepted his dicta.

Italian immigrants brought these attitudes—including anti-clericalism—and religious practices with them to the United States, much to the horror of the more ascetic Irish Catholics who preceded them. The physicality of Italian Catholicism seemed vulgar and blasphemous to the Irish; Italian veneration of the Madonna and the saints was an affront to God the Father, as was their general lack of respect for priests. However, once in America, most Italian immigrants turned to the Catholic Church as a source of familiar values, language, and practices; rejected by both cultures, the immigrants sought to shape a Catholicism that would accommodate and accept their needs.

Many Italian-American writers, including many of the women in this study, use this conflict in their work to communicate not only the real struggles between Irish and Italian immigrants, but also to symbolize the larger struggle to assimilate into American culture. Many writers express the self-hate that many Italian immigrants and their descendants came to feel; the embarrassment caused by ostentatious displays of *italianità*—including "the gaudy, overwrought, paganized pageants of saints with which Italian Americans annually annoyed their Irish clergy in some parishes" (Barolini, *Dream Book* 20)—frequently resulted in the fierce desire that some immigrants had "to separate [their] children from a culture that

[they] had learned to despise" (Claro 78).

The Church's role in defining and controlling female sexuality is also of essential concern to these writers. Economic oppression and physical and emotional abuse of women is often justified by what German theologian Uta Ranke-Heineman argues is willful misinterpretation and manipulation of the Bible, particularly the writings of Paul, by men. Citing, for example, Thomas Aquinas's famous dictum spelling out the duties of women, "Kinder, Küche, Kirche," she argues that this "idea continues to be the Catholic hierarchy's primary theological position on women" (88). An important part of this issue is the debate over abortion, which for several writers in my study is a primary locus for questions surrounding sexual equality and oppression.

Another concern for these writers is the intertwining roles of work and education. Several theorists, such as Max Weber and Doreen Alvarez Saar, have noted that work was used as a yardstick for measuring the "Americanness" and, by implication, the moral worth of other cultures. Sociological texts documenting the Italian-American experience point repeatedly to evidence of the immigrants' perseverance, ingenuity, and skill in achieving economic success. Nonetheless, during the late-nineteenth and early-twentieth centuries, images of Italian immigrants as lazy, drunken thieves and murderers developed and persisted, despite most evidence to the contrary. Two factors partially explain this phenomenon. First, the number of Italian immigrants rose dramatically during this period; Italians were more visible and therefore more threatening to both nativists and to immigrant groups that had already established themselves, however tenuously, in American society. Second, the earlier Italian immigrations were largely composed of the intelligentsia fleeing the political repercussions of Garibaldi's revolt. The later wave was composed almost entirely of the poor, illiterate peasantry from the South, for whom "the culture that produced Dante and Michelangelo was almost as alien as the one they encountered in [America]" (Oliver 6). The irony is that many of these later immigrants succeeded despite cultural and language barriers, and exploitation by those who took advantage of their ignorance (including some of their own countrymen who were already acclimated to the New World).

For Italian immigrant women and their daughters, work usually meant work within the home; if outside, it was usually connected to a family enterprise. As Mary Jane Capozzoli shows in her 1981 study of three generations of Italian-American women in Nassau County, New York, it was extremely rare for Italian immigrants to allow their daughters to go outside the family to obtain work. Thus, Italian-America women do not have the history of domestic service that is common to many immigrant and ethnic groups, such as the Irish, Germans, African Americans, and Chicanas. In the fiction discussed in this study, women interrogate their roles as workers in a culture in which "worth was measured by material achievement, visible riches, and success" (Barolini, *Dream Book* 20). These writers recognize the limitations of such measures of worth, but they also protest the ways in which access to these measures were denied to women by both the Italian and the American patriarchies.

The role of education is another essential concern to many Italian-American writers. Throughout U.S. history, education has represented (or been represented) to the immigrant as a key to the riches America has to offer. For the nativists of America, the public school system was crucial for the assimilation and acculturation of thousands of immigrant children. However, as the excerpt from Maria Mazziotti Gillan's poem at the beginning of this introduction demonstrates, public school was often a place of shame and humiliation for the ethnic child, one that fostered the self-doubt and hatred that haunted second and third generations.

Southern Italian immigrants, typically, had a mixed response to this mode of Americanization; desire for success conflicted with a deep suspicion of education and intellectual life, and fear of a force beyond the control of the family. Helen Barolini points to a common peasant expression: *Fesso chi il figlio megio di lui* ("It's a stupid man who makes his son better than he is") (8). For daughters of these immigrants, resistance to education was multiplied, because they were defined and confined exclusively by their role(s) within the family. To seek education was to look beyond the family, to reject it—the ultimate cultural sin for any Italian, but especially for a woman. Thus, in the case of many of the novelists in this study, that peasant expression may be more accurately rendered "It's a stupid man who makes his wife (daughter, sister, etc.) better than he is." Additionally, Alexander DeConde points out in *Half Bitter, Half Sweet: An Excursion Into Italian-American History* (1971) that the "anti"-education attitude of many Italian immigrants was fostered by American reverence for material success, or, at least, by the conviction that material enrichment was a necessary first step and thus more important than cultural or intellectual enrichment. By the late nineteenth century, most American businessmen had achieved success without formal, higher education, so that the general attitude in America was geared toward material rather than educational success (109–111).

Finally, any scholar of Italian-American experience must also consider the geographical, social, and cultural differences that sharply defined (and separated) the identities of northern and southern Italians. The class system of Italy traditionally ranked northern Italy over southern Italy, and northern Italians bore strong convictions about their status; they "considered themselves superior because of their higher standard of education, their greater contact with the industrial revolution [the benefits of which were focussed in the north], their greater accumulation of capital wealth, and their misconception that the Southerners were gay and shiftless" (Iorizzo & Mondillo 4). Typically, northern Italians were taller, with lighter complexions and features than southerners, and these physical differences were also regarded as a mark of superiority.

In contrast, the social and economic conditions of southern Italy bred misery and fatalism. Jerre Mangione and Ben Morreale reflect upon the image of the donkey as the dominant metaphor for the suffering of the southern peasant of "a poverty so dire it could not be faced directly and could only be described through animals" (35). The land was rocky, overworked, sun-baked, and prone to violent natural outbrusts—floods, earthquakes, etc. A very rigid class system had the unfortunate consequence of in-fighting—the peasants frequently turned on one another because they could not fight those in power. The vendettas that so repulsed northern Italians (both in Italy and in America) were supported by a code of justice based on "a chivalric code introduced to [southern Italians] by the Normans in the eleventh century" (Iorizzo and Mondillo 6). The "real" government was completely ineffective in redressing wrongs, so *mafiosi* (law enforcement offices) were established to enforce some kind of justice. Even some of the prejudices of the north found their way into southern thinking. As Patrick Gallo notes, "The southern peasant remains 'an African' (racially different) in the eye of the northern urbanite" (25). Yet even Neapolitans (and inhabitants of all other regions, for that matter) held Sicilians in low esteem; they were not "real" Italians.

The differences between southern and northern Italians were not lost in the process of immigration. Northerners (who dominated the early wave of Italian immigration) were met with some prejudice and discrimination, but as southerners became more dominant as an immigrant presence, "Americans of North Italian background . . . aided by proponents of Anglo-Saxon Teutonic supremacy, quietly integrated into the mainstream of American life" (Rolle 37). Northern Italians came to be regarded as "sober and work-oriented" (65), and were viewed as preferable to "greasily rhetorical, operatic South Italians" (65). Northern Italians resented being lumped together with southerners, and likewise resented the fact that the physical characteristics of southerners (shorter stature, dark hair and skin, etc.) represented the "typical" Italian to most Americans. Indeed, immigrants of northern Italian origin regarded the great waves of southern Italian immigrants with as much alarm and distaste as native-born Americans and engaged in calls for a halt to such immigration. Southern Italians, for their part, "saw northerners as 'tight' and 'mean,' a bit like shrewd but graceless Yankees" (Rolle 65).

Ironically, it was northern Italians who were more aggressive, more likely to give a padrone trouble, organize unions, and engage in anarchist political activity. Nonetheless, most native-born Americans "thought of the southerner as more violent, addicted to stiletto and revolver, quarrelsome, feuding, even murderous" (66). Northern Italians engaged in social activism, advocating formal education of the poor, medical assistance, and an end to child labor; a number of northern Italian immigrant social aid societies were established in cities such as New York and San Francisco throughout the 1850s and 1860s. Southern Italians were more likely to cling to the familiar and safe institution of the family in order to survive the changes and hardships wrought by immigration.

It is clear that all of these themes—silence, the roles of family and the church, work, education, and North/South conflict—intertwine and overlap in a variety of ways as they shape the experience and writing of Italian-American women. The novels examined in this book represent only a portion of the works that constitute this tradition; unfortunately, many have gone out of print, or are not readily available. However, as scholarship and criticism of this tradition grows, many of these "lost" works are being revived; for example, Tina DeRosa's novel *Paper Fish* (1980), out of print for almost fifteen years, was reprinted in 1996 with a critical foreword by Edvige Giunta, a scholar/critic who has been instrumental in garnering serious attention for Italian-American women's art, film, and fiction.

The first chapter, "Making America, Making Fiction: The Autobiographical Roots of Italian-American Fiction," explores the autobiographical underpinnings of Italian-American literary tradition. The beginnings of this tradition grew out of many immigrants' desires to tell their own stories, to counter stereotypes, and to resist definition by the larger American culture. Though Italophiles abounded among the American intellectual elite in the mid- to late-nineteenth century (including Margaret Fuller, who passionately supported Garibaldi's revolt), by the early twentieth century, this enchantment had largely eroded, and works such as Jacob Riis' *How the Other Half Lives* (1890) and Anna C. Ruddy's *The Heart of A Stranger: A Story of Little Italy* (1908), with their depictions of Italian immigrants as either childish innocents with "colorful and picturesque" (Oliver 10) customs, or as brutish, hot-headed, murderous anarchists, dominated and documented American perceptions of Italian immigrants. Thus, life stories such as *Rosa: The Life of An Italian Immigrant* (1970) were meant, in part, to act as a corrective to the false perceptions of Italian immigrant life, and to reclaim what the immigrants valued about their *italianità*. I chose this particular work for discussion for practical as well as literary reasons. First, *Rosa* is a rarity because it tells the immigrant story from a female perspective; though several chartings of Italian-American autobiographies exist, such as the extensive bibliography included in Rose Basile Green's study of the Italian-American novel, and William Boelhower's *Autobiography in the United States: Four Versions of the Italian American Self* (1982), they focus exclusively on male autobiographies. From a literary standpoint, *Rosa* clearly illustrates the autobiographical beginnings of the Italian-American literary tradition. The chapter examines the relationship and similarities between autobiographical writing and fiction, and explores Rosa's life story as an instance of identity construction that is simultaneously "real" and "fictional."

Chapter Two, "The Right of Passage: The Ethnic Narratives of Mari Tomasi and Marion Benasutti," examines two novels that have clear roots in this autobiographical tradition. This part of the Italian-American women's tradition includes works such as Julia Savarese's *The Weak and the Strong* (1952), Octavia Waldo's *A Cup of the Sun* (1961), Tomasi's second (and last) novel, *Like Lesser Gods* (1949), and Marion Benasutti's only novel, *No Steady job for Papa* (1966). The latter two, though published nearly twenty years apart, bear distinct similarities in the ways in which they engage with both the American literary tradition (and the novel as a genre) and their authors' Italian heritage. Tomasi's first novel, *Deep Grow the Roots* (1940), is unique in the history of Italian-American fiction in that it is set entirely in Italy, and does not treat the issue of immigration; rather, she focuses on portraying simple village life just prior to Mussolini's invasion of Ethiopia. *Like*

Lesser Gods deals directly with the processes of immigration to the United States and the sometimes painful assimilation to its culture; it is generally optimistic about these processes, and is actually a kind of *apologia*, for Tomasi is clearly interested in defending the Italian presence in America, and in depicting the enthusiasm with which Italian immigrants embrace American values, while preserving the best of their own cultural past. Benasutti's novel is also in immediate touch with the experiences of immigration and assimilation. More importantly, in her protagonist/narrator, Rosemary, we see explicit concern with the intertwining forces of gender and ethnicity in identity formation; Benasutti's treatment of these concerns foreshadow later, more detailed and in-depth treatments such as Helen Barolini's, Dorothy Bryant's, and Carole Maso's. Both Tomasi and Benasutti are engaged with the realist tradition and technique; however, while Tomasi employs the strategy of a seamless narrative, Benasutti's technique is fragmented and episodic, and anticipates the postmodern approach of later writers.

Chapter Three, "Dorothy Calvetti Bryant: The Subm/Version of Ethnic Identity," examines two novels by this prolific writer. Her significance lies in both her prodigious output and in her wide experimentation in content, genre, and style. Her engagement with her ethnic heritage in her novels varies, which makes her an important contrast with the writers studied in the previous chapter; I chose to examine two novels that, while sharing thematic concerns, engage with explicitly Italian immigrant experience differently. Other novels, such as *The Test* (1992) examine both the comfort of and demands exacted by close family ties in a contemporary San Francisco setting; her most recent novel, *Anita, Anita* (1993) is an imaginative biography of Ana Ribiero, Garibaldi's Brazilian lover. In addition, Bryant has circumvented the blocks of the economics of publication by establishing her own press, Ata, to ensure that her works remain in print, while The Feminist Press has acquired rights to two of her novels. In this chapter I focus on her second novel, *Ella Price's Journal* (1972) and on one later novel, *Miss Giardino* (1978). *Ella Price's Journal* is the only one of her works that was widely reviewed upon publication; it was part of a wave of what critic Lisa Maria Hogeland calls "consciousness-raising" feminist fiction of the 1970s. While the novel does not deal explicitly with the Italian-American experience, elements of that experience constitute the subtext of Ella's conflicts over identity and gender roles; however, it has not been considered critically as an "ethnic" novel. *Miss Giardino*, as the title indicates, is explicitly engaged with the Italian-American experience; thematically it is very close to *Ella Price's Journal*. Both novels are somewhat experimental stylistically, and are engaged with postmodern literary techniques. *Ella Price's Journal* is just that—a series of journal entries that chronicle Ella's intellectual and emotional development, while *Miss Giardino* intertwines a journalistic day-by-day account with long passages of flashback to imitate the reconstruction of the memory (and the identity) of the novel's protagonist.

Chapter Four, "Creating a Context: The Fiction and Criticism of Helen Barolini" examines the novels of this prolific poet, critic, and fiction writer. Her first novel, *Umbertina* (1979), it has been argued, is the first Italian-American novel by a woman to deal explicitly with the intertwining themes of gender and ethnic identity. Barolini herself sees this novel as feminist rather than as an ethnic novel (a significant contrast to Bryant, who disavows any direct connection to feminist activism or theory). Barolini employs the techniques of the sweeping historical epic, a dominant form of popular fiction (including romance novels), chronicling, in varying degrees of detail, the lives of four generations of Italian-American women; in doing so, she traces the political, social, and economic factors that have shaped Italian-American women's writing and experience. Her second novel, *Love in the Middle Ages* (1986), in comparison to *Umbertina,* has had very little critical attention, other than a few reviews upon its publication. This novel explores the complex conflicts between gender and ethnicity in the context of a romantic relationship. The scale of this novel is much more intimate than that of *Umbertina*, focusing on a single protagonist and her struggles with both her ethnic and sexual identities. Barolini has also been instrumental in the recent efforts to call both critical and popular attention to Italian-American literature, particularly the literature of women; she is also among the first scholars to identify herself as an Italian-American, as well as a feminist, critic.[3] Her work in the *Dream Book* anthology has had a two-fold effect; first, it has unearthed a wealth of writing by Italian-American women writers. It offers a valuable starting point for scholars and interested readers in the field, both in terms of its critical insights and its extensive cataloguing of a variety of Italian-American women's writing. Second, it has given impetus to similar projects which foster the ongoing process of building an Italian-American literary tradition as well as critical recognition of that tradition.

The final chapter, " 'Solving the Mystery': The Third-Generation Narratives of Lisa Ruffolo, Mary Caponegro, and Carole Maso," explores the work of three contemporary authors. While most works written before 1980 are more explicitly concerned with articulating and validating the immigrant experience and perspective, the works studied in this chapter demonstrate a removal from the immediacy of immigrant experience, what Italian-American critic Fred L. Gardaphé sees as a "renaissance" of third-generation Italian-American writers who no longer need to rely solely on immigrant experience for literary material. These authors are also more explicitly engaged with postmodern concepts of identity, subjectivity, and voice. Lisa Ruffolo's short stories have been widely published individually; I focus on her only collection, *Holidays* (1987) and the short story "My Grandfather's Suit." These stories, while primarily realist in technique, demonstrate Fred L. Gardaphé's description of third-generation novelists, whose work exhibits "a more distant historical perspective . . . gained by removal from the ethnic experience" ("Italian-American Fiction" 71). Her protagonists deconstruct and reconstruct identities, often in the context of relationships to friends, spouses, lovers, parents, and children.

Mary Caponegro's collection (like Ruffolo, this is her only collection of works), *The Star Café and Other Stories* (1990), while addressing many of the same issues as Ruffolo, is engaged with postmodernist practice and philosophy; she offers profound challenges to to conventional notions of language, knowledge, sexuality, and subjectivity; while none of the stories make explicit reference to Caponegro's *italianità*, they exhibit clear thematic connections to the Italian-American experience. The chapter focuses on the second and third stories in the collection, "The Star Café" and "Materia Prima," as those works which speak most directly to the ethnic and feminist facets of Caponegro's writing. Finally, Carole Maso has written several novels, after first becoming known for her poetry; her first novel, *Ghost Dance* (1986), is discussed for the ways it brings together the Italian immigrant experience with postmodern technique and philosophy. Its complex exploration of the family as a cultural institution reveals the conflicting feelings many Italian-American writers (and women) have for this institution.

I draw from a variety of critical methods and approaches. Some approaches have already been suggested: Fred L. Gardaphé posits a theory of Italian-American literature based on its oral heritage that bears strong affinity with the vernacular theory developed by African-American theorists such as Henry Louis Gates. Lucia Chiavola Birnbaum proposes a design that draws from peasant culture and orature (including its "pagan" Catholicism), the writings of the Italian political left (e.g., Antonio Gramsci) and of theorists of non-violence, and elements of Italian feminism. Helen Barolini suggests a theory specifically focused on Italian-American women writers that is based on the psychoanalytic work of Karen Horney, who argues that self-alienation leads to development and achievement rather than to repression.

In addition to emphasis on the oral tradition that informs Italian-American literature, my readings draw on a variety of feminist thought. I am particularly interested in current postmodern/feminist debates over subjectivity and identity. The question of whether gender is a legitimate category for analysis is central to postmodern feminist theory; categories such as "ethnicity" and "race" are similarly interrogated (for example, by African American critics such as Gates). French feminist theorist Julia Kristeva argues that identity implies subjectivity and vice versa, and that because neither is static (subjectivity is fluid), "woman" does not exist. Postmodernism's denial of a stable identity and subjectivity is useful because it frees us from the Enlightenment (and, as many feminist theorists argue, male) norms of "reason," "judgment," etc. It also allows for consideration of the varying degrees to which identity is constructed and influenced by a multitude of factors. For example, a central question to definitions of "ethnicity" is the degree to which "ethnicity" is externally imposed and to what degree it is chosen. However, the denial of stable subjectivity and identity is also problematic for marginalized groups that are trying to stake a claim for their identities; it has been argued that the idea of a decentered subject simply reinforces a marginal position.

For this reason, I find Marxist feminism useful to my study. Because Marxist analysis is grounded in specific material, historical, and cultural circumstances, it allows for consideration of real, lived experiences. This is not to say that literature is simply a "reflection" of "real life"; rather, such consideration helps to account, in part, for the ways in which one's entry into a literary tradition is shaped. From psychoanalysis I find useful the acceptance of ambivalence and open-endedness; the resistance to closure is a characteristic of many of the writers in this study. Also important to my discussion is the way in which psychoanalysis questions the (gendered) subject/object dichotomy in Western thought.

Finally, feminist application of the work of Mikhail Bakhtin provides an important piece of the theoretical frame of this study. Bakhtin's emphasis on the voice, rather than the gaze, opens the way for a feminist dialogics, a method for examining how "[t]he explicit and implicit interplay of these [social] voices [given by language] reveals the way a specific historical and cultural context fashions the self.... according to gender differences" (Bauer 671)—and, I would add for the purposes of my study, ethnic difference.[4]

Even works that have purported to examine the Italian-American literary tradition (or lack of it) have ignored women's voices. For example, Rose Basile Green's study, alluded to earlier, examines over sixty novelists—only four of whom are women. Gay Talese, in his essay examining the curious "silence" of the Italian-American novelist, refers *exclusively* to male novelists and theorists in answering his question. I consider the writers in this study significant in terms of subject matter and of literary production—but, most of all, for the variety of ways they give voice to the Italian-American woman, not simply in terms of real, lived experience, but in terms of their roles as artists claiming their places in the American literary canon.

Chapter One

MAKING AMERICA, MAKING FICTION: THE AUTOBIOGRAPHICAL ROOTS OF ITALIAN-AMERICAN FICTION

The importance of biographical and autobiographical writing to the beginnings of an Italian-American literary tradition should not be underestimated. The lack of a literary tradition among the first waves of Italian immigrants, coupled with a variety of economic, social, cultural, and psychological barriers[1], ensured Italian-American writers a slow entrance into the American literary tradition. The first steps toward this entrance were usually in the form of biographical and autobiographical writings; some of the earliest novels by Italian-American writers were strongly autobiographical. For example, Pietro di Donato's *Christ in Concrete* (1939), which tells the story of the gruesome death of an Italian immigrant bricklayer on a construction site and its consequences for his family, particularly for his sensitive and intelligent eldest son, is based on the construction accident death of di Donato's own father. In later chapters, works by Mari Tomasi and Marion Benasutti demonstrate a similar, strongly autobiographical origin; Benasutti's first novel, *No Steadyjob for Papa* (1966), for instance, grew out of a writing teacher's advice to "write about what you know." In fact, in the seminal study *The Italian American Novel: A Document of the Interaction of Two Cultures* (1974), Rose Basile Green argues that the first literary "steps" for the immigrant are *necessarily* autobiographical (though she acknowledges that the lines demarcating autobiography from fiction are often blurred). She adds, "to test the veracity and generality of the accounts in both autobiographies and the novels, it was necessary to compare the incidents described . . . with the personal oral accounts of numerous older Italian immigrants who still remembered their early encounter with America" (22). One example of such an account is *Rosa: The Life of an Italian Immigrant* (1970), an "as-told-to" biography by Marie Hall Ets, a social worker from Chicago.

Family memoirs constitute the earliest forms of what may properly be called "Italian-American" literature. The life story of my paternal grandmother, Mary Frances Pipino, is one example. Although I knew much of her story already, there were some pieces missing, and I felt I had only a fragmentary sense of her life. I went to her with a list of questions, and we talked for about two hours; this face-to-face conversation was followed up by two or three phone conversations. Admittedly, the focus of these conversations was factual—names, dates, etc.; nonetheless, I felt very strongly the emotional current my grandmother experienced as she recalled details of her courtship with my grandfather, the early years of her married life, and her experiences as the daughter of immigrants in a new culture.

She was born January 1, 1908, to Angeline and Vincent Rizzi in the heart of the Italian immigrant community created in Niles, Ohio. Coming primarily from six of Italy's nineteen regions (Italian immigrant identity tended to be regional, rather than national) and attracted by the burgeoning industries of the Mahoning Valley, by 1914 "the Italians in Niles outnumbered other ethnic groups three to one" (Nobili 8). Mary Frances is the second of eight children; her two surviving sisters, Angie and Carrie, still live in Niles. Mary's parents came from the same village, Toursi, near Naples in the Basilicata region of southern Italy (the instep of the "boot"); however, their marriage was not an arranged one. The family's immigration pattern was typical; first, Mary's maternal grandfather came over, working for three years before saving enough money to send for his wife and two daughters, Angeline and Julia. Angeline married twenty-six-year-old Vincent Rizzi, a blacksmith by trade, when she was sixteen. In 1921, the Rizzis purchased a small grocery store on Ann Street, a central location in Niles's East End Italian community. Both Italian and English were spoken in the home, though Mary's grandmother spoke only Italian.

All of the Rizzi children worked in the store, while attending Niles public schools; Mary Frances attended school through her sophomore year and then went to work as an apprentice to a dressmaker. Her parents purchased a sewing machine for her to set up her own business (in the home, of course) and Mary contributed to the family's income by making children's clothing; she specialized in creating beautifully embroidered Easter dresses. Over the years her family has been the recipient of beautifully crocheted and knitted afghans, baby clothes, and other items, all of which are treasured as symbols of a rich and not-so-distant past.

In 1926, at the age of eighteen, Mary met Samuel Rock Pipino, a shoemaker five years her elder. With a wistful smile and a distant look in her eyes, Mary remembers meeting Sam just two weeks before Valentine's Day and the red satin robe he gave her as a Valentine's gift. The lavish and personal nature of that present clearly signalled Sam's intentions to Mary and her parents, who were thrilled that such a serious and hardworking young man wanted to marry their daughter. Just over a year later, on June 12, 1927, they were married in Our Lady of Mount Carmel Church.

Sam had immigrated to America at the age of sixteen from Toursi, the same village from which Mary's family had come (Sam's mother and Mary's grandmother were sisters who married a pair of brothers by the name of Masselli). His two older brothers had already left for the States several years before, and when Sam's father died they sent for him. Sam left behind his mother and two sisters; he never returned to Italy (though Mary went there twice, meeting the family Sam had left behind) and, unlike many immigrants, never expressed any wish to return or regrets for what he had left behind. Sam and another boy from the village were stopped in Switzerland and did not have enough money for both of them to go on;

Sam gave all his money so his friend could proceed, counting on him to send more money once he arrived in the States. Sam spent six anxious weeks stranded in Switzerland, not knowing the language (the Southern dialect Sam spoke was quite different from the northern Italian dialect spoken in the part of Switzerland that bordered Italy) and unsure whether the necessary money would be sent.

Sam was already a skilled cobbler when he arrived in America; in typical immigrant fashion, he apprenticed himself to an established shoemaker, saving enough money to purchase his own shop at the age of twenty-one. He and Mary lived for three years with Mary's Grandmother Masselli while he saved to buy their own home (and my grandfather was not to move again for the rest of his life, nor did he travel, save for the 10-mile trip to his eldest son's home in Youngstown, Ohio). Nine months and three days after their wedding, their first child, Donald, was born; seven years later their second child, James (my father), was born.

Mary and Sam preserved many traditions of Italian life in their new home, including making homemade wine with a press stored in the basement. Mary laughingly recalled an incident from their early days in their new home. Despite Prohibition, she continued to make the alcoholic cordials that were an integral part of the ritual of entertaining visitors to one's home; she purchased illegally made "moonshine," mixing it with tap water and flavoring (such as almond or anise). One day, about a week after moving into her new home, Mary had just finished putting up a batch of cordials when she noticed a uniformed man striding up the driveway. Convinced he was a government agent, she hurriedly dumped the sixteen quarts of cordial down the toilet, sure that the door would burst open at any moment and she would be arrested and taken away to prison. Much to her relief and dismay, as she looked out the window again she saw the man cross her backyard and walk through the hedge that separated their yard from the neighbor's—the "agent" was a fireman taking a shortcut to his home after a tiring day!

Another piece of family legend, a story my brothers and I never tired of hearing as we were growing up, was Mary's power to cast the *malocchio*—the evil eye. One day she passed a roadside stand offering watermelons, which Sam loved. Uncertain of the quality, Mary asked the vendor to plug one so she could see the interior; he assured her that they were good, and if she were dissatisfied for any reason, she could return it for a full refund. Upon arriving home and cutting up the melon, Mary was angered to discover a white, unripe interior, and tried to return the melon; the vendor, however, denied promising her a refund. Mary declared, "The next time I pass this spot, you'll be gone!" By the next day the entire stand had disappeared; a terrible storm had swept through Niles, destroying the fruit stand and all its contents. Mary's brother-in-law, Tony, implored (not entirely joking), "Mary, please, never put a curse on me!"

More importantly, Sam and Mary inculcated in their sons an abiding respect for family, hard work, and education. Both were literate in Italian and English, and Sam and Mary both worked long hours in the shoe shop, saving to send their sons to expensive private schools (Donald attended Oberlin College, James attended John Carroll University) and to provide for them a comfortable material existence. A tremendous love and respect for the integrity of family have also shaped their legacy. Despite quarrels and differences through the years, the Rizzi siblings have remained close; their children and grandchildren have retained relatively close ties among a wide network of first-, second-, third-, and fourth cousins, many of whom still live in the Niles area. Enormous family celebrations characterized my childhood—weddings, christenings, First Communions, and even birthdays were occasions for a gathering of extended family and feasting.

Though Mary asserted she never experienced any direct expressions of anti-Italian prejudice, there are subtle reminders of such prejudice in the family's history. She and her siblings went to public school under the Anglicized name of "Rich" in order to disguise their *italianità*; the second eldest son, Joe, later legally changed his name to Rich in order to secure teaching and coaching jobs. Several of the Rizzi children obtained college degrees; the youngest daughter, Carmel (Carrie) obtained a nursing degree and worked throughout her married life. Interestingly, while all eight Rizzi siblings married, all had very small families; Elizabeth, the oldest, had the most children (three sons).

As with many immigrant communities, the church was the physical and spiritual center of life. St. Stephen's Church was established in 1865 to meet the needs of all Catholics in the community; nonetheless, anti-Italian prejudice, fuelled by the Great Panic of 1873, led to the desire on the part of Niles' Italian community for a church of their own (Nobili 19). As stated in *A Legacy,* a parish-written history of Niles's Our Lady of Mount Carmel Church,

> [Italian immigrants] came to America with hope and faith. As their numbers grew, so did their need to establish a church of their own. The traditions of the Roman Catholic faith were important to these people, along with their spirit of family and their sense of pride. Churches were a part of their culture. (12)

Part of this desire was to have an Italian-speaking priest, as well as the freedom to celebrate festas without the interference and objections of the primarily Irish-Catholic St. Stephens. In 1906, the bishop appointed an Italian immigrant priest, Fr. Vito Franco, to organize an Italian parish in Niles; a formal church was begun in 1923 and completed six years later, the construction and funding provided almost entirely by Niles's Italian immigrant community (Nobili 24–33).

Mary and Sam, of course, were deeply involved in the spiritual and social life of the parish. They and both their sons married there; Mary and Sam were active in a variety of parish groups and activities, including the annual summer festival that raises a large part of the church's operating funds. Mary's devotion to this service was such that, at age seventy-six, just six weeks after undergoing surgery for colon cancer, she was in the basement kitchen of the parish school, helping to prepare the hundreds of pizzas that were (and still are) a major source of the festival's revenue. Mary saw nothing remarkable in such service; she simply saw herself as giving back to her parish and to God part of the life given to her and her family. In the later years of her life, she was no longer able to participate as she once did, but her name remains among those of the "old generation" who built and fostered Mount Carmel's legacy. She died on August 25, 1997 (my grandfather Sam died on December 19, 1983, an emotional blow from which my grandmother never recovered), at the age of 89. She was eulogized by her nephew, Monsignor Nicholas Mitolo, who remembered how she valued her family and her church above all else in her life.

This brief life story of my grandmother constitutes an important part of my own history; my role in shaping and transcribing her story is, in one sense, a transcription of part of my own (particularly since I am named after her). I was conscious very early in my life of my *italianità*; though I am close to my maternal relatives (who are of German-Irish origin), there was little that was overtly "ethnic" characterizing our gatherings. Thus, my desire in eliciting my grandmother's story has deeply personal as well as scholarly motives behind it. The choices I made in arranging my memories of stories told to me throughout my childhood and the material garnered from my "interviews" with my grandmother were dictated both by a desire to preserve a part of our family's history that is now gone, as well as to explore the relationship between autobiography and fiction in the formation of a distinctly Italian-American literary tradition.

The relationship between biographical/autobiographical writing and narrative fiction has been much discussed by theorists in recent years. In the past, the two categories had been seen as mutually exclusive, one recognized as a record of "truth," the other as constructed, or "made up." Increasingly, however, commentary on the genre of biography has explored its fictive qualities. Roland Barthes has remarked that biography is "a novel that dare not speak its name" (qtd. in Heilbrun 28), while Jeff Todd Titon's essay "The Life Story" asserts, "The life story told to a sympathetic listener is a fiction complete in itself" (291).

Oral histories such as Rosa's and Mary's constitute a crucial part of Italian-American literature. *Rosa* is a compelling example of several complex issues surrounding biographical and autobiographical writing. It relates the life story of Rosa Cassetteri (Cavalleri in the book), from her abandonment as a newborn at a charity hospital in Milan to shortly before her death in 1943. She is raised by foster parents in the silkmaking region of Bugiarno in northern Italy; at fourteen she is forced into an arranged marriage to a much older (and, as we learn, violent and abusive) man from her village. Later he sends for her from America, where, Rosa is told, even poor people can become educated and successful. She eventually leaves her husband, moves to Chicago, and remarries, finding work at the settlement house where she and Ets become friends.

Considerable theoretical attention has been given to the genre of autobiography, seen by many critics and scholars to be a uniquely "Western" form of literature. Some critics claim, in fact, that "only Westerners can write autobiography"

(Kaplan 118). For example, in "Conditions and Limits of Autobiography" (1956), George Gusdorf asserts that autobiography is possible only in those cultures/societies which possess "a conscious awareness of the singularity of each individual life" (29). He writes,

> Autobiography is not to be found outside of our cultural area; one would say that it expresses a concern peculiar to Western man; a concern that he has been of good use in his systematic conquest of the universe and that he has communicated to men of other cultures; but those men will thereby have been annexed by a sort of intellectual colonizing to a mentality that was not their own. (29)

Any study of the history of this genre, in fact, traces its origins to Renaissance Europe and the rise of the recognition of the value and glory of the individual.[2] However, there is the current strain in theory that examines the ways in which non-Western cultures tell stories about themselves, for example, in Arnold Krupat's work on Native American autobiography.

One major concern for critics and theorists taking structuralist and post-structuralist approaches to the genre of autobiography is the very recognition of its fictive qualities. For works like *Rosa* this concern is magnified by the "as-told-to" aspect of the work. The critic must decide what the "translator" has imposed of his/her own ideals, world view, etc. on the narrative; likewise, one must also consider what has been deleted or altered by the once-removed teller. One important work which clearly demonstrates these concerns is the landmark Native American autobiography, *Black Elk Speaks: Being the Life Story of a Holy Man of the Oglala Sioux* (1932). It is relevant to my discussion of *Rosa* for several reasons; first, like *Rosa, Black Elk Speaks* is an as-told-to life story, rendered as a first-person autobiography. Second, it is valuable not only as "the finest, most authentic picture of the life and mind of the Plains Indians available in print" (Holly 119), but also as a work of literature. Third, there are cultural similarities at work in both of these life stories. As Robert Sayres notes in "Vision and Experience in *Black Elk Speaks*," Natives Americans lacked "concepts of *life, self*, and *writing*," all of which are fundamental for autobiographical work (qtd. in Holly 120). Rosa, like many Italian immigrants, was illiterate; additionally, traditional Italian culture was strongly rooted in communal, rather than individual, identity.

Increasingly, too, *Black Elk Speaks* has served as a model for discussion of the fictive qualities of autobiographical writing, thanks largely to John G. Neihardt's own commentary in prefaces to the work and in interviews about the creation of this text. As Carol T. Holly points out, in "*Black Elk Speaks* and the Making of Indian Autobiography," most informant-based Indian autobiographies were anthropologically based (and thus geared to satisfy the demands of the researcher rather than to be an accurate representation of a life) and characterized by "numerous distortions" of Native American life (119). However, Holly argues, *Black Elk Speaks* represents an exception:

arrangement and partial writing of the first and final chapters, both unifies the narrative and lends it an authenticity unequalled by the Indian life stories recorded for the purpose of scientific study. For, in the first place, his chronological arrangement of chapters and the stress he puts on Black Elk's role as autobiographer accentuates the unity of vision implicit in Black Elk's perspective on his life. Secondly, just as the structures of such Western autobiographies as Augustine's, Franklin's, Malcolm X's and Nabokov's reflect the individual identities of their authors, so does Neihardt's structure for *Black Elk Speaks* reflect and define Black Elk's identity, one consisting of a union of his personal . . . identity and his nation's collective . . . identity. (120–121)

This passage is relevant to my discussion of *Rosa* for several reasons. First, Holly's assertion that an external point of view unifies, clarifies, and authenticates a life story is arguable, to say the least. Nonetheless, it raises significant questions about the concept of authenticity: Where does authenticity in a life story lie? In its congruence with historical (and therefore verifiable) fact? In corroboration or validation from an "expert," external source? Second, her statements raise the issue of the unified and coherent self. Some critics argue that a crucial component of autobiography is the imposition of a pattern or a sense of coherence on a life; does the imposition of such a pattern imply an essential faith in a coherent self, a concept challenged by postmodern theories? Finally, Holly's use of only male autobiographies as touchstones for her discussion points to a gap in autobiography criticism that has concerned feminist theorists and critics in recent years.

Jeff Todd Titon argues that "The life story tells who one thinks one is and how one thinks one came to be that way" (290), while Carol T. Holly asserts, "The form or design of autobiography in turn reflects and defines the autobiographer's self-concept" (129). In other words, a life story invents a coherent self and then proceeds to explain the genesis and development of that self in a coherent narrative. This description of the life story is evident in *Rosa*. Because Ets chose to use the first person "I" (that is, as if Rosa herself recorded her own story), additional attention must be paid to Sidonie Smith's observation that "Because the autobiographer can never capture the fullness of her subjectivity or understand the entire range of her experience, the narrative 'I' becomes a fictive persona" (*A Poetics* 46). Rosa's "fictiveness" (that is, she is "created" by Ets' narrative) and her role as artist/storyteller within her own story make this particular autobiography an important instance for study, much in the way that Black Elk's is significant for the study of Native American autobiography.

Ets's own introduction to the work sums up many of these issues. She recounts the circumstances of her first meeting with Rosa, or Mrs. C., as she is known at the settlement house. Ets, at the time a war widow in her twenties, relates:

> I had just moved into the [Chicago] Commons and was in my little room at the top of the annex when Mrs. C. found me there weeping. I never mourned except when I was alone, but this time I was caught. She had come through the men's side of the

[T]he shape that Neihardt lends to Black Elk's narrative, particularly through his building where she had been cleaning and I had not heard her. Rosa's efforts to comfort me seemed strange at first—she just sat down and started telling me one of the folk tales she knew from her childhood in Italy. From that day on Mrs. C. and I became staunch friends. (3)

This passage emphasizes the communal spirit out of which women's autobiographies often grow; despite differences in age, culture, and language, the two women connect. It also reflects an observation made by Jeff Todd Titon about the shifting nature of so-called "informant-based" life stories; he speaks disparagingly of the "hit-and-run field-worker," whose collection method "is like [that of] the botanist who brings back a great variety of specimens for analysis and preservation" (289). He notes, however, that such methods are falling out of favor with folklorists:

But as folklorists increasingly come to develop friendships with their informants over several months', even years', time, the word "informant" becomes inappropriately impersonal. As those friendships deepen, the opportunities for life story conversations increase. Seeking cultural information, the folklorist is likely to conceive of these conversations as life history. But if he is interested in his friend as a person, and what it is that makes him or her a tradition bearer, he will look to the life *story* as an expression of personality and self-conception—the who and why rather than just the what and how of his friend's life. (290)

Initially, Ets's literary interest in Rosa grew out of Rosa's reputation and skill as a storyteller. Ets had successfully published a children's story, and Rosa offered to share her own folk stories for publication. However, Ets comments that "when written down these stories held little that would interest moderns" (7). This comment interests me for its ironies. On the one hand, much of Rosa's personal attraction and popularity in the settlement house lay in her storytelling abilities; Ets even relates one occasion when Rosa's storytelling dominates an important gathering at Hull House, where speakers including Jane Addams and a " 'big somebody from Washington' " (5) fail to hold the audience's attention, while for Rosa "the audience came to life" (5). On the other hand, Ets's observation that Rosa's stories lost something when written down points to Walter Ong's assertion that "orality operates with the sort of commonplace formulary expressions and clichés ordinarily despised by fully literate people" ("Literacy and Orality" 197).

While Ong's assertion and Ets's comment may be read as narrow rejection of less "sophisticated" oral cultures by literate ones (which clearly is *not* Ong's perspective), they do point to an important element of orality, clearly illustrated in Rosa's case. Orature depends largely for its impact on performance—the interaction between the storyteller and a visible, participatory audience. Ets tells us in the introduction that much of the interest in Rosa's stories lay in her improvisational skills, her ability to change stories with each telling by adding or deleting details, and her ability to use her body and her voice to add drama and life to each telling. Additionally, we learn that Rosa's skill is a combination of natural talent (her birth mother was a famous actress) and the storytelling she observed during her childhood in Italy. Rosa sees nothing extraordinary in her abilities, though throughout her narrative we see her pride and happiness in her ability to entertain others. Too, we see as the narrative progresses the importance for the dual forces of community and orality for Rosa's life; it is the community's influence and its body of oral wisdom accumulated over centuries that direct Rosa's life and give the pattern and coherence to her life story that many critics see as a crucial ingredient to this genre. Thus, Ets's shift in interest from Rosa's *stories* to Rosa's *story* may be read in light of Jeff Todd Titon's observation about the true source of interest in any life story: "What is it about this person, we ask, that makes [her] an artist in the face of all pressures to stop? What makes [her] an exceptional artist?" (291). Additionally, Rosa demonstrates Carol Boyce Davies's assertion that "The critically defining feature [of life stories] is that they blur the boundaries between orality and writing" (7).

One final important element of Ets's introduction is her description of the narrative's development and transcription. Because Rosa could not write in English (and was barely literate in Italian), Ets had to rely on conversations during which Rosa would tell her incidents, recording them as Rosa spoke. Because these incidents were given to her without benefit of chronology, Ets had to impose order on them herself. Thus, in a very real sense, Ets is responsible for the shape and progression of Rosa's narrative. Additionally, she tells us,

> First I took down her words in heavy dialect, as she spoke them. But this proved too difficult for the reader. Thus in this more recent version I have corrected and simplified the text, trying at the same time not to lose the character and style of her spoken words. (7)

In other words, Ets's work enacts the difficulties of transcribing oral performance. Obviously, she (and Rosa's storytelling audiences) had little difficulty understanding Rosa's "heavy dialect" when face-to-face with her. However, the elements of performance—gestures, facial expression, and voice inflection that enhance meaning and clarification—are lost when orature becomes "literature." However, Rosa's stories are not "lost." Rather, Ets interweaves folktales, songs, and religious folklore with incidents in Rosa's life, thus emphasizing the orature's importance in Rosa's life and her life story.

Rosa's story opens with her account of her abandonment as an infant at a charity hospital in Milan. She explains the system of the *torno,* a kind of one-way turnstile on which the mother placed the baby; the purpose was to preserve the mother's anonymity (because she was either not married or simply did not have the financial means to care for the child). However, if the mother intended at some point to reclaim her child, she simply pinned to the child's clothing half a square of cloth, with some distinctive pattern, and kept the other half as evidence of her claim. Rosa also explains that too many babies were injured on the *torno*, so city government outlawed its use. Thus, she claims, she was the last baby placed on the *torno* before its abolishment.

Interestingly, this claim to minor distinction characterizes the rest of her narrative. Though, as noted earlier, Rosa's narrative emphasizes the importance of community for her, her narrative is characterized also by frequent assertions of her difference and special skills. These apparent contradictions may be read as a tension between Rosa's Italian and American identities, a tension that is common to many works by Italian-American writers. This aspect of Rosa's life story also points to issues surrounding the production of biography and autobiography to which feminist critics and theorists have turned their attention. In the introduction to *Writing a Woman's Life* (1988), Carolyn G. Heilbrun comments on the relative lack of critical attention accorded women's biographies (11).[3] Sidonie Smith points out in the introduction to *A Poetics of Women's Autobiography* (1987) that criticism of autobiography demonstrates a similar androcentric bias, which "[is] restrictive, prescriptive, and inappropriate to a reading of women's autobiographies" (9). Smith cites, for example, George Misch's "normative" definition of autobiography, which emphasizes the writer's relationship to and participation in public life. This definition, Smith argues, renders the concept of "women's autobiography" oxymoronic, because men have usually denied, or at least limited, women's access to public life and discourse. Conversely, if a woman dares to claim a public identity and power, "she transgresses patriarchal definitions of female nature by enacting the scenario of male selfhood. . . . To take a voice and to authorize a public life are to risk loss of reputation" (8,10).

Additionally, Misch also insists upon the "representative" nature of autobiography if it is to be considered "good" (that is, worthy of critical attention). Most (male) critics of autobiography insist on conflating "male" with "human"; thus, Smith asks, "How might the tension between the ideal woman and the ideal man manifest itself in women's autobiography?" (8). Paradoxically, most of these (male) critics also emphasize "a conception of individuality that privileges singularity and autonomy" (9), a conception which "demands the individual's willingness to challenge cultural expectations and to pursue uniqueness at the price of social ostracism" (9). Smith points out that such rebellion on the part of a male subject is made possible and acceptable only because "he and his public assume his significance within the dominant order" (9), whereas for a woman such "rebellious pursuit is potentially catastrophic" (9–10). Furthermore, this model of "(hu)man" personality formation (with its emphasis on autonomy and separation), as theorists such as Nancy Chodorow, Dorothy Dinnerstein, and Jane Flax have argued, is quite opposite to the formation of female identity, which is dependent upon connectedness rather than separation.

Thus, a clear parallel exists between Smith's poetics of women's autobiography and that of ethnic/non-Western autobiography laid out by Carol T. Holly cited above. Both approaches emphasize and insist upon a departure from the traditional argument that a "good" autobiography highlights the individuality of its subject and that subject's process of separation/distinction from the community.[4] Susan Stanford Friedman notes that "The emphasis on individualism as the necessary precondition for autobiography is thus a reflection of privilege, one that excludes from the canons of autobiography those writers [women and non-whites] who have been denied by history the illusion of individualism" (39). That is not to say, of course, that all women's autobiographies thus become interchangeable; rather, it means that a recognition of the communal nature of women's autobiographies is essential to critical and theoretical approaches to them. As Friedman argues in "Women's Autobiographical Selves: Theory and Practice," "Women's sense of collective identity . . . can . . . be a source of strength and transformation" (39). Carol Boyce Davies, in "Collaboration and the Ordering Imperative in Life Story Productions," notes that women's life stories are sites where "private, familial issues" [i.e. "women's" issues] such as rape, wife beating, and childbirth can find their way into public discourse, from which they were formerly barred" (15).

Critics and scholars of Italian-American experience have repeatedly emphasized the role that communal identity plays for the Italian and the Italian American. Such identity begins with the family, followed by local (that is, the village) and, distantly, by regional (but not national) identity. Assertion of difference and of any degree of independence was to invite misfortune, particularly for women, whose roles as daughters, wives, and, above all, as mothers, entirely defined and circumscribed their existence. Helen Barolini explains:

> [The Italian woman] had little choice but to put herself under the protection of a man. Women outside the family structure were scorned as deviants from the established order; they were either wicked or pitiful, but certainly outsiders. Unmarried or widowed women . . . were thought . . . to be consumed with envy toward women with men, and full of spite, [and] were thus commonly held to be the primary casters of the evil eye. . . . In a patriarchal society, any female whose life was not defined by a man's would be suspect. (*The Dream Book* 7)

This system of identity with the family worked well in the context of localized, agrarian life; it was, in fact, the only source of security and protection from a complex system of oppression by the rich (present in both the northern and southern regions of Italy, though more pronounced in the South) and by the Catholic church. The rigid code of familial identity included the inculcation of total, unquestioning obedience to one's elders; this code of family rule (called *l'ordine della famiglia*) was coupled with the inculcation of an equally rigid social hierarchy. Rosa tells us frequently about the intense fear the poor had of the rich, so that a poor person would not dare look into the face of, let alone speak to, a wealthy person.

The utter and absolute control of the rich over the poor is paralleled by assertion of the same control of men over women. Much of Rosa's social indoctrination revolves around her increasing awareness of gender relations in her culture.

Rosa relates the story of Mariana, mother of two of her playmates, who sells some of her hair, against her husband's wishes, to get the money to buy wool for a new shawl. When Rocco, her husband, finds out, he beats her severely; Mamma Lena, however, "didn't scold that husband. She said the man is the boss and he has the right to beat his wife" (29). Rosa relates another story about Pietro, the boss at the silk mill, who breaks his wife's arm when she dares to talk back to him. When the doctor charges five lire for his services, Pietro gives him ten, telling him, " 'You keep it all, doctor. Then when my wife talks back to me again I will break her other arm and have the doctor already paid' " (80). Rosa, still a child, wonders, " 'Why are the men always so mean?' " only to be told by her aunt, " 'The woman is made to be the servant of the man. . . . The man is the man and the woman must obey him, that's all' " (81). Later, Rosa talks over her confusion about these rigid gender roles with the village priest, who tells her

> "God gave the man the right to control the woman when He made him stronger, Rosa. . . . It's a sin for the wife not to obey. Only God and the Madonna come first. Only when the husband wants his wife to sin against God and the Madonna she must not obey him. Remember that, Rosa." (82)

This exchange is important to the narrative. In addition to highlighting (for the reader) and reinforcing (for Rosa) the "natural" roles of men and women in this culture, it demonstrates the pervasive influence of the Church and the role of the village priest in rural peasant life. The degree of control the priest could have, particularly over a woman, is measured by the effect Don Domenic's words have on Rosa; she swears she would never obey a husband who urges her to sin, " 'even if he kills me!' " adding, "And I made the sign of the cross" (82). Second, it acts to foreshadow Rosa's future, and to prepare us for her response to her husband's violence against her later in the narrative.

Finally, it points to a crucial aspect of religious belief among Italian peasantry: the central role played by the Virgin Mary. While her elevated role was based on very traditional constructions of womanhood—Mary is revered because she is the ultimate mother figure—it is also quite subversive because she is treated as coequal with God the Father. Her influence and power were so tremendous that, as Helen Barolini notes, "that it is not to God that Italians cry out in their need but to those interchangeable figures, the Madonna or *mamma mia*" (10). The power and influence of the Madonna is a controlling theme in Rosa's life story, as she enumerates incidents that confirm her own belief in her special protection by the Madonna; in fact, one entire chapter of the early part of the narrative is given to stories of miracles, wrought by the Madonna's intervention, experienced by people in Rosa's village. The Madonna's influence on Rosa's life is made evident early in the narrative, as Rosa relates how she came to be taken in by Maddalena Cortesi, a childless woman who had just lost a foster child (also named Rosa) when her mother reclaimed her. Rosa was being cared for by Marietta, an elderly woman, who decides when Rosa is four that she will no longer be able to care for her. Marietta turns to Maddalena, who initially refuses. However, Marietta insists, assuring Maddalena that Rosa is " 'a daughter of the Madonna. . . . She was born on the *Purificazione di Maria'* " (10). Rosa adds, "Maddalena didn't want to think about me but the Madonna made her" (10–11).

The dual themes of the fear that dominated the lives of these peasants and the centrality of the Madonna are closely interwoven throughout Rosa's narrative. She relates several stories of what she calls "scares" she and other villagers experience to illustrate the extent to which superstition and intensely felt fear affected her life in Italy. Rosa connects this theme of fear to the previously discussed theme of the Madonna's intervention in her life; that is, despite the fears and "scares" that overshadow her childhood experiences (including several experiences with death), Rosa sees in them confirmation of her status as a true child of the Madonna, a beneficiary of her special favors and protection. For example, she relates an incident that took place when she was about five or six years old, when Angelina, an older girl in the village, invites Rosa and another playmate to accompany her to gather wood. Along the way Rosa gathers some wild roses to place at a shrine for the Madonna she knows they will pass. Though Angelina insists they have no time to visit the shrine, Rosa does so anyway. Later, a terrible storm arises, and Angelina is struck and killed by lightning when she takes shelter under a tree. Rosa is saved, however, because she turns back. Rosa reflects:

> The little Madonna in the field had made a miracle to save me and Caterina from the lightning. The Madonna was the Mother of God. She talked to God. The Madonna prayed to God for all poor women and children. Me, I was a daughter of the Madonna—born on the Madonna's day. The Madonna would take care of me always, just as She had today. (38)

This passage makes the reason for the Madonna's importance very clear: She is the only protector of those who are most defenseless in an often brutal physical and social environment, "poor women and children."

The theme of Marian protection and intervention is important for two reasons: first, Rosa emphasizes her own fearlessness and independence as a small child; she tells us "Mamma Lena said I was the daughter of the poor and the daughter of the Madonna and I should be humble and quiet. But she didn't know how to make me. I kept right on laughing and shouting and running from one mischief to another" (25). She also relates an incident when she dares to speak directly to their landlord, a man they called *Signore* (a title of respect) "because he was higher than us" (18); she says, "When I was little I was not yet afraid of the high and the rich" (18). She does, however, gradually learn to be afraid of many things as she grows older, and it is to Mary she turns for comfort and relief. In fact, her complete faith in Mary's power and in God's intentions for her life enable her to endure (and even remain somewhat cheerful about) some terrible experiences. Her exposure to American ideals gradually undoes this fear—another important theme of her story:

> Only one wish more I have: I'd love to go in *Italia* again before I die. Now I speak English good like an American I could go anywhere—where millionaires go and high people. I would look the high people in the face and ask them questions I'd like to know. I wouldn't be afraid now—not of anybody. I'd be proud I come from America and speak English. . . . I'd scold them like that now. I wouldn't be afraid. They wouldn't dare hurt me now I come from America. Me, that's why I love America. That's what I learned in America: not to be afraid. (254)

The examples and experiences by which Rosa learns to assert her independence, while preserving her essential love for communal ties and her intense religious faith, then, become the pattern which dictates the unfolding of her life story. In other words, her life story may be viewed as one example of the immigrant's attempt to integrate her Italian and American identities, to reconcile the tensions between a culture that values conformity, communal identity, and unquestioned obedience to higher authorities (the parent, the husband, the wealthy, God), and one that values independence, autonomy, and individuality. In *Rosa*, the form of the life story/autobiography becomes the means by which these tensions are examined and worked out in the immigrant's life.

One significant pattern that develops in Rosa's narrative is the tension between the rigid and narrow roles prescribed for women in this culture, and the actual lives of several women who influence Rosa tremendously as she matures. The first and most formidable female influence on Rosa's life is Mamma Lena, her foster (and, eventually, her adoptive) mother. Her character and her influence demonstrate the paradox and contradiction of Rosa's life. From the first, Mamma Lena insists on total obedience to authority (particularly hers) in Rosa, and instills in her intense religious devotion as well as acceptance of traditional social hierarchy (particularly of male superiority over female). Mamma Lena's own life, however, stands in stark contrast to these traditions. As a young woman, she rejects the rule of her older brother (who became head of the family after the father died) and moves out with her mother into her own home. Her relationship to her husband, Papa Lur, reverses traditional roles. Mamma Lena's word is final in all matters, because, as Zia Teresa says, " 'Giulur is a saint. . . . He takes everything and keeps still' "(24). When she and Papa Lur buy an *osteria* (pub), "Mamma Lena didn't have to go to the silk mill anymore. She just stayed home and took care of the *osteria* and was her own boss" (23); the rest of Rosa's story strongly suggests that this is the real lesson Rosa learns from Mamma Lena's example.[5] Additionally, Mamma Lena insists on learning to read "like the rich people" (23), and, by learning Latin prayers from the village priest, and reading Biblical stories, becomes a kind of priestess in the village, preaching and praying to the other women in the square (a skill she passes on to Rosa). She is a well-known and formidable figure in the village; Rosa tells us, "Everybody was afraid of Mamma Lena. Me too" (18). Thus, Mamma Lena enacts some of the same contradictions seen in the role of Madonna; while she upholds traditional gender roles as mother and wife, she is also powerful enough in her sphere to assume a relatively high degree of control and authority, in addition to her spiritual power in the village.

A second, though lesser, influence on Rosa's life who challenged traditional gender roles was her birth mother, who, at fourteen, bore Rosa and gave her up to the charity hospital in Milan. When Rosa is six or seven years old, her natural mother ("Diodata" in the narrative) comes to reclaim her, and takes her to live with her, her lover (an artist named Nicolo), and their child, Carlo, in Milan. Though distressed at Rosa's unrefined, peasant appearance and speech, Diodata recognizes Rosa as her child and, delighted to discover Rosa's talent for public performance, resolves to put her on the stage. The people of Rosa's village (and Rosa herself), though awed by Diodata's beauty and fame, are distressed by her profession and her intentions for Rosa. When Don Domenic urges her to reconsider, telling her that "it would be a sin for her to take [Rosa] away from . . . Bugiarno. . . . [where she] had been brought up to fear God and love the Madonna" (60), Diodata refuses. Rosa is astonished: "That Diodata wasn't afraid of anyone—not even the priest!" (60).

Rosa's time with Diodata is brief; she rejects Diodata's attempts to "civilize" her and raise her level of sophistication in appearance. Earlier in the narrative, Mamma Lena scolds Rosa as she tries to braid her hair: " 'It's pride that you don't want your hair in the style of the poor. . . . You know your hair is beautiful and you want to show it off. Pride is a sin. . . . God and the Madonna will punish you for pride' " (17). However, when Diodata attempts to style Rosa's hair in a manner that will highlight its beauty, Rosa resists, insisting on keeping it braided, peasant style, and on wearing the headkerchief and wooden shoes of the country. Eventually, Rosa is returned legally to Mamma Lena and Papa Lur, ironically, because she speaks out for herself in public and takes action to get what she wants. When a stranger on a crowded train asks her why she is crying, Rosa insists that her "real" mother is in Bugiarno, and that Diodata has kidnapped her. Diodata is arrested; later, Rosa runs away in the night and is returned to Bugiarno, and a court investigation of Diodata is followed by legal adoption by Mamma Lena.

Clearly, Rosa's insistence, even as a child, on remaining true to her community's customs and values "saves" her from Diodata. Her persistence in maintaining a peasant appearance surely offers something of a comical contrast to the expensive dress of Diodata and her child; however, it is precisely because Rosa looks like she does not belong to Diodata that the strangers on the train believe her claim that she is being kidnapped. Through her entire time in Milan, Rosa keeps by her side a small statue of the Madonna, and prays to it, again emphasizing the degree to which, at least from Rosa's perspective, her life is protected by Mary.

The pattern of leaving and returning to Bugiarno becomes a marker of significant events in Rosa's life throughout the narrative. Immediately upon her return to Bugiarno, Rosa is put out to work in the silk mills by Mamma Lena. Silkmaking was the economic lifeblood of the region, emphasized by a fairly lengthy interpolation in the narrative (presumably by Ets) which explains the delicate process by which the silk worms were cultivated in the peasants' homes every year. The degree of their importance can hardly be overemphasized; during the storm which kills Angelina, some of the worms are also killed, while the rest are so frightened they refuse to eat—an event regarded as far more catastrophic than Angelina's death. As was common to many regions in Europe in the late-nineteenth century, Bugiarno's silkmaking industry was largely unregulated. Concerns about child labor were unheard of; in fact, the agility and small size of children, as well as their easier exploitation, made them crucial to the industry's success. Rosa's first job in the mill is to wind the silk on spools, and, she tells us, "if we didn't tie fast enough [the supervisor] would hit us" (75).

Rosa describes the terrible working conditions of the mill, where she earned about eight cents a week, with remarkably little bitterness or horror. She does, however, relate several incidents which continue to develop the pattern of her lifestory—her fearlessness and determination to learn, and her faith in the Madonna's protection. Rosa tells us that she did not know why at first she had to simply wind the silk from one spool to the next, so she decides to ask the male boss, against the advice of her fellow workers: " 'Oh, no Rosa!' [Caterina] said, and all the little girls started shivering. 'You can't talk to Arturo! He's higher than us! He will slap you in the face!' " (76). Rosa ignores their warnings; to her delight, Arturo answers her, "And he didn't even take his hands from the belt to his trousers" (76). She relates another incident when, after a scolding and severe shaking from the supervisor, her hair is caught in the machinery: "I didn't even have time to pray. But the Madonna helped me anyway. She made my head go all around with the wheel so it would come out again at the end. (Sure, it was the Madonna! I didn't know myself to do such a thing! The Madonna is the best friend I have!)" (76).

The parenthetical inclusion of this last assertion suggests Rosa's recognition (and Ets's editorial acknowledgment of that recognition) of her audience's skepticism regarding her claims of divine protection and intervention. Italian peasant Catholicism grew largely out of pre-Christian elements such as worship of and sacrifice to a variety of greater and lesser deities, place worship, and various rituals associated with the cycle of the seasons, planting, etc. The practices of saint adoration, village shrines, *festas* (elaborate festivals devoted to the celebration of the birthdays of saints and important dates in Mary's life), and Marian devotion were the result of grafting Catholic dogma onto already established peasant customs. When transplanted to America, these practices horrified the firmly established Irish-American Catholic church, whose priests and congregations regarded the elaborate statuary and gaudy relics, as well as the various devotions to Mary and the saints, as blasphemous affronts to God the Father (Barolini 19–20).

The next major event of Rosa's life is her three years of education at a convent in a nearby city, when she is eleven years old. Mamma Lena, alarmed by Rosa's sudden physical maturation and the attention she begins to attract from men frequenting the *osteria* (and Rosa's mild encouragement of this attention), decides "that was just the place for me" (88). Rosa's education is "completed" at Canaletto; she refines her silkmaking skills (the benefactor of the institution owned a silk mill near the convent and, in exchange for the girls' labor, fed and clothed them). She becomes the best worker in the mill and also perfects her performance skills. In fact, her storytelling quickly distinguishes her in the eyes of the other girls; Rosa becomes their only real source of entertainment at the institute. Her skills also gain the attention of the nuns; during the institution's annual show for the townspeople, Rosa is asked to entertain the restless crowd while the girls get ready. She is so successful that one wealthy patron offers to buy enough wool to make shawls for all the girls of the institution if Rosa will just sing one more song.

More importantly, however, she learns what her roles as a woman and as member of the poor peasant class really mean in her culture. Rosa's awareness of her sexuality (which, even to the end of the narrative, after she has been married twice and borne several children, remains quite muted) begins to grow at this point in the narrative. However, as was conventional, the girls at the convent, even those older than Rosa, remain largely ignorant and are made to feel a vague sense of shame about their bodies. The nun fitting Rosa for her uniform is shocked by her developing body and scolds Rosa for having such clearly defined breasts at such a young age; Rosa reflects, "I had never thought about my breasts before and she made me feel ashamed, but I didn't know what to say. So for once I kept still" (89). Later, simply out her enjoyment of talking and entertaining the other girls, she remarks that the Virgin Mary "was born like other babies" (96), only to be interrogated by the Mother Superior as to how she came by such knowledge. When Rosa confesses that " 'I just said what came into my head' " (97), the *Superiora* tells the girls that Mary was born from a kiss between her parents. Rosa tells us,

> When the Superiora was gone the girls all started asking questions. How could a baby come from a kiss? And what was the sin between the husband and the wife that *Superiora* talked about? What did the man do to the woman when he married her? What did other babies come from and how were they born? Nobody knew. "Only the husband can tell a girl those things. A girl is not allowed to know until she is married. No, she is not even allowed to ask! It is so bad you get punished if you ask!"
> Me, I had never known before that the husband did anything to the wife except sleep in the bed with her. So now I had something new to think about. (97-98)

Despite this initial candor about her sexual ignorance, Rosa is quite circumspect throughout the rest of the narrative about sexual knowledge. The secrecy and shame with which it was surrounded, particularly for women, follow Rosa right up to the birth of her first child, when she is about fifteen: "How that baby got in there I couldn't understand. But the thing that worried me the most was how it was going to get out! . . . Probably the doctor would have to cut me" (157). When she asks Mamma Lena for advice, she is told "to pray to the Madonna. If you pray to the Madonna with all your heart maybe the Madonna will make a miracle for you and let the baby come out without the doctor cutting you" (158). This, of course, happens, reaffirming Rosa's sense of protection by the Madonna. More importantly, however, this portion of the narrative stands in stark contrast to the candor of the rest; Rosa reports falling into a sort of coma, and when she awakens, the baby is born. Subsequent reports of childbirth are equally muted; even when Rosa gives birth alone in a Missouri cabin to her second child, she does not remark at all on the pain and fear she must have experienced, and expresses little, if any, shock over finally acquiring the knowledge she and the other girls sought at the convent.

Tied closely to this theme, of course, is Rosa's consideration of the roles open to her in her culture: wife/mother or nun. The roles of prostitute or actress, regarded by many as one and the same, were not even admitted as possibilities for Rosa (as we see in her rejection of Diodata as her mother earlier in the narrative). While at the convent, Rosa witnesses the lives of two women who elect different roles and who each have a tremendous influence on her perspective. The first is Sr. Vincenzo, a young nun loved by the girls for her beauty and kindness. The daughter of a wealthy family, she rejects her heritage to take the veil of one of the strictest orders. Inspired by her example, Rosa resolves to join the convent, but is rejected because she "has the father *ignoto*—unknown" (115). Rosa laments, "Poor me, I didn't know who I was so I couldn't be a Sister of San Vincenzo!" (115).[6] Thus Rosa begins to understand more fully the implications of the class and gender hierarchies under which she lives.

Rosa's lack of paternal authority and legitimacy illustrates an important difference between the traditional, male-normed construction of autobiography and the female. Sidonie Smith argues that autobiography is "ultimately an assertion of arrival and embeddedness in the phallic order" (40); the father gives his name (and, therefore, legitimacy and "author"ity) to the child, but the child/autobiographer must "invest his name with new potentiality and then interpret it for the public" (40). She goes on to argue that the male autobiographer must work to repress all traces of the female and the feminine in order to "exert power over the uncontrollable and unnamed side of human experience" (40); thus, autobiography has become a central literary form "because it serves as one of those generic contracts that reproduces the patrilineage and its ideologies of gender" (44). Thus (despite her lament of "Poor me"), Rosa's narrative disrupts and perhaps even nullifies this contract, precisely because she does not know her father's name, and because the mother figures of Mamma Lena, and to a lesser degree, Diodata, give her identity, legitimacy, and "author"ity.

Another important female influence Rosa encounters at Canoletto is Beata, an orphan raised by the nuns at the institution. Beautiful and lively, Beata has only one goal in life: to marry a handsome man. Her wish is realized at fifteen when the mill owner's nephew sees her and falls in love. After he comes to ask for her hand, Beata's life changes; she is immediately separated from the other girls until her wedding day (which takes place within a day of the proposal) because she has, with her engagement, acquired an adult female identity. Though the girls are permitted to witness the wedding ceremony, they are not allowed to speak to Beata or say goodbye to her. A year after the wedding, Rosa goes to visit her; Beata is living in a fine home, with servants to wait on her, Rosa tells us, "But she was not our Beata. She was a sad lady dressed up in black. . . . I was wishing I hadn't come. . . . The jolly lively Beata I had loved so much was gone" (110).

Rosa's return to Bugiarno after her three years at Canaletto catalyzes the next major shifts in her narrative. Papa Lur has died during her absence, and she is now entirely under Mamma Lena's control, without benefit of his gentler nature and intervention. The next two chapters detail Rosa's full entrance into adult social and sexual roles; she takes the job at the silk mill, where her skills make her the object of much attention. She also receives marriage proposals from several men, including Signor Cosimo, from a wealthy family in the next village. Mamma Lena's refusal of this proposal again reflects the strong communal and class prejudices of rural life: "You can't trust a man from another village. And a rich man like that—what does he want with a poor girl like you?" (124). Rosa eventually falls in love with a village boy, Remo, but Mamma's Lena's strictness leads her to keep their relationship secret.

At this time Rosa begins to notice the constant presence in the *osteria* of Santino, an older man who clearly commands even Mamma Lena's respectful servitude. Rosa attracts his attention with her storytelling and performing but remarks, "Who he was I didn't know, but I knew I didn't like him" (116–117). Later, he reveals her secret relationship with Remo to Mamma Lena, who becomes so angry that she arranges marriage for Rosa to Santino, despite Rosa's objections: " 'I could not let you marry one of those boys who like you so much. They would let you have your own way. You need someone to control you. You need an older man to make you meek and save you for heaven in the end' " (152). She also favors Santino because he is (relatively speaking) wealthy and past the age of mandatory military service to which the younger men of the village are subject. Rosa insists she will not marry Santino; however, feeling betrayed by Remo's refusal to risk punishment by leaving the army and running away with her, she inevitably capitulates:

> For three days [Mamma Lena] was beating me and would give me nothing to eat. But it was not the beating and the starving that made me stop saying no. It was the fear of God. By defying Mamma Lena I was offending God and the Madonna. For a child to disobey a parent is a terrible sin. If I died while defying Mamma Lena I would go straight to hell and there would be no chance for me ever. (152)

Rosa returns, now with more urgency, to her questions about marital relationships but can find no one to answer them. The wedding ceremony is a sober and anxious affair for her, and she takes care to let the reader know that she never actually assented to the marriage; the priest, being nearly deaf, declares them married without hearing Rosa's "Yes."

The circumspect attitude that characterizes Rosa's revelations of sexual knowledge and her use of pseudonyms in her narrative are also characteristic of her inclusion of her first husband, Santino, in the narrative. Though she relates unflinchingly the many beatings she suffered at his hands, at several points in the narrative, she stops, insisting, "The things he did to me are too bad to tell.... I have to leave that man out of my story, that's all" (174, 205). These statements indicate to me that Rosa is able to relate the physical abuse she suffered because it was culturally accepted. Mamma Lena steps in to defend her against Santino only after she becomes pregnant; later, in Missouri, the men Rosa cooks for at the mining camp, though disgusted by Santino's behavior, do not intervene when he beats her. However, her refusal to tell all the "bad things" he did may indicate that she also suffered sexual abuse, about which she could not bring herself to elaborate, whether out of a sense of propriety or of religious spirit.

Not long after Rosa becomes pregnant, Santino leaves for the iron mines in Missouri; later, when he sends for her, Mamma Lena tells her she must go, for "[h]owever bad that man is, he is your husband—he has the right to command you. It would be a sin against God not to obey" (160–161). Compounding Rosa's pain, Mamma Lena insists that she leave her baby behind, and Rosa is left with no choice but to obey mother and husband (and, therefore, God) and move to America. Despite Santino's brutality and infidelity, the challenges of learning a new language and customs, and hard physical labor, Rosa comes to love life in America. Shortly after bearing her second child, she is summoned back to Italy to reclaim Francesco from Mamma Lena, who is too sick to care for him. This time, when Mamma Lena tries to make her leave the new baby behind, Rosa refuses; she has already learned not to be afraid of authority. Her visit to Italy, in fact, reflects a phenomenon seen in other returning immigrants: she is not afraid to speak to strangers, and she has begun to let go of some the old superstitions, such as belief in the *malocchio*. She sees Remo again but has no feelings left for him; in fact, she compares him to Gionin, one of the men at the mining camp who is clearly in love with her:

> Gionin couldn't dance at all, but Gionin was ready to sit in jail for the rest of his life to save me from Santino. He was even ready to die. Remo had been afraid.... Gionin was not pretty like Remo and he didn't care about nice clothes. But Gionin was bigger, stronger, safer. Gionin had never even tried to touch my hand, but the gentleness that came into his fiery eyes when he looked into mine! Just the thought of Gionin made me stop shivering and feel more calm.... [and] Gionin was crazy for the children. (194)

Shortly after her return to Missouri, she learns that Santino has purchased a bordello and expects her to run it. Rosa refuses, proclaiming, " 'I belong to God and the Madonna!' " (199). Though Rosa has been taught that to disobey her husband is a sin, she also remembers Don Domenico's assertion that it would not be a sin to disobey her husband if he wanted her to sin against God. Nonetheless,

Rosa knows that, with no money and two small children, her options are limited. Gionin helps her escape to Chicago, where she is taken in by the Tuscan immigrant community. Though life in Italy taught her to mistrust the legal system, she has heard (and included in her narrative) several stories of poor people who have received justice in America. Thus, despite her fears, her ignorance of the American legal system, and the fact that she understands little of the language or proceedings, she goes to court against Santino and is granted a divorce. She and Gionin marry (though because of the divorce, they are not permitted to marry in the Church) and settle in Chicago.

The remainder of Rosa's narrative is concerned with her integration into the new multiethnic community in Chicago. Though her life is still dominated by economic struggle, the loss of children, and displacement, her narrative nonetheless possesses a tone of joy and gratitude for what America has given her. Two themes emerge strongly in this section. The first is the transferral of folklore to an urban setting. Rosa's faith in miracles and in her status of special protection by the Madonna is undiminished; in a chapter that complements the one cited earlier, she relates a series of incidents that demonstrate God's power to reward and punish and that offer evidence of saintly intervention.

Rosa, of course, also brings her storytelling to Chicago, linking the importance of her orature to the second important theme, that of community. Though Rosa is at first bewildered by, and slightly mistrustful of, the variety of neighbors she lives with, she comes to embrace her new community and to share with it her stories. On the one hand, her views reflect the regional prejudices of her life in Italy, as well as the necessity for overcoming these prejudices in order to survive:

> The people from *Toscana* they're not good like the people from *Lombardia*. But they're not bad like the people from *Sicilia*—I should say not! The people from *Piemonte* are a little more bad than the people from *Lombardia,* but they come next. *Lombardia* is the last in the world to do wrong things. The Italian government made that investigation and they said so. Gionin was not like the other *Toscani* in Chicago, but they were all *paesani*—they all stuck together and helped the other. (209)

However, through her experiences at the settlement house, Rosa realizes that her love and need for community are far more important that any regional or national differences, and despite any language or cultural barriers. It is through her storytelling that she is linked to her community: "I loved to tell the stories. I never said no" (235).

In her present, she mourns the loss of that old community several times near the end of her narrative. She says:

> The residents in the settlement house now are not like in those old days. Now they all have their own work and go their own way. They're all pleasant and nice.... But it's not like the old days when everyone was one family.... I just love the Chicago Commons. I hope I'll never stop coming. But it's different now. The old Commons,

when everybody was like one family, is gone. (234, 240)

Despite this sense of loss (including the deaths over the years of her husband and three of her children), Rosa's narrative ends on an optimistic note, and its final paragraphs unite the dual themes of her religious faith and her joy in shedding all the fears she grew up with. She has weathered serious illness and is unafraid to die, but "I'm never wishing to die. I like to live" (253). She has succeeded, finally, in following Mamma Lena's example and celebrates her independence: "I have it like heaven now. I'm really in heaven—no man to scold me and make me do this and stop me to do that.... I have it like heaven—*I'm my own boss*. The peace I've got now it pays me for all the trouble I had in my life" (253) (my emphasis). However, as if to remind her audience that she did not achieve this peace only by her own effort, she adds,

> The Madonna is the one to take care for us poor women. You've got to have faith in your heart—you've got to believe. But it's true and true: if you pray with all your heart and beg God and pray to the Madonna you get help for sure. You get happy again. The Madonna, She helped me all through my life, and now She gives me peace. (254)

The structure of the narrative's ending places "America" in the role of a secular Madonna for Rosa; just as the Madonna gives her happiness and spiritual peace, from America she learns "not to be afraid" and is thus satisfied that she is successful in "making America." In other words, Rosa has constructed a coherent self and a clearly patterned narrative that explains the person (and the artist) she is now. In his preface to *Rosa*, Rudolph J. Vecoli argues that

> In my judgment, *Rosa* has literary as well as historical value. It bears more resemblance to the fictional accounts of immigrant life than to immigrant autobiographies. The latter tend to be "success" stories, often with a personal or ideological ax to grind. Rosa has more in common with Willa Cather's Antonia or Ole Rolvaag's Beret than with Mary Antin or Bella V. Dodd. (vi)

Vecoli's observation again highlights the role that life stories such as Rosa's play in their blurring of generic boundaries. His alignment of Rosa with two "fictional" characters over two "real" women, furthermore, points to the relationship between autobiographical writing and the development of an Italian-American literary tradition. Literary "descendants" of Rosa and her experiences are evident in works studied in subsequent chapters, particularly in Chapter Two, which examines novels that arose directly from their authors' lives, and in Helen Barolini's *Umbertina*, studied in Chapter Four, which is based on the author's retelling of the lives of her female ancestors. *Rosa* is particularly important, of course, for the way it gives a voice to the woman's immigrant experience; Vecoli's observation underscores the link between the Italian-American women's literary tradition from its beginning to the rest of American women's tradition. In this study, Chapter Three, for example, examines *Ella Price's Journal* (1972), by Dorothy Calvetti Bryant, as both an example of the feminist consciousness-raising novel and as an immigrant novel.

Rosa's story redefines the notion of a "success" story, I think, as Vecoli seems to be using it and as it is commonly used. Too, I would argue that this redefinition is tied to the notion of "making America," the peasant expression that refers literally to the idea of achieving social and economic success in the New World (that is, the conventional notion of the "success story" as applied to immigrant fiction). Rosa's sense of "success" is based, not on financial success or social status, but on the dual notions of achieving autonomy ("I'm my own boss now") and of establishing herself within a new community. In other words, her success is the result of integrating two seemingly contradictory impulses—a step that many scholars of Italian-American literature and history regard as crucial to the immigrant's full integration into American society (discussed more extensively in Chapter Three). Finally, such integration must include entrance into "American" cultural institutions, including its literary tradition; thus the ideas of "making America" and "making fiction," as well as the notion that the life story itself is the "making" both of a coherent self and a work of literature, become bound together by Rosa's story in a particularly feminist way.

Jeff Todd Titon, in "The Life Story," wonders why more life stories aren't "presented and interpreted as fiction" (289) when one must acknowledge the fact that

> no matter how sincere the attempt, remembering the past cannot render it as it was, not only because memory is selective, but because the life storyteller is a different person now than [she] was ten or thirty years ago. . . . The problem of how much a person may change without losing his or her identity is the greatest difficulty facing the life storyteller, whose chief concern, after all, is to affirm [her] identity and account for it. So life storytelling is a fiction, a making, an ordered past imposed by a present personality upon a disordered life. (290)

Titon's call to his colleagues in anthropology is paralleled by a call by Edvige Giunta, in an article entitled "Crossing Critical Boundaries in Italian/American Women's Studies," for a specifically Italian-American literary criticism, one that "explore[s] possibilities for a broader dialogue that, while recognizing the creative potential of multiple intersections [i.e. ethnicity, class, and age, as well as gender], breaks barriers and crosses borders" (14). Thus, while Rosa's story is certainly valuable as a "historical" document—that is, as the account of one female immigrant's experiences—it finds even greater value in the recognition of its importance to the beginnings of Italian-American literature, of its exploration of the integration of immigrant/ethnic sensibility with American culture, and for its presentation of "the relationship of woman's experience to her linguistic and discursive alternatives" (Smith 11).

The relationship of Rosa's narrative to the Italian-American literary tradition becomes clear in the next chapter, which examines two novels: Mari Tomasi's *Like Lesser Gods* and Marion Benasutti's *No Steadyjob for Papa*. Both of these works, though clearly intended to be interpreted as fictional, are strongly autobiographical. Both Tomasi and Benasutti construct a fictional self to present a version of the Italian immigrant experience, though the selves they construct and the purposes for which they construct them are different. Tomasi uses a third person omniscient narrator in order to defend and evoke sympathy and acceptance for the Italian immigrant presence in America; Benasutti's use of a first-person narrator (a strategy which gives *No Steadyjob for Papa* the veneer of true autobiography) is also meant to garner sympathy and acceptance, but has embedded within it a critique of the sexual, ethnic, and class prejudices harbored by mainstream American culture. Just as F. Scott Fitzgerald "usurped" Zelda's narrative, writers such as Anna Ruddy and Jacob Riis usurped the narrative of the Italian immigrant; the writers in this tradition seek to reclaim their narratives and to "write what has never been."

Chapter Two

THE RIGHT OF PASSAGE:
THE ETHNIC NARRATIVES OF MARI TOMASI
AND MARION BENASUTTI

In *Ethnic Passages: Literary Immigrants in Twentieth-Century America* (1993), Thomas J. Ferraro writes,

> The turn to ethnic narrative is an attempt on the part of the writer to negotiate the terms in which the greater freedoms of the United States are to be accepted: on the one hand, to dispel the charge by the clan of having undergone the essential and traitorous assimilation; on the other, to dispel the charge by the culture at large of possessing predispositions of mind and heart inappropriate if not antithetical to the developing concerns of a national literature and culture. (10)

The works of Mari Tomasi (1910–1964) and Marion Benasutti (1908–1992), both daughters of northern Italian immigrant parents, are examples of the ways in which Italian-American women have negotiated their way into national literary identity. The works discussed in this chapter, Tomasi's *Like Lesser Gods* (1949) and Benasutti's *No Steadyjob for Papa* (1966), represent, in a sense, a transition stage in the development of a specifically Italian-American tradition, a move from the purely autobiographical narratives and transcriptions of oral histories discussed in the previous chapter, to an engagement with the forms and conventions of the realistic novel. Both women made a conscious decision to become writers—a decision that, as Ferraro's passage points out, was not without risks as well as rewards.

Both novelists represent the link between autobiography and fiction studied in the previous chapter. These novels grew out of Tomasi's and Benasutti's personal experiences, growing up as daughters of immigrants in small ethnic communities (Tomasi in Barre, Vermont among granite workers, Benasutti in Philadelphia's Little Italy). Additionally, both writers are working within the realistic mode, and generally portray the immigrant experience, including the assimilation process, in an optimistic and uplifting manner. However, the seventeen-year gap between the publication dates of these novels accounts for an important distinction between them. Tomasi's sentimental portrayal of the Dalli family reveals her primary interest in garnering sympathy for and acceptance of Italian immigrants by American mainstream culture; however, Benasutti's portrayal of the poverty and prejudice endured by Rosemary's immigrant family reveals the subtle influence of ethnic and feminist movements gaining ground in the 1960s.

Mari Tomasi was born around 1910 in Montpelier, Vermont, of Piedmontese (northern Italy) immigrants; her parents' ancestral land became the setting for her first novel, *Deep Grow the Roots*. Tomasi experienced an injury as a baby that kept her confined to a wheelchair for most of her first eight years, and consequently spent much of her time observing and listening to the immigrant stonecutters who patronized her father's fruit store; this community became the inspiration for and subject of her second (and last) novel, *Like Lesser Gods*. Tomasi attended college, but was forced to drop out when her father died unexpectedly; she supported herself by teaching in a country school, writing for the Montpelier *Evening Argus*, and publishing her short stories. She worked for the Federal Writers' Project in Vermont in the thirties, participating in the production of a nonfiction, unpublished work entitled "Men Against Granite"; the research for this project, at least in part, fuelled the writing of *Like Lesser Gods*. One other significant work, published shortly before Tomasi died in 1964, is "The Italian Story in Vermont." While this work "reveals a mine of information about Italian immigrants in Vermont" (Mangione and Morreale 372), it is also noteworthy for what it lacks: an examination of leftist and unionist activities among the Italian immigrant workers, which was largely responsible for the adoption of safety measures in the granite quarries.

While the *New York Herald-Tribune* named *Deep Grow the Roots* "one of the ten most outstanding first novels of the year 1940" (Mangione and Morreale 371), other reviews were mixed. One critic found this first effort " 'drenched in an atmosphere of sunshine and poetic writing' " (qtd. in Mangione and Morreale 371). *Deep Grow the Roots* (1940), unlike most novels by Italian-American writers, is set entirely in Italy, and makes no reference to the immigrant experience; the title suggests, of course, the still-powerful connections that many Italian-American immigrants feel to their "motherland." Rose Basile Green calls Mari Tomasi's second novel, *Like Lesser Gods*, published eight years after her first, "a colorful weaving of the Italian ethnic experience into the American tapestry" (137). While this work generated a good deal of attention and praise when it was published, little critical work has been done on it; like much literature by Italian-American women, it has largely been ignored. It is significant, however, that in the chapter on Italian-American literature in Jerre Mangione and Ben Morreale's *La Storia: Five Centuries of Italian American Experience*, Mari Tomasi is the only woman mentioned among the group of fifteen writers discussed; though a later chapter of their work does address the writing of other Italian-American women, none receives the commentary that Tomasi's does.

Even Green's characterization of *Like Lesser Gods* reflects the bias that criticism of ethnic or immigrant literature has often exhibited. Though she includes her analysis of *Like Lesser Gods* as part of her "documentation of the interaction between two cultures," her primary interest lies in analyzing the way the novel presents (and preserves) Italian folkways within an "American" setting. As Ferraro points out in *Ethnic Passages*, pre-eminent American critics such as Leslie Fiedler and Irving Howe often dismissed literature by or about immigrants with the labels of "local color" or "regional" literature.[1] The merit of and interest in such works lay in their value as "sociological" tracts documenting the folkways of colorful ethnic minorities that had no relationship to any, particularly an American, literary tradition.

Clearly, a reading of Tomasi's novel demonstrates its connection to American realism. However, close reading also reveals a strong streak of romanticism in Tomasi's representation of Italian immigrant life in the 1920s and 1930s. In her 1988 study *The Social Construction of American Realism,* Amy Kaplan offers an explanation for this seemingly peculiar blend. She notes that Lionel Trilling, the dominant post-War critical voice, held the strongly anti-liberal view that realism like Theodore Dreiser's, which critiqued capitalism by showing the lives of the underclass, was "endorsing Stalinism" (4). She adds, "To represent class difference in America, implies Trilling, is to impose a politically dangerous and aesthetically disingenuous literary mode" (4). Thus, according to Kaplan, Trilling and likeminded critics favored the romantic rather than the realistic mode, as truly representative of "American" culture and, Kaplan argues, thus shaped the post-World War II canon of American literature.

An examination of *Like Lesser Gods* cannot ignore the loving attention to the detail of Italian immigrant life—detail that is a hallmark of realistic literature. However, her inclusion of such detail is frequently imbued with romantic, even mystical, elements. Take, for example, the poetic evocation surrounding the preparation of an ordinary dandelion salad:

> Mister Tiff sliced a garlic kernel in two, and rubbed the moist sides to Minna's salad bowl. He diced a small onion and the hardboiled eggs. These he put into the bowl with the greens. And over the whole he let trickle a thin flow of olive oil. A heavier stream of vinegar broke up the golden globules of oil and sent them shimmering between the greens. . . . He urged Minna to try it. (44–45)

Other passages in the novel reveal Tomasi's interest in documenting, describing, and, in some respects, romanticizing the customs and beliefs on which Italian immigrant life rested. Kaplan argues that the use of such descriptive detail in realistic fiction (which some critics regarded as excessive) "often appears in inverse proportion to a sense of insubstantiality, as though description could pin down the objects of an unfamiliar world to make it real" (9). Thus, Tomasi's use of descriptive detail, such as in the passage cited above, may be read as her attempt to make the Italian presence in the New World "real," both for the immigrants themselves and for the larger "American" culture.

Like Lesser Gods examines the community formed, in part, by northern Italian immigrant craftsmen and laborers in Granitetown, Vermont (the fictional name given by Tomasi to her home of Barre, Vermont). The title reflects Tomasi's essential concern with cosmic order and the human place within that order—an order she views as generally harmonious and good, and subject to the authority and will of a central, patriarchal power. The primary, controlling theme of the novel is *form*; many of its tensions and contradictions arise from the fact that patriarchal notions of "law," "rule," and "form" dictate its pattern. From this standpoint, then, it is no surprise that Tomasi has made the novel's central character (and, seemingly, her mouthpiece) the *maestro* Michele Tiffone, an immigrant and a voice for Old World values and traditions. His title of *maestro* is no accident; though translated in the novel as "teacher," it can also be literally translated as "master."

The novel's title comes from Greek mythology: "On Olympus lived the greater gods; and below, the lesser" (166). It expresses the conviction of stonecutter Pietro Dalli that, when he creates a memorial, he is participating in God's design:

> "I carve the name and I say to myself, 'From up there in heaven the *Dio* creates new life; and when he sees fit to take it away, when we stonecutters on earth take up where he left off . . . we make a memory of that life. Almost boy, it is being like— like—'. . . . [Gino] murmured quietly, 'like lesser gods.'" (166)

The title also conveys Tomasi's concerns with attention to form and to rules: there exists a definable, unsurpable hierarchy of which humans are a part and to which they are morally obligated to conform. Such obligation may incur suffering; "lesser gods" must always subordinate emotional responses to the rational dictates of form, or suffer the consequences.

Pietro and his fellow stonecutters are not the only "lesser gods" with whom Tomasi is concerned. Though she moves in and out of the minds of a wide cast of characters, the central figure is Tiffone (nicknamed "Mr. Tiff" by Petra Dalli). Mr. Tiff's function in the novel is that of intermediary; he rights wrongs, intercedes to correct moral mistakes, and sets straying lambs on the "right" path. Though Mr. Tiff is not completely above an occasional peccadillo—for example, he smuggles a pint or two of bootleg whiskey, even as he tries to dissuade Pete Rocco from getting caught up in smuggling activity—Tomasi clearly means him to function allegorically and symbolically in the novel. The obvious parallels to his patron saint, Michael, reflect *contadini* reliance on intermediaries (Mary and the saints) to intercede on their behalf with God the Father, rather than on direct appeal. Additionally, Mr. Tiff's teachings to Petra about the saints, and his emphasis on their importance in the cosmic order, layer the symbolism surrounding his character.

Tomasi manipulates Mr. Tiff's presence providentially at times; he is, in fact, seemingly omnipresent (as divine intermediaries must be) and also hidden from view of other characters, as when he happens to overhear the reason for Asa Conway's eagerness to purchase Vitleau's house and land, or Pete Rocco's plans to make money smuggling whiskey. Thus, Mr. Tiff, as a *character* in this novel, replicates the role of Tomasi as *novelist;* Amy Kaplan argues that "the realist [writer] participates in the panoptic forces which both control and produce the real world by seeing it without being seen in turn" (7). However, she goes on to assert, realism is also a "production of the real as an arena in which the novelist struggles to represent reality against contradictory representations" (7). Thus, Tomasi's struggle as a novelist to produce and manipulate reality is replicated by Mr. Tiff's attempts to manipulate those around him to conform to his ideals of reality—attempts that sometimes fail. For example, his decision to stow away on the bootlegging mission, rather than simply try to talk to Pete directly, leads, indirectly, to Pete's death.

Such failure has several implications for Tomasi's work. First, while she may merely be commenting on the limits of human attempts to influence cosmic order, she may, perhaps, be offering similar commentary on any possibility for such mediation, such as that of the saints. Second, she may be expressing an implicit recognition of the limits of her role as novelist to both produce and record "reality."

The relationship of this novel to the "labor" or "proletariat" novel of the 1930s must also be considered. The novel's opening, which depicts a labor strike at Granitetown's quarries, indicates that *Like Lesser Gods* will be about the labor activities of immigrant workers during the 1920s and 1930s (the period in which the novel is actually set). The novel demonstrates concern for the unsafe conditions under which the stonecutters labor, and the disease and death that these conditions cause. Early in the novel, Tomasi portrays the agonizing death of Italo Tosti from silicosis developed over his years of stonecutting in the sheds; in doing so, she foreshadows Pietro Dalli's death years later. She details the working conditions that foster the disease: the enclosed, airless sheds, the lack of ventilation and dust-removal equipment. She makes clear, too, that this disease is as foreign to the Italian stonecutters as the land to which they have migrated; in Italy the cutters worked in open air sheds, and the stone with which they worked was softer (and thus created less dust).

Tomasi also addresses the activist aspect of Italian immigrant labor; the novel's opening portrays the stonecutters' strike against the quarry owners, and their reaction to the incoming "scab" workers (who happen to be on the same train as Mr. Tiff as he enters Granitetown). Mr. Tiff, misinterpreting the townspeople's presence at the station, is moved to make a speech to express his gratitude for their warm welcome. However, upon hearing his Italian greeting and recognizing his status as a newly arrived immigrant, the crowd mistakes Tiff for a strikebreaker and pelts him with garbage and insults. After Tiff is safely escorted from the train, he sees a striking worker's daughter (who is later revealed to be Petra Dalli) taunting the child of a strikebreaker with epithets and a stick.

However, the tone of the novel shifts quickly and Tomasi departs from the "proletariat" tradition. Unlike novels such as Pietro di Donato's *Christ in Concrete* (1939), Tomasi is not interested in indicting capitalism or engaging in a critique of industry and its exploitation of workers. There is, in fact, a conspicuous absence of radical/Marxist language in her depiction, and the rest of the novel does not follow up on the opening's focus on the strike. Mangione and Morreale note that

> in the novel, there is a noticeable lack of reference to the radical movement that flourished among Italian immigrants.... [l]acking ... is the role of radical union members in Vermont in applying pressure on employers, which resulted in the adoption of safety measures to prevent silicosis. (372)[2]

Indeed, when these improvements do finally appear in the second half of the novel, Tomasi implies that they were made because of the quarry owner's recognition of the morality of such action (a stance which conveniently ignores the seventeen-year lapse between the first and second parts of the novel); the workers are appropriately grateful for this largesse, and everyone is happy. However, most studies of Italian immigrant history clearly document the unionist activity of stone workers in Barre, beginning in the late nineteenth century, activity so intense and successful that "Eventually, some [quarry] owners refused to work without union men" (Mangione and Morreale 282).

The contradictions within Tomasi's portrayal are evident. If Tomasi is upholding a specific social hierarchy (e.g., the position of the boss/owner above his workers), and presenting a community which accepts such stratification as a manifestation of the "right order" of the world, obviously she could not imply that the owner acted greedily or immorally by refusing to spend the money to modernize the sheds and make them safe, nor that the workers ever expressed anger or resentment for the blatant disregard for their health and safety. Yet labor history of the period documents such greed on the part of the owners, and radical activity on the part of workers against them. The obvious question, then, is why, if Tomasi regards herself as an essentially "realist" novelist, she would chose to ignore a significant aspect of Italian immigrant history in her work. An obvious answer comes out of consideration of the political climate in which this novel was written; by 1948, when the novel was published, the Cold War was well under way, with its accompanying "Red Scare" and anticommunist hysteria in the United States. As noted earlier, critics such as Lionel Trilling rejected as antithetical to genuine "American" experience, anything that smacked of "Stalinism" in American fiction. As an "ethnic" writer (and part of an ethnic group frequently targeted as a source of "anti-American" activity), Tomasi had much to lose by a sympathetic portrayal of leftist labor activity; she was also working against the legacy of the public's perception of Sacco and Vanzetti as "representative" Italian immigrants: murderous anarchists who seek to overthrow the American way of life. Tomasi's difficulty was compounded by the fact that, as noted in the Introduction, many northern Italian immigrants were in fact deeply involved in the labor movement and in political anarchy. Tomasi's struggle as a novelist, then, is to portray the Italian immigrant workers of the 1920s and 1930s, not as "rabble rousers," but as decent, hardworking, "good Americans." Additionally, as David Madden notes in his introduction to *Proletarian Writers of the Thirties* (1968), "[H]aving pursued the radical cause as a crusade based on the ideal world of brotherhood, the American writer, betrayed by the reality, experienced a disenchantment in the Forties and Fifties that was more bitter than his disaffiliation from capitalism in the Thirties" (xxii). In other words, Tomasi's rejection of the leftist sympathies of the proletariat novel of a decade earlier may also imply her recognition of this disillusion on the part of other writers.

Instead, Tomasi engages in the kind of "feminization" of the working class that Rosemarie Bodenheimer discusses in *The Politics of Story in Victorian Fiction* (1988). Bodenheimer asserts that many "social problem" novelists of Victorian England failed to recognize the working class as a potent political force; the result was either excessive romanticization of the worker's life, or a horrified retreat from its squalor. Thus, Tomasi situates her critique, muted as it is, within the context of the family romance. Very little of the novel's action takes place in the sheds; rather, it is set in the homes of the workers and, to some extent, in the social interactions among the families in the community. The family in this novel is, of course, a signifier of traditional Italian identification of the self within the family. However, it also allows Tomasi to critique the negative aspects of capitalism by showing its disruptive effects on the family; the workers are shown in loving (and sometimes sentimentalized) interactions with affectionate wives and obedient, happy children. These interactions are disrupted when, for instance, Italo is destroyed at an early age by silicosis, leaving behind a wife and several young children, or when Pietro is forced to leave his family to find work in another town. This strategy of feminization offers Tomasi a way out of the difficulties she may have created for herself as an "ethnic" novelist seeking acceptance into the literary mainstream. The workers' battles against the owners are seen not as expressions of anarchy and disrespect for authority, but rather as attempts to preserve and protect the family.

Tomasi's portrayal of the painful deaths of stonecutters such as Italo and Pietro, and of the necessity of safety equipment in the sheds, then, demonstrates neither that she is ignorant of the dangers these workers faced, nor that she wishes to pretend they do not exist. "Evil" is indeed present in this world—but it is a disembodied and abstract presence. This stance dovetails neatly with the traditional Catholic belief in Providence—evil exists in the world, evil which God permits but in no way causes. In turn, Tomasi is able to romanticize the response to evil; for example, Italo Tosti's widow Lucia steadfastly resists the romantic attentions of another stonecutter, becoming a metaphorical virgin/martyr figure in her fidelity to her husband's memory. That she successfully raises three boys, one of whom goes on to become a doctor, is testament to and reward for her upholding of her traditional role.

Additionally, Tomasi's portrayal of Pietro Dalli and his fellow stonecutters is not one of interchangeable human parts, laboring anonymously in the industrial machine, but of craftsmen and artisans.[3] Indeed, Pietro's pride in his status as a "lesser god" emphasizes this crucial difference between Tomasi's work and that of novelists such as Pietro di Donato. The stonecutters of Granitetown are portrayed as artists, each having an individual style; Pietro favors the roccoco in his carving, while his friend and fellow worker Ronato is dedicated to simplicity in artistic expression. The ornately carved cross over which Pietro labors in the first part of the novel, his "masterpiece," represents the endurance of his artistic spirit and confirmation of his *destino* (destiny) as a carver. Thus, Maria's destruction of it, in her desperate attempt to get him to leave the sheds and enter into a "safer" occupation, must necessarily fail. Ronato's decision later to take up the carving of the cross himself as a memorial for Pietro's grave completes Tomasi's design and reaffirms the "right order" of the world which the novel represents.

Similarly, Tomasi is not interested in commenting extensively on the ethnic and class differences that are typically part of the labor novel tradition. Tomasi portrays a community of workers of various ethnic heritages—German, Irish, Scottish, and Italian—that is integrated and free of conflict based on ethnic difference. In fact, all of these groups, including the Italians, unite against the incoming Italian immigrant strikebreakers at the beginning of the novel, suggesting that this new, "American" community takes precedence over Old World allegiances. Clearly, Tomasi's vision of America is a kind of melting pot fairy tale; each immigrant group is permitted to retain the best of its Old World traditions, discard the rest, and blend its beliefs seamlessly with those of other cultures. Tomasi makes clear that the one instance in which ethnic conflict appears, the quarry fight between Vetch Dalli and Baldieau (Americanized to "Baldy"), is based on personal animosity rather than ethnic prejudice. Additionally, the quarry owner, Alvah Douglas, though of WASP heritage, is portrayed as a benevolent, even admirable, figure who has his workers' best interests, rather than profit, at heart. Little, if any, resentment or anger is expressed by the workers toward his power and material success.

The closest Tomasi comes to portraying class conflict is the strike at the novel's beginning. The workers are striking not for safer working conditions, but for higher wages, a position which Tomasi critiques via Mr. Tiff. However, this critique makes sense in light of Tomasi's concern in the novel with the "right order" of the world. Mr. Tiff asks Italo Tosti to explain the reasons for the strike; when told that the workers are demanding higher wages, in violation of a contract they had signed the year before, Mr. Tiff reflects:

> Seeing Italo in his bed, his cheeks aglow not with health but with the fever of his illness, it was easy to believe that the workers were justified in demanding more pay. But the kindly, haunting face of old Don Benedetto [Mr. Tiff's superior at the seminary] quickly made a discipline of his mind, and he was forced to admit that whether or not they deserved more pay they should have abided by their agreement, or should not have made it in the first place. For, he was thinking, if man's word is abused, then agreements . . . become so much worthless scraps of paper, and no one has faith in them. The first Word had been duly fulfilled, and faith and hope had been instilled in millions. And surely society must follow this ex-

ample if it wished to live in a world of order. (32)

Thus, for Tomasi's vision to remain consistent, the workers must strike for higher wages, and not for safer working conditions. The latter may be seen as a reasonable, even moral, demand, and a strike in support of such a demand could be viewed sympathetically. However, Tomasi intends the opposite effect; the demand for more money (and, therefore, the strike itself) is immoral for, as noted, it is a direct violation of the workers' contract. Additionally, the desire for more money may be read as a sign of class envy—an implication that Tomasi scrupulously avoids. In fact, the only characters that exhibit such envy are viewed as either demented, as in the case of Aggie Rugg, or unsavory and dishonest, as in the case of Asa Conway. Thus, the workers are seen (and are shown to themselves through the guidance of Mr. Tiff) as merely misguided in their strike activity. Nonetheless, this scene remains fraught with contradictions, which may be why Tomasi felt the need to abandon quickly the tone set by the novel's opening and focus instead on the domestic aspect of the workers' community.

Mangione and Morreale attribute the stance in the passage quoted above to Tomasi's conservative Catholicism[4]; indeed, the allusions in this passage to Christ's ("the first Word") promise of redemption, to faith (both secular and religious), and to the belief that "a world of order" is indeed possible, reflect Tomasi's essentially Catholic outlook. What is important for Mr. Tiff (and for Tomasi) is that "law"—signing a contract, giving one's word—must always override emotional response. Tomasi's Catholicism also explains the resistance to leftist/communist implications in her portrayal of labor-management relationships.

Implicit in Tomasi's portrayal is the traditional peasant belief in *destino*—that is, the "right order" of the world includes a hierarchy of social and economic position, and it is futile, and even morally wrong, perhaps, to attempt to disrupt that hierarchy. Yet, other aspects of the novel undercut this implicit belief, for example, the act of immigration itself, which is often based on a desire for a better life, and the upward social and economic mobility of the Dalli children, particularly Petra, through exogamous marriage and college education. Thus, *destino* may not be an immutable force, but rather one to be negotiated with and perhaps even circumvented. Otherwise, it certainly would be difficult to explain the mass migration of the late nineteenth and early twentieth centuries, as well as to understand the ways in which women such as Tomasi were able to defy the old traditions that dictated women's roles. In fact, it may be that Tomasi's defiance of such roles also dictates her conservative treatment of Italian immigrant history in both her fiction and her nonfiction.

Interestingly, the strongest commentary that Tomasi makes on class difference is also tied to sexual difference; however, this particular instance is also portrayed as aberrant. Through Aggie Rugg, Tomasi offers some comment on the nature of capitalistic activity, the disparities in wealth it can create, and its negative effects; however, because Aggie is also portrayed as mentally unbalanced, once again Tomasi's critique of capitalism is thwarted.

Aggie is portrayed as plain, even unattractive, and as none too bright. Only in her mid-twenties, Aggie is already worn and blighted by a lifelong resentment against the Douglas family, based on her conviction that Alvah Douglas's grandfather swindled her grandfather: "the Douglas family should be blamed for her financial straits, for the unhappy lines in her plain face" (39). Aggie's built-up resentment, coupled with her grief over the deaths of Pete Rocco and Leo Vitleau, drives her to madness:

> There was no crowd to bother Aggie here on Douglas Hill, yet her head suddenly felt as if it were spinning, spinning, and she could not draw her eyes from the yellow-gold of the Douglas house. Had old Douglas built a house of yellow so that it would look gold? Look rich? If he hadn't bought that pasture land [from Aggie's grandfather], perhaps *she'd* been born in just as beautiful a house. Aggie's breath rasped in her throat. She swallowed a sob. It settled in a painful lump in her breast. And it became a violent, aching weight, for the spinning seemed to be draining her head of blood and rushing its added heaviness to her breast. (108)

The surfacing of this long-suppressed resentment impels her to attack Alvah Douglas, in whom she sees the comfortable and happy life of which she has been cheated. Her blightedness includes her sexuality, and her resentment of Douglas is based both on economic and sexual envy. Douglas is handsome, happily married, and has a child, while Aggie's only prospects for romance are represented by Paulie, unappealingly described as dirty and weasel-like, engaging in petty shoplifting and constantly wiping his nose on his sleeve. Aggie's digging of graves for Pete and Leo, portrayed as the pathetic gesture of an insane woman-child, suggests her burial not only of her anger, but also of any hopes she may have held for economic and social mobility. Her acceptance of this truth seems to result necessarily in her madness.

It becomes clear what Tomasi is trying to say about class and economic inequities with this event. She does not fault the Douglas family for Aggie's state; whatever injustice exists, she indicates, has been built up in Aggie's own mind. The townspeople generally agree that Douglas's grandfather acted fairly in his purchase of Eb Rugg's pasture, and that his subsequent discovery of the granite underneath it was purely serendipitous. Thus, she upholds the ideal of the "American dream," that with a combination of hard work, honesty, and, in some cases, good luck, one can achieve (and indeed deserve) social and economic success. She underscores this perception by indicating that Eb Rugg was a lazy alcoholic, unwilling to work the land and make it productive. Finally, she juxtaposes the Douglas success in land acquisition with the example of Asa Conway. Aware of a developer's plan to buy land for the construction of a sanitorium, Conway schemes to take advantage of the grieving Vitleau family, buying their plot cheaply and reselling it at a much higher price. His lack of success in this scheme (prevented by Mr. Tiff's fortuitous, unseen presence) is justified because his means of securing greater wealth is dishonest. Thus, in all instances of potential conflict—class, ethnic, or sexual—Tomasi's novel, like many novels in the realistic tradition, constructs "utopian moments that imagine resolutions to contemporary social conflicts by reconstructing society as it was meant to be" (Kaplan 12).

Ultimately, Tomasi's concern with the situation of immigrant laborers and their social and economic status remains on a personal rather than a political level. The roles that various female characters play in the novel reveal Tomasi's essential interest in the personal, domestic aspects of the immigrant experience. The central female figure, Maria Dalli, represents the crucial role held by the mother within the traditional family structure. However, she is not merely the mother; rather, as Mary Jo Bona notes, Maria Dalli and other mothers in fiction by Italian-American women "expand the confines of female possibility by their belief in themselves to be active, assertive, independent women *within* a familial framework of marriage and children" (*Claiming a Tradition* 28). That is to say, rather than portraying the traditional roles held by women in Italian culture as relatively powerless and restrictive, Tomasi is interested in showing the ways in which women wielded considerable influence from these positions. However, her portrayal of Maria also reveals the underlying contradictions inherent in traditional women's roles.

Tomasi emphasizes the emotional, spiritual, *and* sexual fulfillment Maria experiences in her marriage:

> Now [Pietro] took her by the hand, and together they sat on the edge of the bed, his brown mustache brushing her cheek. As always, a part of her wondered if twenty years from now his touch would still grow these cool little hills of delight along her arm and breasts. (27)

This passage is all the more startling when one considers the degree of sexual ignorance to which young Italian women were held, and the circumspect manner in which sexual knowledge was shared among women, as seen in the previous chapter's discussion of Rosa Cassetteri's memoir. Thus, Tomasi's acknowledgement of the possibility for and importance of sexual pleasure for women (within the confines of a marital relationship, of course) is an important feature of her treatment of Italian immigrant women's experience.

Though the Dalli marriage is painted in rather idyllic terms, it is not free of conflict—and Tomasi portrays a wife who is unafraid of expressing her opinions to her husband. The primary locus for dissent and struggle within the Dalli household is Pietro's work. As noted earlier, Maria's fears for Pietro's health impel her to rail against his stonecarving at every opportunity; Pietro's commitment to stonecarving as his *destino* forces him to reject her pleas and concerns. Neither will bend to the will of the other, and both conspire to marshal support for their position. Indeed, Mr. Tiff is no sooner ensconced in the Dalli household when both Maria and Pietro draw him aside to plead their case against the other. Representing Old World wisdom, Mr. Tiff listens patiently to both, and renders his decision. In keeping with his belief in what constitutes a "right and ordered world," he honors Pietro's prerogative as head of the household to decide what is best. Though he sympathizes with Maria's concerns, and half-heartedly argues these against Pietro's assertion that " 'for me there is no other work but stonecutting!' " (20), he concludes, " 'Sometimes for a man there is only one job at which he can be truly happy, and unless he is happy how can he give the best of service to his fellow man and to God?' " (15).

Maria's reaction to this logic tells much about the conventional gender roles of Italian family. On the one hand, she must be concerned with the preservation of the family; on the other, she faces the demand that she acquiesce in all matters to her husband's will and judgment. In response to Mr. Tiff's assertion, Maria asks, " 'What about service to his wife and children. . . . What service can he give anyone when he is under the ground?' " (15). However, she recovers her composure and reminds Mr. Tiff (and herself) that she knows where her loyalties must lie:

> "What kind of wife do you think I am? Do I love Pietro the less because in this matter he has a mind of his own? Strong willed, my father and mother called me! Yet the moment Pietro touches me, I am no longer Maria—I am Pietro, thinking and feeling as Pietro. . . . " (15)

Thus, Maria, for all of her willfulness, upholds the traditional roles—a man's primary commitment is to God and the larger society, a woman's to her husband and family. Yet, as Maria's dilemma demonstrates, a woman's traditional role may force her to choose between supporting her husband's wishes and ensuring the welfare of her children. Helen Barolini offers this commentary on the place and function of traditional women's power:

> The Italian woman's soul was in her consecration as core of the family, upholder of its traditions and transmitter of its values. In that role her hardships and sacrifices were repaid, her value inviolate, and this gave her a positive sense of her self and her power—power that was, however, often manipulative and always relative, confined as it was to the home environment and not used in the world at large. (*The Dream Book* 12)

In light of this analysis, and of Maria's character, it is easy to recognize her subsequent action as inevitable, its result necessarily inconsequential. Though she seems to abandon her fight against Pietro's profession, she plots a coup. Breaking into the carving shed late at night, she chisels away at Pietro's masterpiece, the ornately carved cross, in the belief that Gerbatti, the boss, will see the damage, blame Pietro for careless work, and fire him (or, at least, that Pietro, angered by accusations of carelessness, will quit). However, by Tomasi's design, this effort is destined to fail; Maria's attempt to exert her power beyond its rightful scope (that is, outside the home, in the public sphere) violates the right order of the world. Thus, Gerbatti recognizes the damage to Pietro's cross as "the intentional butchering of some malefactor" (148).

That Maria's action is a violation of cosmic order is underscored by Mr. Tiff in his role of intercessor. Again, he providentially discovers evidence of Maria's hand in the stone's destruction: a piece of cloth from her skirt caught on the window of Gerbatti's office. Though he assures her that he will never reveal his knowledge of her actions, he reprimands her, reminding her of her place in an ordered world:

> "Since the very beginnings of family, the husband's lot has always become the wife's. And justly so. Remember the wise Ruth who even made her mother-in-law's lot her own.... And the Roman bride of antiquity formally promised her husband—'Where thou art, Caius, there am I, Caia.' In the same measure your own promise... makes Pietro's lot your lot, and must accept it if you would keep his love." (149)

He reinforces his warning by asking her, " 'But suppose God had not been so generous with you? Suppose Pietro himself had come across that all-revealing piece of cloth . . . it would mean the end of everything beautiful and honest between you' " (150). Mr. Tiff's reprimand, and his hint that Maria's actions could drive Pietro into another woman's arms, have the desired effect. Maria's only concern now is "the vital urgency of preserving the happiness that was hers, Pietro's, and the children's" (150)—in other words, the primacy of family and her responsibility to uphold it. Again, Maria (and the reader) is reminded by Mr. Tiff that fidelity to form, to law, to a contractual promise (here, Maria's wedding vow) must supersede all other factors, including her fear of losing her husband to a terrible disease. Essentially, Maria's choices, both dictated by different aspects of her traditional female role, boil down to losing Pietro now, or losing him later.

Thus, for all her belief in adherence to custom and form, Tomasi demonstrates the terrible conflict and contradictions inherent in the traditional role of mother for Italian immigrant women. As Helen Barolini notes, one of the primary sources of conflict for the immigrant Italian woman was the Americanization of her children—a process which she, by cultural mandate, had to resist. Thus, "[un]able to Americanize on the spot, the Italian immigrant woman suffered instant obsolescence . . . and became an anachronism, a displaced person, a relic of remote rural village culture" (13). Thus, Maria's "old world superstitions" are treated as a source of amusement (as in Pietro's response to her insistence on testing wild mushrooms for poison by throwing a silver coin into the cooking pot) or as an occasion for rebellion (as in Petra's resistance to Maria's wish that she wear gold earrings as protection against eye strain).

Maria's adherence to these customs seems to be based not so much on her faith in their efficacy, but on the fact that her ancestors, specifically her *female* ancestors, practiced these same rituals. Petra's staunch resistance to having her ears pierced, then, serves to highlight in particular the *mother-daughter* conflict that immigration and assimilation often produced:

[D]aughters assert a need for self-identity and want to free themselves from the past patterns; in their self-actualization they *must* react against their mothers; and in denying the value of the mother's role by their rebellion against it, they lay upon themselves a heavy and terrible conflict. (Barolini, *The Dream Book* 11)

Petra's rebellion against her mother's will is not portrayed as disrespectful or disobedient; in fact, both Pietro and Vetch support her. Pietro recognizes that pierced ears are a mark of difference that will separate her from her peers and points this out to Maria; he proposes, instead, that Petra be taken to an American eye doctor. When Maria asks, " 'Is she ashamed, then, of her Italian blood?' " (130), he reassures her that Petra is not. However, he also notes, " 'But the day I took my final papers I became American; you too' " (131). Again, we are reminded that a contractual promise must always supersede any other issues. Additionally, Tomasi shows us that the mother's role of upholding traditional values becomes a trap—she has no other option but to do so, yet this very role renders her ineffectual and anachronistic in the eyes of her assimilated children. Thus, while *Like Lesser Gods* demonstrates Tomasi's interest in the preservation and documentation of the old ways, it also demonstrates her awareness of the necessary conditions of transition and loss for the Italian immigrant and implies that she is documenting a way of life that is rapidly vanishing by 1948.[5] Significantly, this transition is captured in the figure that is the primary symbol of the old ways—the Italian mother. Petra's rebellion in the first half of the novel prefigures the radical departure her life will take from her mother's in the second half of the novel. In fact, the first part of the novel concludes with Maria's vow to preserve her family's happiness and unity by submitting her will to her husband's; the penultimate scene of the novel is Petra's acceptance of Denny Douglas's marriage proposal.

Gabriella, the younger Dalli daughter, perhaps comes closest to reproducing Maria's conflict. However, the particulars of Gabbi's situation reflect the conflict and tension produced by the desire of the children of immigrants for assimilation and greater material success. Her insistence that her fiance, Robbie, quit his quarry job before they marry and take a position with the state, is based not on fear for his health but on pride—she is ashamed of his "blue collar" status. Like Maria, she vows to take matters into her own hands, much to Mr. Tiff's dismay. Like Maria, Gabbi attempts to usurp the right order, violating the "morals and religious principles into which she was born" (233), when she deliberately becomes pregnant, in the hopes that Robbie will give up his quarry job, which he loves, for the security and higher paycheck of state work in order to support a family. The scene between Gabbi and Mr. Tiff, who again providentially discovers what she has done and counsels her about the right course of action to rectify her mistake, is nearly an exact replica of the one between Maria and Mr. Tiff seventeen years earlier. In the background, figuratively and literally (because the sanitorium overlooks the Dalli home), is the example of Aggie Rugg, whose fate is an implicit warning against envy for money and status.

Given the ways in which Tomasi demonstrates the parent/child (mother/daughter) conflict in the struggle to assimilate, it is interesting that it is Maria's daughter-in-law who is most committed to recapitulating the traditional role that Maria embodies. Vetch's wife, Peggy Riley, is of Irish immigrant stock, yet she, rather than Petra, embraces Maria's traditional values. This relationship recalls Mr. Tiff's allusion to the Biblical story of Ruth, who embraced the lot of her mother-in-law, Naomi, as her own. Peggy's role as Ruth is captured symbolically in her request for Maria's recipe for spaghetti sauce, because it will please Vetch; later, it is underscored by Peggy's refusal to interfere when Vetch begins to spend his days drinking in the local tavern rather than going to work at the quarry. Though Peggy is pregnant and certainly has the right to object to Vetch's irresponsibility, she does not:

> [S]he was smart enough to know . . . what had attracted Vetch to her. . . . He liked her because she paid no apparent attention to his sullen, restless moods, because she didn't question him, and because she cleverly did not intrude into that aura of independence which he loved. (214)

Unlike Maria, Peggy makes no attempt to thwart her husband and thus becomes a caricature of the dutiful Italian wife—completely submissive to her husband's will and wishes. Peggy's "cleverness," then, is perhaps ironic—or it may be that Tomasi is presenting her as taking the path of least resistance, thereby saving herself from conflict and frustration. Indeed, she says, " '[Vetch] knows his responsibility. And if he doesn't—well, I'd rather lose him than send him away by criticizing him' " (214).

Petra, in contrast to Peggy, is presented as strong, imaginative, and independent from the beginning of the novel. While Maria symbolizes Italian immigrant culture in transition, Petra represents the success of assimilation. Through Petra we see one of the few hints of ethnic conflict presented in the novel. When Mr. Tiff reprimands her for taunting the daughter of a strikebreaker, she replies, " 'Anyhow, I'm glad there's a strike! Once, just once, a smarty-pants boy called me *wop*, but now everyone's too busy calling the [strikebreakers and their families] *bozos* to bother with me' " (18). However, Tomasi mutes this potential ethnic conflict — note that Petra says she was called *wop* "just once." The Vitleaus (the family whose daughter, Jean, Petra taunts) are quickly accepted into the community, and Leo and Jean become friends with the Dalli children. When the Vitleaus are eventually "driven out" of Granitetown it is not because of ethnic conflict. Rather, their departure is caused by the quarry accident that kills Leo, but which Vetch, who "belongs" to the community, survives.

It is also through Petra that Tomasi voices any criticism of the quarry owners for their failure to take earlier action to install safeguards for the workers. Denny Douglas, now back in Granitetown and running his father's company, asserts that " 'The shed and quarry owners have done a lot to help the workers in the past years.

They'll probably do more' " (203). It is significant that "[t]here was a hint of her mother's voice in Petra's" sharp reply: " 'The workers would probably still be waiting for the installation of suction hoses if it hadn't been made compulsory' " (203). Thus, while Maria is interested in protection on a personal level and directs her efforts for change accordingly, Petra's criticism is directed into the public sphere (though in an admittedly limited way).

Petra's friendship (and eventual romance) with Denny Douglas brings the theme of exogamy into the novel, a theme that is an essential piece of Tomasi's assimilationist vision. As Werner Sollors argues in *Beyond Ethnicity,* intermarriage is *the* metaphor for ethnic assimilation in much American literature; for Tomasi, ethnic intermarriage expresses her literal belief in the melting pot as the blend of the best of all cultures. All of the Dalli children marry exogamously; however, Petra not only marries outside of her ethnic group, but also outside of her social class. Tomasi employs the convention of the "two suitor" plot to explore the meanings of exogamy and social mobility through marriage for the second-generation ethnic woman.

Petra's suitors, Gino Tosti and Denny Douglas, represent the choices and conflicts faced by the assimilated Italian-American woman. Tomasi carefully sets up this triangle in the first half of the novel. Gino, on one level, is the obvious choice for Petra's mate. He represents the second-generation son who has "made good" and is a model of immigrant American success. (Italo, conveniently dead, does not have to worry about the old peasant dictum about making one's sons better than oneself; significantly, Pietro dies just before Americo leaves for college). Gino's return to Granitetown to establish his medical practice both upholds tradition—he returns to family and community—and defies it—he becomes the first doctor of Italian descent in the area. Petra's degree in nursing, then, and her cultural heritage, suggest a symmetry that almost demands a romantic relationship with Gino.

However, Tomasi's interest in depicting the successful integration of Italian immigrants into the larger society, as well as her faith in the melting pot ideal, make Petra's decision to marry Denny inevitable. She and Denny are portrayed as *simpatico* from childhood — both are spirited, artistic, and imaginative. In contrast, Gino, though loyal and loving, is depicted as solid and rather aesthetically unimaginative. Though Gino represents a social mobility of sorts, it is not the kind carefully bred over decades that Denny embodies.[6]

Despite Petra and Denny's ethnic, social, and religious differences, little opposition to their union is portrayed; though Alvah Douglas is not happy with Denny's choice, he does not actively oppose the marriage. Minna, in contrast, expresses reservations about Denny's conversion to Catholicism, but on oddly practical grounds:

> "I'm sure, dear, I can't understand why you should want to put yourself in the unpleasant position of considering as sinful something that the rest of us do not.

... Like not going to Mass on Sundays ... and eating meat on Friday. And if you want to be a good Catholic ... why think of all the discomforts you are asking for." (285)

Thus, her objection to her son's decision is based on a caricature of cultural heritage. Implicit here is Tomasi's critique of Anglo culture as having at its heart material wealth and physical comforts, rather than, as Denny says, a " 'philosophic system that seems to remain changeless through the ages ... something to hold on to in a world where everything changes' " (285).

Denny's remark points to yet another contradiction underlying Tomasi's presentation of Italian immigrant life. First, his description represents a romanticization of Catholicism which contradicts its reality as an often oppressive force. Second, it points to a paradox inherent in an Italian immigrant's life, that is, his/her fear of and resistance to change is undercut by the very act of immigration, with its implicit hope for change and improvement of one's lot in life. Thus, Petra's decision to marry Denny is a contrast to the exogamic marriages of her siblings, who choose partners from other immigrant groups and are of a similar socioeconomic background. Denny is a "real" American whose family history in America spans centuries instead of decades.

From Tomasi's perspective, then, Denny and Petra's marriage represents the best blending of the old and the new. The moment of consent between them is consecrated by the quietly euphoric image of "the slanting rays of sunlight ... on the Hill, ... quiet and faintly tinged with the lingering gold" (286). Their marriage literalizes Tomasi's melting pot fantasy; because Petra and Denny represent the best of their respective ethnic cultures ("the lingering gold"), their union promises a shining future that upholds, in a slightly modified way, perhaps, the "right order" of the world.

Of course, Tomasi's northern Italian background may have much to do with the way she chooses to structure her novel and to portray the relationships among her characters. Though northern Italians were more aggressive and were more likely to engage in agitated political and social activity, they also gained respect and acceptance more quickly than their southern counterparts; this acceptance may account in part for Tomasi's essential optimism. Additionally, the sense of superiority that northern Italians held may certainly account for the confidence they had for acceptance and success.

Marion Benasutti's *No Steadyjob for Papa* (1966) has received even less critical attention and commentary than *Like Lesser Gods*. Like Tomasi's work, it is semi-autobiographical and realistic (though it is set roughly ten to fifteen years earlier than Tomasi's novel); it is important for this study because it re-examines many of the themes and issues with which Tomasi is concerned in light of both feminist and ethnic revival movements taking place during the 1960s. Like Tomasi, Benasutti portrays Italian immigrant experience in a manner that is sentimental, romantic, and optimistic (like Tomasi, Benasutti is of northern Italian origin).

However, Benasutti tempers these qualities with clear recognition and explicit depiction of the injustices and hardships induced by class, gender, and ethnic difference. Claiming an ethnic tradition while critiquing the prejudices of mainstream culture was far less risky by 1966 than it would have been in 1948, as challenges to all aspects of "traditional" American life began to develop.

Marion Benasutti was born in Philadelphia, the daughter of northern Italian immigrants. She attended the Philadelphia High School for Girls, and later graduated from business college. Her writing career began during her time at Temple University; at the close of her first (and only) novel she thanks H.P. Lazarus of Temple's English Department, who advised her to turn to her family ("all I know," according to Benasutti) as a source of inspiration for her work. That one's family could be a valid subject for literature was clearly a startling idea for Benasutti (though there is no sense of the hesitation to reveal family "secrets," as seen in many other writers of Italian-American heritage), yet it attests to the power and significance of this institution in Italian-American life and art.

No Steadyjob for Papa is written from the point of view of Rosemary, second in a family of five daughters. The title of the novel is important, for it reflects Benasutti's recognition of and experience with the lack of secure work opportunities for many immigrants during the early-twentieth century. Their choices often limited by prejudice, illiteracy, and ignorance, many were forced to work in occupations that were physically dangerous, seasonal in nature, or dependent upon economic or political conditions beyond their control; even educated immigrants such as Rosemary's father (the eponymous "Papa") were often unable to make use of their education in America.

The title also refers to the temperament of "Papa." Though initially lured to America in 1892 by the promise of "Freedom, Wealth, and the Right to Pursue Happiness," Papa is temperamentally unsuited to "make good" in the American way. It is Papa's "natural hedonism" that makes the idea of a "steadyjob" (all one word in the narrator's household) so unappealing to him. Rosemary tells us:

> Papa was both happy and wise but he did not, alas, inherit from his maternal Italian ancestors the energy and industriousness that Mamma maintained was typical of the northern Italian. As our mother so often said despairingly, "That man! He is as lazy as a Neopolitan!" Really, it was sad that Papa had to work for a living. He would have been quite happy puttering about in his garden, tending to his strays, reading *The North American*, and fighting with Mr. Leopoldi, our neighbor, about politics and the Austrians versus the Italians. (33)

This passage points to several of the novel's central conflicts. Unlike Tomasi, who insists on muting most of these conflicts (though they surface, in spite of her conscious efforts to suppress them), Benasutti recognizes them as central, shaping forces of immigrant experience and literature.[7]

As in *Like Lesser Gods*, the primary conflict is centered in the parental relationship and arises out of competing notions about work. As noted above, Papa is a "natural hedonist," and the idea of a "steady job" is an affront to his nature. However, Rosemary tells us, "Work was [Mamma's] very nature; without it she would have been lost" (188). Indeed, it is significant that in Mamma's vocabulary the words "steady" and "job" are one; to her way of thinking, there is no job worth considering but a steady one. Furthermore, the relationship between Rosemary's parents reflects another dimension of the conflict between Maria and Pietro. Like Maria, Rosemary's mother rejects the aesthetic in favor of the practical; Papa, like Pietro, regards himself as an artist or craftsman. Rosemary sums up her parents' temperamental differences in this way: "Mamma would never, under any circumstances, have sold bread to buy hyacinths, while Papa would cheerfully have given it all away" (20).

Indeed, despite the fact that "Papa" is the central figure in the novel's title, it may be said that the title is somewhat misleading. However, it does point to a central fact of Italian immigrant family life. "No steady job for Papa" indicates that Papa, as male head of the family, is the central figure. However, through the title's use of negation, it becomes clear that *Mamma's* role is central to the novel; she is the touchstone by which various characters are defined. Through her relationship with Mamma, Rosemary defines herself as a woman and as an Italian. Mary Jo Bona, in *Claiming a Tradition*, reads the novel in terms of the conventions of the *bildungsroman*, recognizing the centrality of the mother's role in the daughter's development, awareness, and maturation.

Rosemary chronicles the endless cycle of her father's sporadic employment and his annual winter *dolce far niente* ("good for nothing"), when "Mamma was certain the very elements were in a diabolical conspiracy to keep Papa unemployed" (100). The novel focuses on the period during which the family lives in "Filadelfia," in a shabby house on what is locally known as "The Back Street." Though not the street's actual name, "The Back Street" establishes its position in relation to "The Front Street," "where the houses stood on neat squares of green grass, their front porches illumined at night by lamps on little wooden posts at the foot of each set of steps" (27). In contrast to "The Front Street" (and to Tomasi's idyllic "Pastinetti Place"), "The Back Street" is unpaved, with a muddy ditch running its length, in the part of town referred to as "Goat Hill because the immigrant Italian families who lived there had kept goats" (28).

Rosemary realizes that Mamma, much more than Papa, has an acute sense of the class differences that money (or lack of it) confers. Rosemary remarks that Mamma's hatred of life in the Back Street arises from the fact that "she hated the *feeling* of being poor that the street gave her. It seemed to rob her of her innate dignity; it demeaned her in a way that we, who were happy there, could not wholly understand" (33). Thus, Mamma's goal of securing a beautiful home becomes her obsession, "na bella casa" her battle cry, "money in the bank" her motto.[8] She, not Papa, masters the intricacies of American finance, despite her inability to read or to speak English; she sets up a savings account and purchases insurance policies, making her dream of home ownership a reality by the novel's end.

However, Benasutti emphasizes the painful and maddeningly slow nature of this process for Mamma. Her frustrations with Papa's disinclination to work steadily is compounded by her "curious, stubborn guilt" because she has produced only daughters, a "failure . . . [that] was a continual source of acute personal misery" (102). Mamma sees her five daughters as economic liabilities; not only are they unable to work (although eventually the two oldest, Trina and Rosemary, do so), they must be provided with dowries, however small, when they marry. Though Papa clearly adores his daughters, he too is given to making the frequent observation "that had our mother given him five sons he might have established a Dynasty, A Big Business, and then he would not have to work at all" (102).

Papa's desire to establish a "dynasty" points to a significant theme throughout Italian-American literature. Thomas Ferraro notes in *Ethnic Passages: Literary Immigrants in Twentieth Century America* that in much ethnic literature of mobility (what he calls the "up-from-the-immigrant-colony narrative"), an inherent tension exists between the family or clan identity, and the impulse to individualism that assimilation and capitalist success demand. According to this paradigm, then, Ferraro argues, some immigrant success stories such as Mario Puzo's *The Godfather* are mistakenly read as critiques of capitalist enterprise, and as triumphant romanticized affirmations of the family over the "myth of the self-made man" (13). While it is true that Puzo is refuting that myth, Ferraro asserts, he is also using the model of Italian family identity "to unveil and scrutinize the interpenetration of family and business" (13). In other words, rather than positing family and capitalism as incompatible forces, destined to conflict, writers such as Puzo show the ways in which they are inextricable from one another in the immigrant experience.[9]

Thus, Benasutti presents a similar recognition in *No Steadyjob for Papa*—that family cohesiveness and economic success are mutually dependent. However, she (and other female writers, such as Helen Barolini in *Umbertina*) extend this argument; unlike Puzo, Benasutti explicitly addresses the crucial role that women—grandmothers, mothers, daughters, and sisters—play in ensuring this success. In Puzo's work, the women are relegated to the margins of the story; they are "civilians," kept ignorant of the men's activities and confined to caring for the home and attending Mass to ensure the family's spiritual health—in short, they are models of ideal Italian mothers (even Michael Corleone's WASP wife, Kay Adams, embraces the lot of her mother-in-law, converting to Catholicism, attending daily Mass, and praying for the soul of her murderous husband).[10] Benasutti clearly presents an alternative perspective; in fact, it is the women of Rosemary's household who support the family through the leanest times by their persistence and ingenious ways of generating income. Thus, Benasutti points (though not consciously, perhaps) toward Zillah Eisenstein's assertion that while the patriarchal family supports male privilege, and that social patriarchy (which she distinguishes from familial patriarchy), capitalism, and male privilege are all mutually interdependent, the demands of capitalist success actually undermine the patriarchal family structure when women work outside of the domestic sphere. In other words, male privilege and authority are weakened when women have work opportunities outside the home (204–205).

In fact, it is made clear in the novel that Mamma is the better capitalist of the two parents. When Papa does eventually establish a lucrative and successful business, an essential difference between his and Mamma's natures emerges. Like Pietro, Papa regards his skills in concrete and brickwork not merely as a means of economic success, but as an artistic endeavor. Likewise, his naturally generous spirit impels him to take tremendous care in construction and materials. Thus, Rosemary reports,

> This netted [him] less profit . . . but enhanced his reputation for both honesty and craftsmanship and was probably its own reward, though Mamma insisted that if he would learn how to "cut corners" it might result in larger profits. It wasn't that Mamma wanted him to be dishonest, merely practical. But, as always, Papa gave full measure, brimming over. (146–147)

As Michael La Sorte asserts in *La Merica: Images of Italian Greenhorn Experience* (1985), it seemed to most Italian immigrants that

> the American child was raised to revere the father who could attract dollars to his billfold. A condition of poverty was examined as if it were the symptom of a terminal disease. Only good flowed from the constant acquisition of wealth, and only bad could come from the failure to do so. Work was the path to salvation, and the immigrants were enjoined to work and work and work. America was a nation of pragmatists; unless what one did made the cash register ring, it was not worth the effort. (146)

Max Weber's analysis of the origins of the Puritan/capitalist impulse in America in *The Protestant Ethic* (1958) reflects these immigrant impressions. Weber argues that in America, the pursuit of material wealth becomes a religious duty, rather than merely a matter of economic survival; covetousness is less dangerous than sloth, and poverty is *not* a meritorious state. Thus, in all respects, Mamma is a "better" capitalist (and, implicitly, a "better" American) than Papa. Her unflagging pursuit of "money in the bank," her unconcealed envy of Zia's beautiful house, and her bitter hatred of their poverty are, according to Weber's paradigm, hallmarks of a good American.

The issue of honesty, invoked by Rosemary, is easily handled within Weber's analysis. He asserts that rather than being a virtue unto itself, honesty becomes a practical tool within the capitalist enterprise. According to Weber, Benjamin Franklin's assertion that "honesty is the best policy" reflects the fact that "all Franklin's moral attitudes are coloured with utilitarianism" (52). Certainly, Mamma's morality may be defined in similar terms. Honesty is not valued because it is morally good, but because honesty (or, at least, the appearance of honesty) secures credit and continued business. Thus, for Mamma it is possible to make a distinction between "cutting corners" and "dishonesty" without invoking a moral dilemma.

Finally, Papa's desire for sons to establish his "Dynasty" is both an ironic commentary on the reality of the family's financial situation, and an indicator of the sexism within traditional Italian culture as well as American culture. The devaluation of daughters (and, by extension, women in general) and their roles as workers becomes an important theme in the novel. Benasutti presents the problem of the female worker from a larger perspective than that of the immigrant. Twice, Rosemary encounters genteel, Anglo, middle-class women whose education and socialization have done little to prepare them for the responsibility of providing economic security. The case of Miss Ida Stackpole is particularly wrenching, from Rosemary's perspective:

> Miss Stackpole's father, a retired professor of Romance languages at the University ... was an invalid. Reared like a lady, with all a lady's delicate skills, his daughter, middle-aged and inexperienced, and nowhere to begin to earn their living but in this factory where she folded men's underwear for ten wearying hours each day. (180)

Clearly, the "delicate skills" Miss Stackpole possesses have ill-prepared her for the economic realities of life without male support. Though Rosemary is fortunate enough to escape the heat, noise, and degradation of the mill after only a month, she realizes that "[for] Miss Ida Stackpole it would not pass so quickly, certainly not just yet, and I could not bear to think of her, loving Shakespeare and 'the Classics' as she did, in that small, hot cubicle folding men's underwear all day long, year in, year out" (182). Thus, Miss Stackpole, the elegant, refined, and educated middle-class woman, provides an ironic counterpart to Mamma, who, though illiterate and barely able to speak English, manages to acquire practical knowledge of American politics, history, and finances to provide for her family's needs.

We are led, then, back to the earlier assertion about the novel, the title notwithstanding, that Mamma is the central figure of the family and of the novel itself. She is linked in an essential way to another theme illustrated through Rosemary's narration: the inter- and intraethnic conflict. Frequently this conflict is illuminated by Mamma's actions and comments, though Rosemary herself is not immune from expressions of ethnic prejudice. Surprisingly, the first instance of such expression comes early in the novel, when Rosemary describes the "essential" differences between northern Italians (such as her family) and those of the *Mezzogiorno*:

> I suddenly had this feeling about the Italians from the south who were with us in the wagon, their faces darker, their features thicker, their voices not as melodious as the one I was used to. All at once I felt sorry for them, sitting there a little apart in the cherry pickers' wagon ... while the northerners ... chattered among themselves in

their quick colorful way.... (4)

This acute sense of difference between northern and southern Italians, of course, is a remnant of life in Italy; though it was unified as a country by the time of the greatest wave of immigration in the late nineteenth century, the sense of cultural difference between the northern and the southern regions (and even among the southern regions) was such that national identity meant little, while regional identity was all. Indeed, "[t]he unification of Italy . . . exacerbate[d] the conflict between North and South, and contribute[d] to conditions that would . . . provoke the 'great hemorrhaging' of [Italians]" (Mangione and Morreale 27). Those from the northern regions of Italy were culturally conditioned to regard those from the south as inferior in every way. Thus, Mamma's earlier remark that Papa was "as lazy as a Neapolitan" reflects genuine intraethnic conflict, as well as the prevalence of regional stereotypes that pervaded Italian culture. Of course, ignorance on the part of most Americans caused them to lump all Italians together, regardless of regional origin, a fact deeply resented by all Italian immigrants.

A second site of ethnic conflict is that between the Irish and Italian immigrant communities. This conflict is expressed in Benasutti's presentation of the Lacey family, centered in the relationship between the mothers of the two families. Of course, the primary battleground is the Church; though Mamma considers herself and her family to be good Catholics, her failure to engage in and promote regular practice of the Faith scandalizes Mrs. Lacey, who is "more Catholic than the Church itself" (49). That Mrs. Lacey takes her obligation as a good Catholic to evangelize is evident by her sponsorship of Rosemary and Trina's First Communion, and her active campaign to bring Mamma "back to the Church."

Though Mamma does not object to Rosemary's more active participation in Catholic practice, her suspicion of Mrs. Lacey's "Irish" interference (matched only by her general resentment of the English), and her resentment of the time that both Rosemary and Trina spend at the Lacey home, create tension. The strained relations between the two women are exacerbated by the elopement of Trina and Larry Lacey; Mamma's devastation at the loss of Trina's contribution to the family bank account is matched by Mrs. Lacey's grief over Larry's rejection of the priesthood. Present, too, though not explicitly stated in the narrative, is the fear of change and loss of cultural identity as the result of exogamous marriage—a perspective very different from Tomasi's advancement of the melting pot ideal.

Ironically, peace is made between Mamma and Mrs. Lacey when another of Mamma's conflicts is resolved. The death of Nonna (Rosemary's paternal grandmother, who immigrated with Mamma), as Rosemary notes, ends a relationship that, though outwardly cordial, was strained by mutual jealousy and resentment. Though custom dictates that Mamma prepare Nonna for burial, "there had been too much between them to separate them in life, and now that Gran'ma was dead Mamma could not bear to touch her" (221). Mrs. Lacey takes over this role for Mamma; Mamma's gratitude, coupled with her discovery that her "enemy," the

English, is one that she and the Irish have in common, dissolves the tension between the two families and allows her to accept Trina's marriage.

Though Rosemary seems not to understand her mother's attitudes and conflicts, we see as the novel progresses how deeply she does understand and share them. Part of Rosemary's process of maturation, and the development of her relationship with her mother, involves her eventual recognition of the affronts to her own dignity that being poor, female, and Italian confer. Her confrontation with the wealthy young members of the nearby tennis club makes her inferior status real for her as it never was before:

> *Wop!* It wasn't the first time I'd heard that word but it never before seemed to belong to me. . . . And then it came, the bitter, stifling shame. All at once I was full of hate, of my mother and father, of the place I lived in, which . . . was now, by a single cruel word, made dirty, unclean. (85–86)

First, like other incidents in the novel, it offers a stark contrast to the muted presentation of ethnic prejudice in Tomasi's work. Unlike Petra's experience in *Like Lesser Gods*, Rosemary's shame and bitterness in response to the epithet "wop" are presented in vivid detail. Rosemary's identity becomes conflated with her ethnicity. Her humanity is erased; her mute, startled retreat after she is hit with a switch by the club's caretaker renders her similar to the animal with which her home ("Goat Hill") has become synonymous.

The significance of this event for Rosemary, of course, goes much further; Benasutti's presentation links the difficulty of transition and assimilation to the mainstream culture for the Italian immigrant to Rosemary's transition from child to woman. While running home from the Tennis Courts, she wets herself, compounding her shame further by what she considers a "babyish" response to confrontation. However, she comes to an adult awareness of the consequences of class and ethnic difference, and moves from innocence to experience in one swift moment: "All at once I knew how Mamma felt about this house, the Back Street; her bitterness was mine. . . . Gone was the dreamy time under my tree on the hill. . . . all beautiful, all mine, all devastated" (86). Later that night, Rosemary gets her first period. The emotional pain caused by the incident at the Tennis Courts, which metaphorically awakens her from her naive ignorance of ethnic and racial prejudice, is paralleled by the physical pain of menstrual cramps, which literally awakens her from sleep.

The central figure in helping Rosemary cope with her emotional and physical pain is, of course, Mamma. Her "unassailable logic" gives Rosemary some comfort, as she reminds Rosemary of their Italian cultural and historical heritage and tells her, should such information fail to silence tormentors, to "politely punch them in the nose!" (89). Mamma comes to her immediately in the night, telling her not to be frightened, that " 'It is natural—to become a woman when you are twelve or thirteen' " (95).

Yet, for all this, Mamma is unable to satisfy Rosemary's needs through the mother-daughter relationship. Mamma is unable to express physical affection, though Rosemary makes frequent pleas to her: " 'Hold me Mamma, put your arms around me and hold me!' " (94). Certainly, this portrayal challenges the stereotype of the effusive, overly emotional Italian mother; however, it also emphasizes Benasutti's portrait of Mamma as being the most "American" of the family. As Michael La Sorte notes in *La Merica*, Italian immigrants regarded Americans as emotionally cold and were "struck by . . . [their] inability to express public emotion" (147). This lack is most poignantly felt in the aftermath of Rosemary's devastating encounter at the Tennis Courts. She attempts to comfort herself through her favorite escape, reading; the book she chooses, ironically, is entitled *Rose Marion*. Rosemary's anguished response to the saccharine description of Rose Marion's blue-eyed beauty and impossibly idyllic relationship with her mother reveals the depth of her emotional pain: she hurls the book out of the window and cries " 'Oh Mamma. . . . Love me! Love me! I need you!' " (88).

Rosemary becomes angry at her mother, too, for her failure to prepare her for her sexual maturation. Indeed, much of the novel chronicles Rosemary's largely unassisted coming to terms with sexual knowledge and growth, and the particular meanings these have for women. Benasutti captures both the wonder and the terror of sexual maturation as Rosemary gazes at her naked body in a full-length mirror for the first time:

> But now there was someone else in the room with me. She came toward me as I walked over the soft rag carpet. We met halfway between the room's closed door and the long mirror attached to the closet. Fearful and uncertain, I came closer. Did she look like all the girls in the whole world? Or only unbelievably like herself? Was she, perhaps, beautiful? I did not know. This was the first time we'd met, she and I, face to face. Naked, I did not know myself. (114–115)

Significantly, this encounter between Rosemary and this "stranger" occurs not in her own home, but at the Pierces'. Rosemary's ignorance of herself reminds her of her mother, whose body no one, not Rosemary, not even Papa, has ever seen in the light. Though Rosemary believes her mother "must have had . . . a flawlessly beautiful body," she cannot know for sure, and she reflects, "So much beauty . . . lost to the world. Poor Mamma!" (115).

Two incidents in particular frame her growing awareness of her sexuality. The first is her encounter with Stuart Malcolm. When he takes down Rosemary's hair and kisses her, she experiences for the first time a sense of the sexual dimension (as opposed to the merely romantic) of male-female relationships. His kisses destroy forever Rosemary's naive, fairy-tale notions of innocent romance: "it had robbed me forever of Alex Truelove and his galloping white steed, of Lassiter and of Ronald Coleman and of all the fairy-book heroes who had sustained me in the long dreamy days that were gone" (120).

However, there is a curious other dimension to this incident. Rosemary first takes Stuart's gentle admonition to "Be true to yourself" as a clichéd attempt to humiliate her further for her failure to understand the social conventions of Peggy Malcolm's party—wearing the wrong dress, drinking too much mulled wine, and, consequently, falling during a game of musical chairs. However, his repetition of "Be true to yourself" erases her earlier shame. She is reminded of a fable that her grandmother is fond of telling, about a boy who goes searching for "the house with the golden windows" he sees in the distance, only to realize when he reaches it that his own home is that house. The connection she makes between Stuart's words and Nonna's story awakens in her the knowledge that "there was my world [as opposed to the world of Peggy Malcolm], and that it could be anything, anything at all I chose to make of it" (120). Thus, Stuart reaffirms her self-esteem and sense of her own power and possibility. Her ethnic identity, earlier turned into a source of shame and grief, is resurrected as a source of pride and strength.

Significantly, Rosemary transfers this new sense of herself to a renewed connection with her mother: "I hugged the thought of my mother close to me as I opened the door" (120). Rosemary resolves to "go forward" and help Mamma achieve her dream of "na bella casa": "'We'll be true to ourselves, Mamma, and God will let us have a nice house, just the way you want it' " (121). Thus, the development of Rosemary's identity serves not to separate her from her mother, but to strengthen the bond she feels with her.

However, the second incident which provides Rosemary with new insight into male-female relationships reveals an aspect of sexuality that is negative and ugly; her sense of self, as well as her identification with her mother, are undermined once more. Papa's client's attempt to molest her when she goes to collect his bill bears marked resemblance to her encounter with Stuart Malcolm. He, too, takes down her hair and tries to kiss her, but instinctively Rosemary recognizes a difference between his and Stuart's actions. The powerlessness of her situation — she is young, female, and from a poor immigrant family from Goat Hill—dawns on her fully after she has escaped more or less unharmed. Again, her emotional response is directed toward her mother. Her first thought is how she will explain to Mamma the loss of her hairpins; suddenly, however, her anger with the client's actions is transformed: "I was suddenly furious with [Mamma]. There was a lone nickel in my pocket. It would never occur to my mother that perhaps I should have some extra change in case of emergency" (198).

Significantly, Rosemary uses that "lone nickel" to purchase some hairpins before returning home, ostensibly out of worry over Mamma's anger for the lost hairpins. However, the act of putting her hair back up also symbolizes her need to regain some dignity and control. The connection between being without money (whether because one is actually poor, or is denied access to it by one who has it) and being female comes alive for Rosemary in a very painful and startling way: "Why did I have to learn about life like a smack in the face?" (198). She begins to see the triangular relationship between money, power, and sex in that instant, realizing that the man feels he may molest her with impunity because he is male and wealthy.

Yet the fact that she is still a child, and still largely ignorant, is made clear when she arrives home. Knowing that she cannot ask Mamma to explain what has happened to her (or, at least, believing she cannot), she turns again to literature to find some answers. Her earlier refusal to read past page 80 of *Tess of the D'Urbervilles*, where the seduction/rape scene occurs, is driven by her unwillingness to accept sexual knowledge—particularly a depiction of sexual violence, as opposed to the dreamy, romantic portrayals of love which were more palatable to her. However, she now seizes the "Song of Solomon," recognizing, though not fully comprehending, its expression of sexual knowledge: "I didn't, and I wouldn't understand it, but I was determined to get educated anyway I could" (199).

Rosemary's ignorance places her in stark contrast with her older sister, Trina, who "really wanted to know" and would "eavesdrop shamelessly" (92) on Mamma and the other women who would come to visit occasionally. Thus, "Trina got to know about things"(93)—"things" being knowledge of the realities of physical maturation for women and its consequences. Rosemary, in contrast, would avoid hearing these conversations, even though she was often openly present in the same room, by reading: "[I] never heard a word, lost as I was in Sir Lancelot and Zane Grey's Lassiter, who was even more romantic than Lancelot" (93). Thus, Rosemary worries about her sister's relationship with Larry Lacey[11]; she reflects, "Trina had never read a book. She did not know about Lassiter and Sir Lancelot. . . . How, then, could she be expected to know about love, romantic love?" (193).

This passage reveals an essential difference between not only Rosemary and Trina, but between Rosemary and Mamma (whom Trina resembles strongly in outlook and temperament). Rosemary's love of words and of the world of the imagination comprises yet another theme in the novel. Her engagement with words and with literature is both confining and liberating. As noted earlier, her naive acceptance of the world portrayed in some of her favorite novels leads to some painful awakenings. Yet her development as a reader and her decision to become a writer also marks a departure from her cultural heritage, and from her mother as role model. Rosemary's aspirations offer an illuminating example of what Thomas Ferraro refers to as "ethnic passage." He writes:

> [I]t takes a profound degree of cultural self-distancing for a member of an impoverished immigrant enclave to be in the position to write in English. . . . When individuals from genuinely illiterate or impoverished backgrounds become writers, they pass through or somehow short-circuit far more common and reliable forms of mobility, freely choosing the special kind of marginalization involved in becoming a writer. (9)

Ferraro's observations confirm what writers such as Helen Barolini have said about their passage to authorship, in particular, the notion that for *women* the degree of "cultural self-distancing" is even greater. As in *Like Lesser Gods*, the most obvious self-distancing occurs in the mother-daughter relationship. *No*

Steadyjob for Papa may be read in part, then as Rosemary's struggle to balance her need to identify with her mother, to support and to be supported by her, with the need to "be true to herself" and make her own way. Despite her overwhelming love for her mother, Rosemary necessarily distances herself from her mother's life and experience, and suffers the painful conflict that such distancing engenders. The gap that develops between Rosemary and Mamma, and the resulting guilt and anger are evident in the following exchange, which occurs while Rosemary is home for the first time after taking her position as a live-in caretaker for Mrs. Pierce:

> "What is it like in that house of the rich?". . . .
> "Oh, Mamma, it's wonderful. . . . Rugs on every floor and a big couch . . . and books—books everywhere, everywhere! And pictures! Beautiful pictures with frames of gold."
> "Books? Pictures?" Mamma said impatiently. "What else? What of the stove in the kitchen? And the stairs to go up . . . are [they] open . . . all polished and shiny and open?"
> "Oh, yes, Mamma . . . [and] I use the back stairs to go up to my room."
> "Like a servant!" Mamma muttered. . . .
> "But I don't feel like a servant, Mamma, I feel like—one of them!"
> "Go!" Mamma cried angrily. "Go back there, then. . . . Now we are not good enough for you, it seems!" (109)

This scene echoes the earring conflict portrayed in *Like Lesser Gods*; Papa steps in to defend Rosemary just as Pietro did for Petra. Yet again we see the ways in which the immigrant mother's traditional role as center of the family inevitably sets the stage for conflict with her increasingly assimilated children. Nonetheless, the conflict here is not as pronounced as it may seem. Though Mamma's practical nature prevents her from sharing Rosemary's love of words, literature, and the fine arts, she supports her aspirations for authorship and for higher education—much to Rosemary's astonishment. Practically, of course, Mamma realizes that a college education will provide greater economic opportunities for Rosemary; ultimately, however, Mamma also realizes that these things satisfy Rosemary's soul in the same manner that having "na bella casa" will satisfy hers.

However, it is also important to note that for most ethnic writers, the passage that begins with distancing the self from its cultural heritage often ends with a *return* to that heritage.[12] For example, Benasutti's presentation of the development of Rosemary's authorship may certainly be read in an autobiographical context. In an author's note at the end of the novel, she reports her inability to discover a subject for her fiction; when her writing instructor advised, "Write about what you know," she replied, "But all I know is my family!" Thus, her novel was born, as she discovered that her family, the family, could be a compelling subject for literature.

Thus, these two novels, taken together, represent what Mary Jo Bona calls in

Claiming a Tradition a "coming of age" for the second generation, in a dual sense, that is, for the fictional characters portrayed in these works (Petra and Rosemary), as well as their authors. Though Tomasi seems to be most interested in affirming patriarchal order and the ideal of ethnic integration, careful examination of *Like Lesser Gods* reveals an acknowledgement of the inescapable tensions and sacrifices created by immigration and assimilation, particularly for women. Likewise, though Benasutti acknowledges more explicitly both the ethnic prejudice and sexism faced by Italian immigrant women in their transition to a new identity, the ending of *No Steadyjob for Papa* undercuts its more "radical" vision, and aligns it more closely with the melting pot ideal expressed in Tomasi's work. Mamma's dream of a beautiful house is finally fulfilled; the novel ends with the family moving into a home in Germantown, owned by an Irish Italophile. The house is covered in wisteria, a plant which, as Papa points out, was named for an Englishman—thus pointing to a truth of life in America: " 'Therefore, one cannot escape the English' " (232). Likewise, Rosemary is left dreaming of dates with the fair-haired college boy who lives across the street. This may be read, of course, in light of Rosemary's essentially romantic nature. However, Benasutti also indicates a faith, similar to Tomasi's, in the virtues of exogamy as the best means of assimilation by portraying Mamma's recognition and approval of this situation: " 'A handsome young man who is probably regarding us as gypsies. You have four daughters yet to wed, Gio. When we come [to the new house] we come without Clara and this—this dead wagon [a horse-drawn hearse]. We come with dignity to Germantown!' " (236).

However, the fact that the novel's last word literally belongs to Mamma (she determines that Zia, the sister-in-law whom she has envied for so long, will be the first visitor to their new home) reiterates Benasutti's challenge to the conventional treatment of the Italian family. This ending, in fact, looks with hope to the future much in the same way that the conclusion to Tomasi's work does. Rosemary reports that the joy and excitement of acquiring a home has transformed Mamma: "Gone was the reserve we were so familiar with. Mamma was a new, exciting stranger" (243).

This "new, exciting stranger" may well represent Tomasi's and Benasutti's sense of themselves as "ethnic" writers, as well as their belief in their works as important contributions to the body of American literature. Both *Like Lesser Gods* and *No Steadyjob for Papa* exhibit the essential optimism that Rose Basile Green asserts "seems to have evolved from the immigrant's successful accomplishment of his immediate goals in America" (19). These authors demonstrate a clear sense of the family itself as a protagonist of Italian-American fiction, amplified by the voices of its various members. By any standards, their output is meager—Tomasi having published two novels, Benasutti only one. However, this fact points to a reality of publication for most of the early figures in Italian-American fiction; interest in their work was limited to a "local-color" conception of their writing, and this in turn resulted in a limited response (or, at least, a belief that the response would be so limited the work was not worth promoting).

Clearly, however, there are some important differences between these two writers. The historical context and political climate in which Tomasi's novel was written dictates her more careful attention to tone and her strong desire to present these immigrants as good Americans willing to embrace a new culture; her determination to mute ethnic conflict and mitigate the extent and effects of immigrant labor activity is clearly a response to fear of accusations of "Stalinist" sympathies. It may even belie a discomfort with her heritage on Tomasi's part, as she strives to depict Italian immigrant life in an essentially romantic (and therefore non-threatening) manner.

Benasutti's work is also marked by an essential optimism for immigrant success and acceptance in America. However, her optimism is tempered by an open acknowledgment of the ethnic prejudice, gender oppression, and violence that sometimes accompanied the assimilation process. The shift in context, which entailed a surge in ethnic pride and growing criticism of the dominant Anglo-Saxon social order allowed Benasutti to be more open in her presentation of immigrant family life. Thus, Benasutti's novel is a "bridge" work in this chapter, for she exhibits strains of Tomasi's earlier romanticism and optimism, while pointing to future directions in Italian-American women's fiction. Her work bears important relationships to novels studied in subsequent chapters; the work of Dorothy Bryant, studied in the next chapter, examines more explicitly the sexual and ethnic prejudices that inhibit and limit the roles of women, a theme taken up by all of the writers studied in later chapters. Nonetheless, both Tomasi and Benasutti strive to position their ethnic culture and their "author"ity within the framework of the larger culture by the act of writing and assert their faith in the belief that, by doing so, "there will be a valid record of the literary art of the American people" (Green 25).

Chapter Three

DOROTHY CALVETTI BRYANT:
THE SUBM/VERSION
OF ETHNIC IDENTITY

Dorothy Calvetti Bryant (b. 1930), a prolific writer living in the San Francisco area, has produced works of fiction, nonfiction, and drama, and has received awards for her novels, dramas, and publishing (she began Ata Books in 1978 to ensure publication of her books). Bryant's significance for this study lies in the ways she defies categorization—both in terms of the variety of her output, and how she sees herself as a writer. She writes,

> "Italian-American" writer is one of several labels that, at one time or another, are attached to me [by critics such as Helen Barolini, Fred Gardaphé, and Mary Jo Bona], like "Woman writer," "Feminist writer," "Bay Area writer," "California writer," "working class writer," and so on. I am all of these things when I draw on experience denoted by them, and none of these things when anyone attempts to confine me with a label. (Personal correspondence)

Despite her insistence on downplaying critical perception of her as an "Italian-American" writer, Bryant's works represent crucial moments in the development of the Italian-American women's literary tradition. Indeed, her assertions about her identity as a writer bear remarkable resemblance to Chicana poet and theorist Gloria Anzaldùa's notion of a "mestiza" or "borderlands" consciousness:

> Cradled in one culture, sandwiched between two cultures, straddling all three cultures and their value systems, *la mestiza* undergoes a struggle of flesh . . . of borders, an inner war. . . . [she] copes by developing a tolerance for contradictions, a tolerance for ambiguity. . . . Not only does she sustain contradictions, she turns the ambivalence into something else. (*Borderlands* 78–79)

Bryant was born in 1930 in the Mission District of San Francisco, in what she describes as "a working class, immigrant neighborhood." Her immigrant parents were born in Balangero, in northern Italy; like Rosa Cassetteri, the members of both families worked in the textile mills from an early age. Bryant's paternal grandmother came from a comparatively upper class family; she married a man who left for American shortly after the birth of their first child (Bryant's father). Bryant writes, "It took [my grandfather] ten years and three trips to persuade my grandmother . . . to come to America with him." Bryant adds, "Perhaps she hoped that if she held out, he would return, as many others had, finding life in America much too hard."

Her maternal relatives followed a similar pattern of immigration. However, her maternal grandfather (who seems to be the model for the brutal immigrant father portrayed in *Miss Giardino*) was "considered shiftless by my father's family." Both families gradually made their way across the United States, following "a network of *paesani*" to California, where Bryant's parents eventually met and married, much to his parents' dismay. Bryant grew up in the Bay Area, achieving a level of educational achievement not seen before in her family, completing college and acquiring teaching jobs in San Francisco and the East Bay.

Bryant's experiences as the child of immigrants, and the conflicting messages she received in such a household, are reflected in the novels she writes, particularly in the two novels discussed in this study. She notes that while her parents were both literate and valued education, there were no books in their home; thus, the library became her source for reading and learning about the world beyond her tightly-knit family. She notes how the centrality of family, and the woman's role in preserving its integrity, was instilled in her at an early age:

> [Women] not only cooked and cleaned and supervised the children, wrote all letters. . . . they worked at jobs full time and saved all their money to set their husbands up in a business that they, the women, took responsibility for managing. They were more literate and better educated than the men. . . . but they always deferred to the men in decision making. My mother often said "Your family comes first," and she usually added that a woman must give more than a man to make a marriage work. She was both proud and bitter at carrying this burden. (Personal correspondence)

Bryant notes that while her observations about the women in her family taught her that "women were strong, capable, responsible, educable, and able to do pretty much whatever they tried to do," she also realized that these qualities were valued only insofar as they worked to "the benefit of the family."

The two novels examined in this chapter, *Ella Price's Journal* (1972) and *Miss Giardino* (1978), have the strong autobiographical roots seen in works studied in the previous two chapters. However, Bryant's novels are more explicitly engaged with feminism and demonstrate greater awareness of the negative impact of immigration and assimilation than the novels examined in the previous chapter. They bring together the ambiguities and contradictions of the contemporary Italian-American woman.

Ella Price's Journal, Bryant's second published work, chronicles the emotional and intellectual development of a thirty-five-year-old Bay Area housewife. Though widely reviewed when published in 1972, there has been almost no critical work on *Ella Price's Journal*. The one exception is Lisa Maria Hogeland's reading of it as an exemplar of the feminist consciousness-raising novel, a term Hogeland created to examine a genre that includes works such as Erica Jong's

Fear of Flying (1972), Allison Lurie's *The War Between the Tates* (1973), and Marilyn French's *The Women's Room* (1977). Hogeland takes the term "feminist consciousness-raising novel" from the process first outlined by Kathie Sarachild, which in turn evolved from the so-called "rap sessions" formed by small groups of women, beginning around 1966–67 (Morgan xxvi).[1] Ella describes herself initially as "an average person with a nice home, a good husband, and a lovely daughter. I lead an average life" (18). Significantly, Ella does not come from an Italian background; nonetheless, the novel demonstrates an explicit concern with dominant themes in Italian-American women's fiction which were outlined in the introduction: traditional gender roles, education, and the centrality of family.

While it is obvious that this novel embodies the development of consciousness raising, it is also true, as Hogeland points out, that

> it does not make explicit its allegiance to the WLM, indeed does [not] mention Women's Liberation at all.... The echoes of Friedan and de Beauvoir suggest that Bryant knows feminist writings, but chooses not to show Ella reading them. (187)

Bryant herself disavows any direct influence of feminism on her work; she writes:

> I don't really see myself as being much influenced by feminist thought. I see myself as being encouraged and fostered by that thought, which brought me readers.... But the ideas and rebellions pushed by the young feminists of the 1960s and 1970s were not new to me.... I don't want to minimize the effects of activist feminism. It made me feel freer to say the things that were on my mind, but I don't think it put new Ideas in my mind, that is, not that came into my fiction. (Personal correspondence)

While such disavowal may seem disingenuous, at best, particularly in light of Hogeland's observation that Bryant's novel seems to be taken directly from Sarachild's outline of the consciousness-raising process (187), it points to a different angle from which to examine *Ella Price's Journal*. That is, while Ella's story may certainly be interpreted in relation to the development of feminist thought and fiction during the late 1960s and early 1970s, it may also be read as the response of an uneasily assimilated immigrant to the contradictory demands of two cultures. Recognition of Bryant's ethnic background and the relatively recent immigrant history of her family leads to recognition of the parallels between the structure and theme of the consciousness-raising novel, and what Thomas Ferraro calls the "up-from-the-immigrant-colony" novel, a tradition out of which many "ethnic" authors work. Examples include Abraham Cahan's *The Rise of David Levinsky* (1917) and Anzia Yezierska's *Bread Givers* (1925); Ferraro includes more recent works such as Mario Puzo's *The Godfather* (1969) and Maxine Hong Kingston's *The Woman Warrior* (1976) in his own study of the genre, *Ethnic Passages: Literary Immigrants in Twentieth-Century America* (1993). Such novels, Ferraro argues, are not merely chronicles of generational transmission; rather, they are "improvised strategies to deal with the unequal distribution of wealth, power, and status" (21)—a strategy shared by the consciousness-raising process and the consciousness-raising novel.[2]

Ella's initial characterization of herself as an average, contented person is underscored a few pages later in her journal. In response to an assignment to write about "A problem you are struggling with," she writes:

> My biggest problem right now is finding time to go to the beauty parlor—or should I give up looking like a Barbie doll? I don't have any real problems. I'm healthy. I have a happy marriage. My daughter is pretty and happy. No problems. No real problems. (26)

However, Ella's somewhat defensive protest is almost immediately undercut in an entry made two days later, in which she admits, "There's something wrong with me. I was all right until about a year ago, but then . . . no that's not true. I was never all right" (27). She goes on to describe an experience that, as Lisa Hogeland points out, bears all the hallmarks of Betty Friedan's "problem that has no name" (187).

Many scholars of Italian-American experience and literature have identified various phases of both literal and literary assimilation; the descriptions of these variously identified stages bear strong resemblance to Kathie Sarachild's formulation of the consciousness-raising process. Rose Basile Green, in her seminal work on the Italian-American novel, outlines five stages in the development of this literary tradition. The first, which she calls early impact, is characterized by a need to explain and examine the problems surrounding the immigrant's introduction to American culture. The second, the need for assimilation, reflects the desire of the immigrant to embrace and be embraced by the larger culture (a process which, Green notes, may be accompanied by violence); this stage is followed by a "revulsion" (Green's term) into non-Italian themes. The fourth stage, counter-revulsion, reverses the previous stage; while returning to Italian-American themes and subjects, it demonstrates a greater degree of integration with the national culture. The final stage, rooting, is the creation of a "mature fiction" that reconciles the old culture and traditions with the new (23–24). Carol Bonomo Ahearn, in an essay entitled "Definitions of Womanhood: Class, Acculturation, and Feminism," outlines a similar four-stage process she applies specifically to the writings of Italian-American women; her paradigm bears distinct hallmarks of the feminist consciousness-raising process. The first stage, which she refers to as the immigrant stage of trust and hope, is characterized by optimism about one's prospects for a better life, as well as an essential faith in one's cultural values. The second stage is characterized by shame and doubt about one's heritage, while the third, role confusion, examines the conflicting demands made by two cultures. The final stage, integrated autonomy, is a resolution of the competing demands (126).

Both of these categories of novels are literary stereotypes—the consciousness-raising novel represents a general feminist notion of what women (and, it has been argued by feminists of color such as Alice Walker, bell hooks, Cherie Moraga, and Paula Gunn Allen of what *white, middle-class* women) go through, and the "up-from-the-immigrant-colony" novel represents a general ethnic notion of what immigrants go through. Both are highly undervalued subgenres as well, frequently dismissed by critics as formulaic and parochial. However, as Ferraro argues of the immigrant success story, it is crucial "to read . . . instances of the genre so well on their own terms that one wonders how any of them were ever taken to be mere formula stories" (17); the same must be said, in this instance, about the feminist consciousness-raising novel. Bryant's intention in *Ella Price's Journal* is to illustrate the ways in which traditional constructions of "the female" and "femininity" restrict and limit middle-class women and deny them status as intelligent, autonomous beings; she also means to illustrate the process by which these limitations can be challenged, a classic theme of feminist literature. While Ella's transformation is depicted as liberating and exhilarating, it is also traumatic; the fears that Ella expresses in her journal, as well as the fears of those around her, particularly of her husband, reflect in important ways the immigrant's fear of transformation and change. Thus, I would argue that Bryant chose to use the form of the consciousness-raising novel (though she does not make explicit use of that term) to foreground her concerns regarding gender identity, but also because she recognized the parallels between American women and the immigrant in their respective struggles for identity and for social, political, and economic power. The fear of transformation, and the loss of old ways of thinking and living, is an important element of both feminist and ethnic fiction.

As explained by Richard Gambino in *Blood of My Blood: The Dilemma of the Italian-Americans* (1974), *la via vecchia* ("the old way") sums up the world view of the poor Italian immigrant. However, *la via vecchia* was not merely clinging blindly to tradition (though, in its worst manifestations, became simply that), but a manner of living carefully cultivated over centuries. It was developed in response to and as a defensive posture against a seemingly endless parade of oppressors. An essential component of *la via vecchia* was *l'ordine della famiglia*, "the unwritten but all-demanding and complex system of rules governing one's relations within, and responsibilities to, his own family, and his posture toward those outside the family" (3). One's family became the only institution that merited complete loyalty and trust; included in this code of rules was a careful delineation of gender roles, particularly that of the mother, whose identity as a sexual being was often muted or denied by her position as the stable center around which *la via vecchia* revolved.

The all-consuming importance of preserving *la via vecchia* naturally became very difficult in the face of pressures induced by immigration and the demands of assimilation. Indeed, the very fact of the mass exodus of poor peasants, particularly from southern Italy, in the late nineteenth century is astonishing, given the generally fatalistic acceptance of *la misèria* (the terrible political, economic, and physical conditions of southern Italy) that characterized the outlook of that region. A Sicilian proverb, cited by Gambino and other scholars of Italian-American experience, expresses both this fatalistic attitude and the urgency felt by most Italians to preserve their way of living: *Chi lascia la via vecchia per la nuova, sa quel che perde e non quel che trouve*—"Whoever forsakes the old way for the new knows what he is losing but not what he will find." Thus, Bryant's portrayal of a woman's exploration of the new takes on dimensions of both ethnic and gender difference.

Though not of Italian descent, Ella possesses an ethnic/immigrant identity that establishes her marginality early in the novel. Originally from Nebraska, her family migrated to San Francisco in search of work during the upheaval of World War II. They are labelled by established Bay Area residents, including the Irish Catholic family of her husband Joe, as "Okies"—barely a step up from the black and Italian families who have similarly migrated to California.[3] Her family's "immigrant" status (underlined by the subtext of Bryant's own Italian immigrant heritage in the novel) must be recognized as a force with which Ella must contend in her struggle to define herself and to establish her identity. Her process of growth and transformation through education reproduces a tension found in many immigrant texts; while on the one hand it frees her, exposing her to new ideas and possibilities, it also separates her from her family. At first, she feels guilty for leaving them behind (metaphorically) and for making them feel "dumb" in comparison; ultimately, this guilt and shame are transformed into resentment of and anger over their stubborn refusals to change and dogged attempts to hold her back.

At the beginning of the novel, Ella's world is firmly centered on her family—her husband Joe and daughter Lulu; her identity is circumscribed entirely by the terms "wife" and "mother." As noted earlier, Ella asserts that these relationships are satisfactory and fulfilling; however, it becomes evident that these traditional roles leave a gap in her existence—hence her decision to go to college. As Ella becomes more deeply involved with words, ideas, books, and the discovery of her own intelligence and strength, she recognizes how the roles of wife and mother confine and limit her as an individual. She also feels societal pressure to maintain a sexual identity, one that, as her professor puts it, demands that she look like "an aging Barbie doll" (23). An early entry in her journal hints at the confusion she experiences as the result of these demands, which seem contradictory because of the ways motherhood and female sexuality are presented to her:

> You know, if you're a woman you can be nice and decent and intelligent. . . but if you're not attractive to men . . . you're a failure. And to know that, after a certain age, no matter what you do you're not going to be attractive to men anymore—what do you have left, motherhood? That doesn't last long, unless you keep having one child after another. . . . Don't you see that women wouldn't look like female impersonators if they had something else to do? (37–38)

This passage clearly demonstrates Ella's recognition of the conflation of "beauty" and "sexuality," and the way that such standards for beauty distract (or, at least, attempt to distract) women from developing their intellectual lives. It also emphasizes Ella's belief that for women there are only two choices—the sexual Barbie doll or the asexual mother (an oxymoron if ever there was one)—neither of which is realistic, fulfilling, or permanent.

Part of Ella's difficulty initially is her inability to separate her being/existence from that of her husband. Joe Price is portrayed as handsome, lackadaisical, physically strong, but with little interest in the life of the mind. Their marriage, at first glance, seemingly enacts the "equal marriage" archetype described by Annis Pratt. Joe characterizes himself as "stupid," reminding Ella constantly that they are a perfect match: " 'brain and brawn' " (216). He professes to value her intelligence, asking her " 'Who wants to live with a stupid woman?' " (216) (Never mind that she must live with a "stupid" man.) Thus, he gives Ella the illusion of equality, the illusion of a complementary partnership. However, the reader recognizes quickly what Ella comes to know gradually: that Joe actually fears her intelligence as it becomes clear that she is leaving him behind. What he really values about her is her weakness, insecurity, and dependence. Long believing herself to be "sick and neurotic," (a self-concept Joe strongly, if silently, supports), she depends on Joe completely—a role he relishes and is loath to relinquish. Thus, we (and Ella) see that it is indifference, and eventually, fear, rather than genuine stupidity, that hold Joe back as Ella progresses.

Ella's transformation, however, is painful and slow. Initially, her journal entries reflect a rigid, fearful, and defensive approach to her English class. She wants to study grammar; she is dismayed by the book requirements for the class, which include *The Autobiography of Malcolm X,* and is fiercely resistant to the journal assignment. She is upset by class discussions that challenge her traditional middle-class values. In her journal, the only medium through which she feels she can safely challenge her professor, she writes:

> I think you encourage young people to be disrespectful toward their elders and leaders. After all, doesn't disrespect for leaders account for most of the disrespect for law and order and decency in this country and in this college? (22)

Clearly, Ella is entrenched in a way of thinking and living that she considers decent, moral, and, above all, safe. Indeed, it is remarkably like the world view expressed by Mari Tomasi in *Like Lesser Gods*. Founded on respect for and obedience to authority, and centered in the family, Ella's perspective reflects that of traditional Italian culture as it has been "whitewashed" (Barolini 26) by American assimilation. Her suspicion of the conduct of her professor and the content of the class reflects what Helen Barolini calls "the Pinocchio personality—so much emphasis and energy are given to being transformed into conventionalized 'good guys' that life is distorted . . . real live people . . . have become dummies of virtuous platitudes" (26).

Joe's character perhaps best embodies the results of such complacency and convention. Ella tells us several times that Joe is perpetually happy and is very popular due to his good looks and happy-go-lucky attitude. His philosophy summarizes his "simple" needs for contentment: " 'I'm happy as long as I can eat, drink, and screw' " (44). Ella values and admires Joe's simplicity, seeing in it the stability and constancy she believes she cannot achieve on her own. Her anxiety, in fact, arises in part from her inability to be satisfied with Joe's three basic needs and her belief that something is wrong with her, that she must be "sick and neurotic" (a phrase she applies to herself frequently) for wanting more. Thus, in response to her professor's assertion that "anyone who could live in this world and not be sad, let alone anxious . . . must be either stupid or evil" (38), she defends Joe's disposition by arguing "that being unhappy isn't necessarily a virtue, that maybe it's a sign of weakness or sickness"(38).

Subsequent journal entries reveal the depth of Ella's dissatisfaction and anxiety. She confesses, for example, to thoughts of suicide. Though she concludes with the claim, "I don't think I really mean it" (41), her writing reveals the desire to escape her family and her "normal, happy" life; it also reveals the psychic burdens induced by the pressure to assimilate. In one entry Ella writes: "I wouldn't feel that I had to work so hard to be normal, at least on the outside" (40). In another entry, she relates a favorite activity: perusing the For Rent ads and imagining herself living alone, "sitting in a chair, surrounded by a few of my own things, only my very own things, and hearing distant sounds of strange people" (42). She also relates another fantasy, in which she comes home to find the house burned to the ground, her husband and daughter trapped inside, gone, "and every single thing that was a part of my life with them" (43).

Ella's mental activities are clearly the deepest violations imaginable under traditional Italian thought. Thoughts of being free from the family, in traditional Italian culture, is betrayal of almost unthinkable enormity, especially for a woman. Ella has positioned herself (at least outwardly) as the ideal Italian female figure — her identity is circumscribed by her roles as wife and mother, and she is totally dependent on male support (financially and emotionally); however, Bryant is intent on portraying a woman capable of breaking away from tradition. Indeed, Ella's revelation that she has frequently taken part-time jobs to pay bills incurred by Joe's periodic bouts of extravagance points to a theme already discussed in *No Steadyjob for Papa*—that is, the crucial role that women often play as wage earners outside the home. In this case, however, working outside the home is not merely a matter of survival, or of securing necessities; rather, it is the result of the desire for the trappings of middle-class suburban life and the rampant consumerism such desire invokes.

The novel's theme may, in part, be summed up in a quotation from Albert Camus that Ella cites in her journal: "Beginning to think is beginning to be undermined" (25). The journal, in fact, documents the consequences of "beginning to think"—that is, as Ella begins to examine her life and the beliefs by which she has lived, her life begins to come apart. Ella's fear of the psychological consequences of such unravelling is reflected in the following passage:

> Suppose a person has the feeling she's done everything just the right way, and hasn't made any mistakes to speak of . . . And then one day, she wakes up in the morning and she says, "Oh, no, this was not the way to do it at all. My whole life has been a mistake." But it's her whole life, and it's over, so wouldn't it be better not to know? (36)

However, Ella quickly concludes that, yes, it is better to know, and she realizes that fear is part of the process: "You can't be brave unless you're afraid" (43). Nonetheless, at this point in her development she is still afraid of being afraid, which reinforces her sense of herself as "sick and neurotic." She is thankful that she has a "sane" man such as Joe to "take care of [her]" (44).

Ella and Joe, in fact, represent two responses to transformation and change. Ella presents Joe initially as her safe haven; she can count on the predictability of his responses to any situation. However, the reader recognizes that Joe actually represents utter stasis and dull conventionality. This stasis is symbolized by "a joke he tells all the time, the only joke he knows" (44), about a soldier wandering about, searching for some unknown thing, picking up random items and saying "That's not it." When served discharge papers for mental incapacity, the soldier gets what he's been searching for.

While it initially captures the absolute stasis of Joe's existence, the joke comes to represent Ella's transformation in the novel; it also makes direct reference (though not consciously, perhaps) to the Sicilian proverb cited earlier. Ella's vague feelings of dissatisfaction, and her searching for solutions are like that of the wandering soldier. The "That's it!" for Ella — her "discharge papers" so to speak — come in several forms. The first is her journal; the writing she does allows her to examine the source of her dissatisfaction, to speak of those things which she cannot discuss with Joe (or anyone else in her family), and to reflect honestly, and to question openly everything she has taken for granted. The second form is the novels that she reads; as Hogeland notes, "Consciousness-raising becomes novelized in *Ella Price's Journal* — not just, that is, the structural device of a novel, but also a process Ella undergoes by reading novels and measuring her life against them" (187). Finally, her ultimate "discharge papers" come in the form of her divorce from Joe.

Like the soldier in the joke, Ella is viewed by those around her as "crazy," for leaving a "happy" marriage, "abandoning" her daughter and husband, and having an abortion. Significantly, from her family's perspective, her "insanity" is caused by her education. This formulation of education as exposure to "disease" reflects the deeply ingrained Italian immigrant mistrust of education, indeed of any institution that challenges or threatens the family, particularly for women. Helen Barolini writes:

[A]n educated woman was (is) looked on with deep suspicion: the emancipation of the mind put her outside familial control, beyond male authority, and that had to mean intolerable license. The psychological warfare between the family and its progeny is still in fierce engagement. (9)

Ella experiences the ferocity of this "warfare" frequently throughout the novel. As her awareness develops and her beliefs are altered, she makes the mistake of trying to share her new awareness with her uncomprehending and unaccepting family. Consequently, family gatherings become ideological battles; for example, she quarrels with her brother-in-law at a Thanksgiving dinner over U.S. involvement in Vietnam. Ella is anxious "to show off what [she's] learned," but quickly realizes that "It didn't matter what I told him, he didn't want his ideas shaken" (74). The rest of the family becomes "resentful of [Ella] as a troublemaker"; later, when she attempts to apologize to her mother and explain her position against the war, her mother says, "But you don't have a son, and your first duty is to your family, not to get mixed up in other people's problems" (74–75). Later, when Joe informs her parents of her decision to have an abortion, their reaction is predictable:

My duty to my family. Shirking my responsibility. Doing something then trying to escape the consequences. What would Joe's parents think? What had she done wrong in raising me? I had always been . . . etc., etc. (203–204)

It is not only Ella's family who challenge her need to be educated. Because of her age as well as her gender, her desire to obtain a college education is viewed as a source of both suspicion and amusement by others. Other women who, like Ella, are middle-class housewives and mothers, resent her growth, and disguise their resentment with snide observations about " 'neglect[ing] my family' " or " 'tak[ing] classroom space away from some young person' " (73). Even fellow students seem to resent her presence in the classroom; they frequently react sarcastically or impatiently to her participation in class discussion. To other professors, she is a cliché: "Another bored suburban housewife" (173).

While Bryant generally presents education in a positive light, clearly demonstrating faith in its power to free an individual from restricting circumstances, there is also an underlying critique of education as an institution in the novel. Typically, in immigrant experience (and literature), public education is represented (or represented to them) as the key to Americanization, the means by which aspirations for social and economic success could be fulfilled. A classic statement of immigrant faith in the riches offered by public education is captured in Mary Antin's autobiography, *The Promised Land*:

The apex of my civic pride and personal contentment was reached on the bright September morning when I entered the public school. The day I must always remember, even if I live to be so old that I cannot tell my name. To most people their first day at school is a memorable occasion. In my case the importance of the day was a hundred times magnified, on account of the years I had waited, the road I had come, and the conscious ambitions I entertained. (198)

In this novel, however, Bryant questions the reality behind the democratic ideals and impulses of American public schooling. The junior college at which Ella takes courses is infused with pronounced gender, racial, and class conflict; the student cafeteria is the site where difference becomes spatially arranged. There, Ella encounters several students who, like herself, feel marginalized by their social or economic circumstances. They point out to her, in hostile tones, the "black" table, the "jock" table, the "Greek" table, and their own group, " 'the so-called intellectuals, which means we actually mention books and ideas while we drink coffee' " (64).

However, the students are not the only ones who recognize the social and economic divisions that characterize the college, and the ways in which they act as barriers to real education. Dan's cynicism is rooted in his recognition of the same hostility that Ella has witnessed; as a professor, he believes that he, too, is fighting a losing battle. He reflects:

"[Students] come to me, asking to learn how to read and write better so that they can get a place in the system. But there is no place for them. It was all decided, a long time ago, who was getting a place in the system and who wasn't. . . . They [support] all the lies that they're victims of: that competition is great because it weeds out the unfit, that if everybody got an education they'd all have good jobs, that they're free. . . . Oh, the poor bastards." (97–98)

In this presentation, "Americanization" via education becomes nothing more than indoctrination into the exclusionary practices of America's gender, race, and class structures. This is re-emphasized as other students question Ella's motivation for being in school. One young woman asks her, " 'Why do you come . . . you don't need a job or anything. You got a husband to support you and you're on that hill; what else do you want? You got everything you need' " (64). They scorn her desire for "learning for its own sake"; to them, the purpose of a college degree is " 'to-help-my-people' " or " 'to get me a good job' " (65). As Dan bitterly notes, " '[They're] furious at the quality of this place, but [they're] part of it too' " (66).

Bryant's critique of higher education becomes linked in crucial ways to her critique of gender roles in the novel. The novel interrogates the role that is the heart of the Italian female's existence: that of mother. Though as Lisa Maria Hogeland notes, "Bryant's critique of marriage and motherhood here is rather mild" (190), it is nonetheless deeply ingrained in the narrative. Through her reading, Ella begins to question the maternal role and its "natural" status in female existence. First, Ella knows that her Catholic mother-in-law views the fact that Ella has only one child as "too obscene for words" (89); however, Ella herself is an only child, her own mother proud of the fact that she did not have many children like "cheap white trash." She is constantly compared to her sister- and brother-in-law, "now up to five children and with all the moral superiority of being such superparents" (89).

Early in the novel, Ella's relationship to her daughter Lulu is represented as less than ideal. Though Ella loves her daughter, a curious tension between them is evident. Lulu is much like Joe; she is attractive and popular, all Ella was not at the same age. At first, Ella assures her reader (and, obviously, herself) that she is relieved and happy that Lulu will not have to endure the kind of isolation and self-doubt that she experienced as a teenager. However, we gradually come to recognize that Lulu's self-assuredness is born out of an essentially selfish and spoiled nature. Like Joe, she is uninterested in and eventually threatened by Ella's return to school; for example, Lulu is angered when Ella informs her that she cannot work for extra money for the customary extravagant Christmas presents because of her classes. Later, Ella finds Lulu on Joe's lap, "looking not like a little girl but seductive, wheedling, manipulating . . ." (85).

Ella's fury with Lulu after this incident may be read as latent jealousy over Lulu's social ease, intensified by her startled recognition of Lulu's incipient sexuality, and Lulu's manipulative use of it in her relationship with Joe. However, Bryant presents Ella's anger in terms of the incident's potential effects on her education: "But if [Joe] did give her money, that means we'll be getting behind on the bills again, and how can I go to work and school both?" (86).

In wondering "aloud" about her relationship to her daughter, Ella examines and exposes several myths surrounding maternity. She, in fact, relates her experience of motherhood in largely negative terms; she also begins to question motherhood as the "natural" and inevitable consequence of female sexuality:

> I remember how I felt about [the pain]. . . . shock that it was so great. . . . And then I was resentful, angry that I was to be torn apart in this way as part of the normal course of events. . . . And I remember that when I got pregnant I was angry. I pretended to be happy and all the rest of it but I wasn't. I hadn't decided—it had happened to me, in spite of being careful. (70–71)

It is significant that Ella's journalistic reflections on motherhood arise out of her response to novels she is reading under Dan's direction, such as *Emma Bovary*. Though Dan insists that she read Emma's story (and others like it, such as *Main Street* and *Anna Karenina*) as indictments of provincial and stifling societies, and cautions her against "just being sentimental [in] want[ing] the survival of the character as if she were a real person . . . [and] just want[ing] a happy ending" (77–78), Ella cannot help but react to the novels on an emotional level, using the stories of their protagonists as a way to understand, analyze, and articulate her own frustrations. She characterizes Emma (= Ella?) as "a very stupid woman who created most of her problems" (68), and criticizes her for having an "unnatural" attitude toward her child, "never paying any attention to her" (69). But as she stops in her journal to reflect on Dan's question about her own "maternal feelings," she admits, "After [Lulu was born] I had another feeling . . . a nagging feeling that there was something else I should be doing instead of doing things with Lulu" (71). Significantly, she adds, "I don't feel that way when I'm studying." Thus, Ella's use of literature to effect (at least in part) her intellectual and emotional transformation parallels the phenomenon studied by Ferraro in *Ethnic Passages*: "the cultural transformation of the literary immigrant" (7).

Ella's conflicted experience of motherhood, and her sense that this role is *not* what a woman's life ought to be about, is also tied to her own role as a daughter. She recalls her mother's frequent observation that raising a child is the most difficult job in the world; Ella knows "that sentence was full of meanings. It meant, 'I worked so hard raising *you*.' It meant, 'Nobody could ever be as good a mother as I was.' It meant, 'Now you must sacrifice yourself as I did' " (71). In other words, a "good" daughter can best repay her mother's sacrifices by *reproducing* them in her own adult life. Torn between two "martyr-mothers," Ella feels both guilty about and resentful of her feeling that she is a failure as a woman.

Interestingly, the real changes Joe observes in Ella as an individual are accompanied by perceived changes in their relationship. As Ella becomes increasingly involved with her academic life, Joe accuses her of losing interest in sex: " 'You never feel like it anymore. . . . You'd rather read a book or something' " (80). Ella's response is predictable; she feels guilty for having "neglected" him, apologizing and promising "I'd devote more time to him and Lulu while I was on vacation from school" (81). Yet, when she stops to consider his remark, she realizes "that it isn't true. . . . [w]e make love once or twice a week just the way we always have" (81). Clearly, then, Joe, either deliberately or subconsciously plays upon Ella's fears of failure—in this case, failure to be a "good" wife, and to fulfill her duties in that role. By challenging their sexual relationship, too, Joe also challenges Ella's sense of her womanhood. She writes, "Any time that I don't enjoy sex much, I feel ashamed of myself for feeling that way. . . . Once women were ashamed if they enjoyed sex. Now women are ashamed if they don't. In one way or another the shame is there, but the rules change" (81).

Ella's conflicted feelings about motherhood, daughterhood, and her sexuality become tied in significant ways to her education. I would argue, in fact, that her sexual attraction to Dan Harkan is based on intellectual, rather sexual, awakening; however, she confuses the one for the other because it is still easier to see herself solely as an object of physical desire. This self-perception is confirmed when Ella relates a recurrent dream about giving birth to a girl, which Dan interprets as a manifestation of her love for him: " 'When a woman is in love she wants a child by the man she loves. . . . your deeper instincts, the *real woman* [emphasis mine] in you, comes out in this way—in dreams' " (162). Thus, though Ella does not realize it, Dan undermines her earlier realization that female sexuality and maternity are not "naturally" and inevitably linked.

The coincidence of the development of Ella's sexual attraction to Dan and her newfound willingness to take intellectual and emotional risks in her life develops significant themes in the novel. Her participation in the anti-war march is a defiance of authority that both terrifies and thrills her. She begins to speak out in her classes, and to challenge her family's traditional beliefs. Her inability to challenge Dan, however, is evident when she relates her insight into the "failures" of Emma Bovary and Anna Karenina: they were created by male authors who could not ultimately accept the notion of a successfully rebellious woman, so "[the authors] had to destroy them" (79). However, when Dan rejects her insight, Ella accepts his verdict, feeling "shot down again" (80).

Ella's unquestioning acceptance of Dan's rejection of this insight reveals the limits of Ella's progress. While she sees their affair as a defiant acting out of her own desires, it inevitably leads to frustration and disappointment. She finds herself once again lamenting the unequal share of sexual responsibility she must bear in order for their affair to be consummated; sitting through a seminar on contraception at Planned Parenthood and resenting Dan, she recognizes the Catch-22 of her position: "It was up to me to take care of all these indelicate things . . . so that our love affair could be safely impetuous!" (161). In the end, Dan proves inept as a lover, and the affair fizzles out in a morass of awkwardness and embarrassment. Ella learns that she is just one in a string of Dan's affairs, a joke and a cliché to other professors on the faculty.

Ella's friendship with one these other women, Laura Wilkens, is the only relationship Ella experiences that is based on common interests, and in which she can express her ideas openly without fear of ridicule, censure, or indifference. Second, Laura represents, in a sense, a progression a few steps beyond Ella's; she has already passed through the stages of growth and resistance that Ella is currently experiencing. Though one critic argues that Ella's consciousness-raising process "is depicted as individual and private" and that Bryant "isolat(es) Ella from the WLM" (Hogeland 195), Laura's own involvement in feminist social activism, as well as her role in supporting and advancing Ella's transformation, does bring the Women's Liberation Movement into the novel, if only tangentially.

Most significantly, Laura allows Bryant to refer to her own ethnic background and to reinforce the "immigrant" theme of the novel: " 'My maiden name was Locatelli. Does that tell you anything? My family is so shocked at having a divorced woman in it that they hardly speak to me' " (140). Laura's painful present offers Ella a glimpse into her own future, and brings the reader back to Ella's earlier question: "[W]ouldn't it be better not to know?"

That question, and the introduction of Laura's character, reflect both the consciousness-raising and the "up-from-the-immigrant-colony" strategies and themes of the novel. As noted, Laura effects, in part, Ella's consciousness-raising process; this parallels a common strategy in immigrant novels, the depiction of the newcomer's relationship to a more experienced predecessor who acts as an agent of the acculturation process. Second, Ella's fears of forsaking her old life in pursuit of the new, and her frustration with the unsatisfying results of her attempts to change so far, are similar to what Carol Bonomo Ahearn identifies as the third stage in the acculturation process, which she describes as one of "role confusion, where the goals of one's heritage, one's personal goals, and the the goals of the new culture ... all seem to be irrevocably at odds with each other" (126). Finally, Laura's experience as an Italian-American woman—her husband's jealousy over her pursuit of independent goals, her family's horror at her divorce, the neighborhood husbands' view of her as easy sexual prey—brings to mind two concepts relating to traditional Italian constructions of womanhood. The first is that of *mala femmina*. Literally "bad woman," *mala femmina* connotes bad in a dual sense: such a woman is not only morally deficient, but a failure *as a woman*. The second concept is that of *puttana*, a term for prostitute, but also used to refer to any woman "who do[es] anything without [her] husband" (DeSalvo 94).

Laura's story also introduces another important theme of the novel: a "sweeping" critique of the psychiatric profession (Hogeland 191) and its crippling and manipulative effects on women who turn to it for help—a theme that is repeated in Helen Barolini's *Umbertina* as well as in other novels in the feminist consciousness-raising tradition. Laura's experience when her son Marty turns to therapy to help him cope with his discovery that he is gay reveals a primary quarrel that Bryant (and many feminists) have with psychoanalysis:

> "[I]f a boy is homosexual, we all know whose fault it is.... I know that whatever factors operate in this, my son has chosen this *at least partly* as an ingenious method of torturing me.... [But] if I say it, it stands as proof of my paranoia, my neuroticism—proof that I did ruin my children." (142–143)

Clearly, Bryant critiques the ways in which society's (and, by extension, traditional Italian culture's) placement of the mother at the center imprisons women in a role that offers a false sense of power—power that is, paradoxically, both illusory (because her hold and control over her children often become tenuous, at best) and all-encompassing (because she is held responsible for every aspect of her children's lives).

Ella's own experience with psychiatry reiterates and enlarges Laura's. Her decision to go into therapy, like the immigrant's decision to embark on a voyage to a new country, is born out of frustration over what she perceives as failed efforts to change her life. Significantly, she also decides not to return to school. In many ways, her relationship to Dr. Redmond is much like her relationship to Dan; her first session is about reading his face and reactions to see if she is giving the "right" answers to his questions. Over the course of several sessions, Ella is "taught" the importance of being able to read her past, especially her childhood and her relationship with her mother, on whom all her current problems are blamed: "my overseriousness, guilt about sex, my undeveloped maternal feelings" (180). She now reinterprets her recurring baby dream as a "manifestation of stifled feminine part of me, resulting from mother's indoctrination" (182). She writes, "Dr. said nothing, but I could tell he agreed" (182).

Ella's response to this "revelation" is "I've always known I wasn't much as a woman.... Never knew how much it poisoned my whole life" (182). Thus, her dream is appropriated, first by Dan, and now by Dr. Redmond, to reflect meanings that suit their particular purposes. Significantly, in both cases the dream's meaning boils down to Ella's "failure" to be a "real woman." Ironically, it is Ella's socialization as a woman that allows her to accept these interpretations without question. She is adept at what Elaine Showalter dubs "double-voiced discourse." Showalter argues that "all language is the language of the dominant (male) order, and women, if they speak at all, must speak through it.... [their voices] always embod[y] the social, literary, and cultural heritages of both the muted and the dominant" (262–263).

The muting of Ella's voice takes several forms. Her acceptance of Redmond's interpretation of her experience reveals how effectively the dominant-muted relationship between them is established; his authority is such that he can remain silent, allow her to speak, and remain confident that his own ideas will come out of her mouth. She has not only given up school, she has ceased writing in her journal. Her one attempt to link her academic life to her present proves ineffective, because Redmond has not read the books she refers to, and because of her belief that she's "too far away from all that" (182). Just how far Ella has moved "away from all that" is underscored by her discovery that she is pregnant. Though happy at first because she believes her dream is fulfilled and that she is recapturing her true feminine nature, she quickly realizes that having a baby is the last thing she wants: "The great solution to everything. Get pregnant. Then you don't have to think about anything anymore.... Why didn't I see what I was doing?" (190).

Ella's decision to have an abortion opens up yet another battleground. Her family's reaction is one of shock and disgust. While her mother worries about how Ella's decision will reflect on her as a mother, Ella's father believes "This is something she must have picked up at that place [college]" (204). This formulation of education as exposure to "disease" reflects the belief that education is a force which disrupts the integrity of the family, particularly the role of the woman.[4] When she turns to Dr. Redmond for information about obtaining an abortion, she meets more resistance, a resistance that is more powerful and frightening because it is institutionalized, and has the full force of the law behind it. Her reanalysis of her baby dream as an attempt to give birth to "a new me" (193), rather than as an attempt to "recapture her femininity" is met with stubborn lack of comprehension on Redmond's part. Just as Dan rejects her readings of Emma Bovary and Anna Karenina, Redmond authoritatively dismisses her interpretation of her dream. He tells her that in order to get an abortion she must provide "letters from two psychiatrists stating that bearing a child would be dangerous to your mental health" (194), and refuses to give her such a letter until they discuss the matter further to determine if that is what she "really" wants. Ella realizes that not only can he make legal determinations about her mental stability, but that, "[h]e could decide whether or not I was to have a baby.... [and] I could see ... that he was enjoying his power"

(195). Ella's rage at this abuse of power is magnified when she learns from Laura that he lied to her; because " '[l]ast month a county judge declared all abortion laws unconstitutional,' " Ella can now get an abortion on demand at any hospital.

Ella's decision to assert her voice in the matter of the abortion is accompanied by a return to journal writing, as well as a decision to return to school. Finally, she makes the decision to which the novel has inevitably led: to end her marriage. Her resolution to "[do] the real job, whatever that is" without the crutch of husband or family is, of course, a tremendous violation of traditional Italian culture. That is, Ella (and Bryant) chooses not to define her "womanhood" as relative to her roles as wife and mother, accepting the (implicit) labels of *mala femmina* and *puttana* in exchange for autonomy.

Symbolically, the novel ends shortly after midnight on the day after Christmas, the holiday which conflates and reifies both religious and secular images of family and motherhood. Ella lies in a hospital, prepped for the abortion, feeling simultaneously "like a sacred virgin . . . prepared and purified according to ancient rule" and "a plucked chicken about to be gutted" (227). These conflicting images capture the duality of female sexuality as an entity to be simultaneously worshipped and plundered; they also echo the Italian/Catholic underpinnings of Bryant's background, by which the female body takes on characteristics of the host, ritualistically consecrated and consumed by the male priest. Finally, these images emphasize Ella's ambivalence about the abortion and her decision to leave Joe, and the uncertainty of her future.

The recognition of the parallels between the traditions of the immigrant success novel and the feminist consciousness-raising novel offers one explanation for the tensions at work in *Ella Price's Journal*. Nonetheless, the question of why Bryant chose to depict Ella as she did, downplaying her ethnicity and foregrounding a feminist agenda and form, remains difficult to answer. Personal discomfort with explicit exploration of her ethnic heritage is one possibility; many Italian-American writers, both male and female (including Bryant), have related the pressures they have experienced not to "betray" the family by revealing its inner workings to "outsiders." A final consideration is the sociological concept of creative ethnicity, by which one "us[es] one's ethnic heritage as a starting point upon which to build one's identity in a selective and critical way" (Barolini 14). Thus, Bryant's depiction of Ella Price and her journey of transformation links the limitation and oppression of women in both traditional Italian and "American" cultures.

Miss Giardino (1978), Bryant's third novel, like *Ella Price's Journal*, focuses on the changes wrought in a female protagonist over a period of time (in this case, however, the transformation takes place over the course of a week). Like *Ella Price's Journal, Miss Giardino* may be read as part of popular female literary stereotype: that of the older woman looking back and taking stock of her life. In this novel, however, unlike *Ella Price's Journal*, Bryant engages explicitly with her Italian heritage, drawing on the stories of her "mother's sad childhood"; she states that doing so made her "[feel] good about making something good out of her terrible ordeal" (Personal correspondence). The novel begins with the protagonist, Anna Giardino, a former high school teacher in her sixties, awakening in a hospital bed, recovering from an attack by an unknown assailant. The rest of the novel traces not only the reconstruction of her memory, temporarily lost due to the blow she suffered, but also her settlement of unresolved conflicts and issues from her past. In the piecemeal process of regaining her memory, Anna is forced to confront her past and make important decisions about her future.

Though at first glance Ella and Anna seem to have little in common, close examination of both novels reveals Bryant's essential concern with several recurrent themes: ethnic and racial identity, gender roles in traditional Italian culture, and the role of education in American culture. As they do for Ella, these issues becomes intertwined in shaping Anna's life and perceptions of herself and the multiethnic society in which she lives. Bryant's narrative interweaves Anna's present—a week in 1972—with long flashbacks chronicling significant moments in her childhood, her college years, and her forty years of teaching at Camino Real High School.

Anna represents, in a sense, both the reverse and extension of Ella's experience. In many ways, too, Bryant's work is a re-vision of Marion Benasutti's *No Steadyjob for Papa*. The child of extraordinarily poor Italian immigrants, Anna has fought her way past the barriers of language, ethnic prejudice, and gender limitations to create a life which she desperately needs to believe has significance and value. Significantly, the first memories Anna recovers in the hospital are of her turbulent (and frequently violent) childhood as part of an itinerant immigrant family. Like the family in Benasutti's novel, the Giardinos' lives are dictated by the endless search for steady and secure work—which, for illiterate Italians such as Anna's father, was more or less an impossible dream. Anna reflects:

> The others say, "Mama, let's go back home." They tell me about home, but I don't believe them. Home is, the world is, a cabin on a muddy road up the hill to a mine. It is called Illinois, Colorado, Utah, Montana. We move, but it is always the same cabin, road, mine. We move west, going to California, always going to California. But it stays the same, always the cold, the pot of polenta to stir on the stove, the muddy road between the cabins, the men on the road, walking, coughing. (6)

The physical dangers and spiritual frustration engendered by the hardships of coal mining quickly take their toll; in contrast to the generally sentimental and optimistic portrait painted by Benasutti's Rosemary, Anna's memories of this period are dominated by images of her father's verbal and physical violence, his frequent alcoholic binges, her mother's mute and passive acceptance, and the unsuccessful attempts of her siblings to resist his tyranny. Their strategies are various; the oldest, Mike, leaves the house whenever their father's rage threatens to overwhelm the household, while Alfonsina clings to their mother and cries with her. Victorina takes up a weapon to confront him, but it is Anna who is best able to handle his rage, staring him down and refusing to let him see her fear. She also resolves to speak to him only in English, because

> [s]omehow I know the words in English will hit his eyes like a whip. . . . The new language, the language of the people outside the family, outside the cabin. The language of the people who own the mines. It is my language too. I alone in the family speak it without accent, read it, think in it. (8)

Thus, Anna begins fairly early to separate herself from the stranglehold of culture and family. The hardships of immigration have corrupted and inverted the family's power; rather than being a safe haven against the oppressive forces from the outside, the family itself has become the site of brutality and oppression, and institutions outside the family, normally regarded as threatening, represent freedom and safety. Anna's conscious decision to think, speak, and read in English may be viewed as a positive step toward successful assimilation and upward mobility; however, it also violates every rule of Italian life: she defies her father's authority, looks beyond the confines of the family, and engages in intellectual and academic activity that is undesirable, particularly for a female. As a result of this confrontation, her father no longer calls Anna by her name, but begins to refer to her mockingly as " 'the American' " (8).

Thus, Bryant shows the ways in which the move to America disrupts the centuries-old pattern of *la via vecchia*. The father's position as breadwinner, provider, and primary decision-maker was a cornerstone of the old way; however, according to *l'uomo di pazienza*—the ideal of manliness based on patience, strength, discretion, self-reliance, and constancy—this role did not entitle a father to brutalize or bully his family. Bryant's portrayal of Anna's father (based, in part, on her maternal grandfather) demonstrates the terrible consequences that immigration often produced. Because Anna is the only one of the four children born in America, her only experience of her father has been of his alcoholic abuse and rage, born of frustration over denied opportunity, and the terrible work choices and conditions he must endure. Anna's siblings have memories of a laughing, loving man who *"sang and was happy"* (7), but to Anna he is *"a monster like the giants in the book of fairy tales the last teacher gave me"* (7). Thus, Bryant is clearly "re-visioning" the father-daughter relationship presented in Benasutti's novel; Rosemary's father, loving, supportive, and optimistic despite physical and economic hardship, is transformed into a "monster" who terrorizes his wife and children.

Anna's role as "the American" in the family is emphasized by her relationship and commitment to education. Like Ella (and like the female protagonists in many novels by Italian-American women), early in life she develops a passion for reading and for learning that sets her apart from both her family and her peers. The public library near their new home in the Mission area of San Francisco becomes a substitute for institutionalized religion; the building itself is for Anna a "palace," a *"quiet hall with its sacred smell of old bookbindings and glue, a smell that gives me a sense of peace and safety that Mama gets from the candles and incense of the church two blocks away"* (12). Education becomes a substitute for institutionalized religion for Anna; to her, her mother's Catholicism is nothing more than "superstition" (28).

Anna's conflicted relationship with her father dominates the first memories she recovers. Even when he is no longer drinking or capable of working, his lungs destroyed by years of coal dust, his rages continue, vented only at Anna; he waves his fists in the air, *"calling on God to witness the curse of his child, the American, thriving in the air that strangles him"* (13). The distance between Anna and her father is increased when compulsory education laws take Anna out of the factory where her mother and sister work, making her *"'A useless mouth to feed, her nose in a book all day'"* (13). However, for Anna this intervention is nothing short of divine, offering opportunity for escape, for knowledge, and for a better future than her father could ever have hoped for. The conflict portrayed in this novel, between the immigrant parent and the child who desires assimilation and a life outside the confines of the family, captures the difference between Italian and American concepts of what it means to be "well-educated." In Italian, the expression *buon educati* has nothing to do with formal, institutionalized schooling; instead "it meant being brought up to value *la via vecchia* in thought and feeling and to honor it in practice" (Gambino 7).

It is ironic, then, that Anna fulfills the role of dutiful daughter, caring for both parents in the days before their deaths. Her father's demand for her presence in his sickroom, and hers alone, even though he refused to see or speak to her while she was at college, underscores the contradictory and complex nature of the conflict between immigrant parents and their children. Their final reconciliation (such as it is), when her father admits he "likes" her, his "American" daughter, reveals the complex web of emotions underlying that epithet for the immigrant father: it simultaneously expresses fear, envy, insult, and, ultimately, admiration.

Bryant's treatment of Anna's relationship to her mother is much more positive than either Anna's relationship to her father or Ella Price's to her mother. Though Victorina criticizes her for failing to protect her children, Anna understands and defends her: " 'But Mama wasn't like us. She couldn't [leave]. It wasn't possible for her even to think of leaving her husband. Surely you can forgive her for that' " (15–16). Anna takes on the responsibility for caring for her mother, providing her with a place to live, sitting with her in the hospital in her final illness. Though her relationship is not characterized by the overt guilt and conflict that Ella experienced, Bryant indicates that these feelings are nonetheless present. Anna preserves her mother's apartment exactly as it was before her death, unable to divest herself of the physical reminders of the hardship and sacrifice her mother endured. Certainly, her mother was not the strong central figure ideally portrayed as the Italian mother; unable to hold her family together, she simply survived and endured.

Like Rosemary in *No Steadyjob for Papa*, Anna, at about age thirteen, takes a job as a "mother's helper" with a Jewish family, the Sterns, in the Mission. While most scholars of Italian-American experience emphasize the rarity of Italian-American women working in a "domestic" capacity outside their own homes (though, interestingly, immigrant Italian women brought strangers into the family, so to speak, by taking in laundry, or housing boarders), female novelists frequently portray characters who do so. Richard Gambino argues that, "For [a woman] to work in the house of another family . . . is seen as a usurpation of family loyalty by her family *and by her*"(13). While statistics show that Italian/Italian-American domestics were indeed unusual, they were not unheard of; additionally, the fictional portrayal of young women who take such positions suggests a good deal about the interest female Italian-American novelists have in examining the myths and strictures surrounding female experience in Italian-American culture. In that light, Victorina's assertion that their mother should have "scrubbed floors," if that's what it took to get the children away from their abusive father, becomes moot; Anna's assertion of the impossibility of such an action takes on deeper meaning—the impossibility stems as much from cultural conditioning as it does from their mother's nature.

Though not wealthy, the Sterns represent to Anna the kind of genteel middle-class existence that she has never known. She enjoys the light housework she is required to do, handling fine clothes and china that she has never had; most of all, she enjoys caring for the books in the study, use of which Mr. Stern generously offers to her. Yet again, in this family, we are presented with a weak and often absent mother; Mrs. Stern is given to "spells" which cause her to retreat to her room for days at a time, leaving Anna in charge of caring for the house and for David. Though David cautions her, " 'You mustn't work too hard' " (28), Anna laughs, *"because life has never been so easy"* (28). Thus, Bryant juxtaposes Anna (and by extension, the entire Giardino family) with David, for whom *"life has been sunny, a paradise"* (29). Though David is handsome and talented, and harbors ambitions for Hollywood stardom, he lacks the ambition and *"the ability to push others aside and grab something for himself"* (30).

The importance of being able to "push others aside" in order to secure success is a minor, yet important, theme in the novel (and, indeed, of much immigrant literature). The ways in which class, gender, racial, and ethnic difference, as well as individual character, interact to promote or deny economic and social achievement haunt Bryant's work. In this novel, Bryant addresses another theme treated in *Ella Price's Journal* : the value and meaning of education in American society. Bryant's treatment of education and its relationship to economic success reflects her personal experience. She writes:

> Those who disdain formal education usually come from homes where there are books, records, highly cultured parents who read to their children every night. . . . I taught such children in a prep school for five years, and know them to be uncon-

scious of the riches that have nourished them. (Personal correspondence)

Anna is, of course, completely committed to the value of education and has devoted her professional life to upholding it. However, as memories of her years as a student and as a teacher flood back, we begin to see the enormous struggle she has undertaken in its defense. In a conversation, Arno reminds Anna of an argument they'd had, begun when Anna "[was] going into [her] usual thing on standards and grades and education being the key to upward mobility" (111). These standards and the compulsory attendance laws, which made it possible for Anna to escape factory life, are characterized by Arno as part of the "comfortable fiction" of the American public education system: " '[It is] a way to keep the poor in their place. The few who rose proved the point, held out hope, but the whole thing was dependent on just a few making it' " (111). In recalling the details of this conversation, Anna suddenly remembers her reaction to Arno's assertions; this response is remarkably similar to Ella's anguished question ("But it's her whole life, and it's over, so wouldn't it be better not to know?"):

> *Oh, God, can he be right? It hits me like a blow.... If he is right, then I made a terrible mistake, turned the wrong way, made my whole.... life's work, a detour. By trying to save a few. That seemed possible.... How could I have faced it every day without a concrete goal? Limited. Reachable. So I pushed them all, preached salvation through education, hoping a few would listen and slip through. And when a few did, I felt vindicated, triumphant... righteous.... I did my best... And now, does it turn out that my best was my worst? Was I only part of a murderous system? But I did my best. What else could I do? I did my best, as I saw it. My best! (112)*

This recollection is just one of many recounting Anna's conflicted experience over forty years of teaching; tales of individual students come back to haunt her and force her to re-evaluate both her past and her present.

Anna is portrayed on one level as the stereotypical "old maid schoolteacher"—unmarried, childless, given to dressing severely, disdaining the conventional feminine trappings of carefully styled hair and make-up. However, as Anna reconstructs her past, we learn of various romantic and sexual entanglements which have shaped her life: her college affair with Arno, which resulted in unexpected pregnancy and an illegal abortion; an intensely felt but unconsummated love for a student in her early years of teaching; a brief affair with a younger man during a trip to Mexico midway through her teaching career. This last memory represents "a door that closed off a part of her life.... the final closing off of the possibility of marriage" (102). Anna admits, *"I am taking him like a pill, a narcotic, to kill my pain"* (101)—the pain of loneliness, of increasingly frustrated ambitions, but also the pain of feeling she *"[had made] a return to a place I have never seen, to a childhood I have never known"* (96). Too, she recognizes in her Mexican lover the stereotypical "gigolo" from which she has carefully distanced herself, and she becomes infuriated with herself for succumbing to what she has criticized other women for, the easy seduction of *"a few weeks of romance by a slightly paunchy imitation of an old Hollywood movie Latin lover"* (95). For Anna, this incident reveals a significant truth about her status in cultures that simultaneously deny and exaggerate female sexuality:

> She could become a ludicrous figure, longing for tenderness and going . . . to buy it in some place distant and poor enough to accomodate her . . . To show her need would be to open herself to humiliation as a silly old sexual beggar. To fight it and deny it only brought new humiliation, [to be] laughed at as a cold, frigid old maid. (103)

More significantly, Anna becomes infuriated with Manuel; her castigation emphasizes both their age difference and Anna's fury with herself for taking the easy route:

> *"My God, if you were my son, I'd rather you became one of the starving peons, digging in the ground, than become one of those men. But it is so easy. So much easier than studying, so easy to be nice to the ladies who keep coming from the North. . . . you must not be taken in, you must resist!"* (102)

Bryant suggests in this passage (and throughout the novel) that Anna's role as teacher has much in common with (and may even be a substitute for) the role of the ideal Italian mother. Anna sees her purpose as a teacher to be the inculcation of certain values—respect for learning, for authority, for hard work, for economic and social mobility. Early in her career, she succeeds, for the most part; the children she teaches primarily come from a similar cultural and economic background as she, and they accept her value system. However, as the student population changes, and generational and racial conflicts are introduced into the classroom, Anna's methods and values are dismissed as hopelessly anachronistic by both her students and by newer, younger teachers, who regard homework as superfluous and any grade lower than a 'C' as *"psychologically damaging"* (116).

As Anna's memory is gradually reawakened and reconstructed, past encounters with students that have challenged Anna's role and goals as an educator return with painful clarity. The case of Willie Fortuna, for example, represents a total violation of Anna's principles; lazy and undisciplined, but passed on because of his athletic ability, Willie challenges Anna at every turn. She is further frustrated by a principal (and former coach) who insists she ought to sympathize with Willie because he, too, is Italian, *"and could be an outstanding representative of your people"* (74). The fact that Willie goes on to "earn" a college scholarship and various job promotions, despite his ineptitude and dishonesty, rankles Anna, for his success disproves the very foundation on which she has built her own life and which she has tried to pass on to her students. Much like the Italian mother who finds her attempts to preserve the old ways and values disregarded or disdained by her more Americanized children, Anna feels increasingly swept aside by changes in the educational system.

The story of Maria Flores offers a slightly different perspective on Anna's role as teacher/mother in the novel. Maria is much like Anna; both are bright, ambitious, praised for their academic diligence, and held up as positive examples for "their people"—a "distinction" both deeply resent. That Maria is a Chicana, rather than Italian, represents the shift in ethnic population; the "new" ethnics, blacks and Chicanos, have, in a sense, replaced the Italian, Irish, and Russian, now considered fully "American" in comparison.

Maria may, in fact, be read as Anna's "daughter," for when she comes to Anna's class, Anna sees in her an opportunity to prove her methods and beliefs valid. Maria has been "patted and petted and praised for years," but to Anna's mind she is "lazy.... [and] had no idea what real work was" (83). Anna's determination to teach her what "real work is," and her enjoyment of her success in doing so, is presented as a tangible reward for Anna's devotion after years of frustration: " 'Maria was the only positive thing in my life just then. I felt old and tired. And Maria responded ...' " (84). However, Anna failed at the time to see the danger in this relationship; like the Italian mother whose rewards for sacrifice are dependent on her children, Anna " '[had] been reduced to getting all [her] satisfaction from one student' " (84). Her subsequent accusation of dishonesty against Maria, based on her mistaken belief that she has been tricked, is a terrible blow to Anna's carefully cultivated image of herself as "teacher." Though Arno tries to reassure her, reminding her of the personal and professional pressures she was under at the time, Anna says " 'That's no excuse, not for a teacher.... a teacher must be fair. That's the highest compliment a student pays a teacher.... No matter what.... [a] teacher must be fair' " (86).

Significantly, Anna's memory of this incident is sparked by Maria's call, a request to come to visit Anna at home. That Maria is now herself a teacher at Camino Real reinforces the "mother-daughter" interpretation of their relationship; Maria, ironically, has replaced Anna in her position in the English Department. Through their conversation, Anna traces years of Camino history—the shifting ethnic populations, the increasing violence and poverty; she also discovers that Maria is experiencing some of the same frustrations and sacrifices Anna herself endured. Maria tells of her initial attempts to make herself as different a teacher from Anna as she possibly could:

> "I hated you.... You were the nasty old teacher who'd been unfair to me.... When I was hired to replace you at Camino, I felt vindicated.... I was the New Teacher: free, pretty, lively.... I just wanted to be popular. I wanted them to love me.... [But] I wasn't myself. Every move, every gesture, wasn't really me." (91)

Maria's recognition of the falsity of her teaching persona leads her to model herself after Anna. And just as Anna was accused in the case of Willie Fortuna of "betraying" one of her own, Maria says, "I was called a traitor to Third World people. Cruel, too demanding. . . . This year, I started out a little better, not a drill sergeant, not their girlfriend. . . . firm, demanding, but *fair*" (91–92) (my emphasis).

That Maria, rather than Willie, is the student with whom Anna connects, and who chooses to pattern herself after Anna, suggests that gender rather than ethnicity is the primary bond in which Bryant is interested; it suggests, too, that ethnic difference is not as troublesome as generational difference. Nonetheless, in addition to their parallel histories of immigration and occupation of the lowest rung of the socio-economic ladder, Mexican and Italian cultures have much in common. Most important, of course, is the ways in which both cultures define the roles of women, particularly the central role of the mother. Thus, Maria metaphorically fills the daughter role to Anna's mother, and in turn reenacts the mother role with her own students. Bryant underscores this "kinship"; Anna says " 'You'll end up like me,' " recognizing "a certain tight lift to [Maria's] jaw" as Maria relates her frustrations.

While Anna is forced to re-evaluate her role as teacher/mother, as daughter, as Italian-American woman, she is led, by extension, to re-evaluate those beliefs and values that have been the foundation of ways of teaching, thinking, and living. Bryant captures this conflict in portraying Anna's reverence for the works of Bertrand Russell, whose works have served as a model for both good writing and thinking for Anna: "the reasonable, kindly voice of Russell had been able to convince her that life could be lived, that learning made living possible" (109). However, after the attack, and after Anna has already begun to question and re-examine her life, Russell "no longer reassures her" (109). Anna puzzles over this sudden change and reflects, "He wrote like a man who had always been listened to, who expected his audience to be attentive, thinking and rational" (109)—a role Anna realizes that she had been desperately trying to fill in all her years of teaching, a confidence she has desperately needed to have. The unspoken difference Anna recognizes at this moment between Russell and herself is, perhaps, that Russell, as a white, upper-class male (like the "standard" male subject of autobiography discussed in Chapter One), could take for granted (and was indeed granted) that "people had always listened to him, admired him and respected him" (109). But Bryant seems to suggest as well that Russell's distance from his audience allowed him to make those assumptions, while Anna, working face-to-face for and with those she hoped to reach, was unable to do so. Anna realizes, "One might be a very different person . . . if everyone always listened" (110).

This revelation comes to Anna after she awakens from a dream, one of a series that has haunted her since the attack. Though the dreams vary in their particulars, they have one significant factor in common: they are always set inside or around Camino Real High School, and the school is always on fire. Like Ella, Anna struggles with the interpretation of these dreams, because, like Ella, she knows that "Dreams would give her the answers . . . even the part she was afraid to remember" (108). On this particular night, Anna has dreamed that students ("recent students... mostly black and brown" 108) are dancing in the school cafeteria, oblivious to the fire raging around them and to Anna's attempts to save them: " 'Stop playing and let me get you out of here. You'll all die in this place!' " (108).

This dream symbolizes several themes of the novel—Anna's role as teacher/mother, her ability to "save" her students through education, the ethnic and generational conflicts that have frustrated her efforts. The fire in the dream is, of course, a reference to the fire that destroyed the school not long after Anna started teaching. Because this fire destroyed most of the school's records, it becomes a metaphor for Anna's "lost" past, but also for her eventual decision to divest herself of the past and the ways in which it oppresses her present. More importantly, however, the dream offers a significant clue for solving the mystery of the reason for Anna's late-night excursion, and the subsequent attack. Just as previous dreams have helped her "remember," for example, Maria's identity, this dream ends with a voice which Anna recognizes but cannot yet identify, a "deep, black voice.... [which] said quite clearly, 'You get'n closer' " (108).

Thus, the discovery to which Anna is being led—why she was out on the night of the attack, and what happened as a result—becomes inevitably linked to the struggles of her life. The novel's air of mystery, of course, depends upon the deferral of Anna's discovery of her reason for strolling the streets at three o'clock in the morning, and her conscious recognition of the identity of her attacker. Again, part of the answer is revealed to Anna in yet another dream; she recognizes her attacker as Booker T. Henderson, a student from her last year of teaching, an angry and bitter boy who resented Anna as a "racist bitch," seeing in her an *"easy, accessible target"* (130) for his hatred. Anna reflects, " 'He was on that edge.... hating me because I threatened to change [him], demanded work ... demanded growth' " (131). Booker, in a sense, replicates the role of Anna's father, his fear of what Anna represents transformed into hatred and insult. Now, however, Anna no longer has the strength to fight; though she recognizes something in Booker that is "teachable," she says "his hatred was so strong" (131) that she could not fight without help from " 'anyone ... who would take him aside and say 'Booker, you're full of shit' " (131).

Though part of the mystery is solved by the revelation contained in this dream, Anna is still unsure of how or why the attack occurred. Her call to Booker's home indicates that Booker is indeed the guilty party; it also reveals that Anna had a secret ally in her struggle to educate him. His mother tells her:

> "I used to tell him, that old teacher, she sound like your grandma; she used to scold and worry us children ... but only to make us do right.... I try to tell him, there's chances for him I never had.... that old teacher just telling you how to read and write.... Don't matter if she's black or white. Don't matter if she don't like you, if she willing to teach you something." (137)

However, like Maria's assurances that Anna had made a positive difference in her life, this defense does little to help Anna: "Did knowing you were in the right help after the car had run over you?" (93).

Thus, because Anna remains unsure of whether Booker's attack was deliberately aimed at her, she is led to an inevitable decision. Despite the best efforts of those who care about her to keep her from wandering the streets at night, she resolves to re-enact the night of the attack in order to understand fully the reasons for what has happened. The discovery to which she is led—that she was intending to set the high school on fire—horrifies her. Her encounter with Booker was accidental; intending to mug an anonymous victim, Booker's attempt to steal her purse is met instead with Anna's intense, hate-filled attack, waged not out of self-defense, but

> "because I recognized him. Because I hated him so.... He was everything I hated, everything that had gone wrong, everything about the school, about my life, everything I hated was.... Booker." (143)

That Booker takes the force of Anna's built-up frustration and rage, and her recognition of her serious intent to set the school on fire, disturbs Anna deeply, for she recognizes in herself the same desperation and loss of hope that fueled the rage of students like Booker, and, more significantly, of her father:

> Now, finally, she understood him. She had learned to understand him by becoming him. He had a vision of a better life and had strained himself to the utmost to go after it.... He had been used and abused by the forces in which he had put all his hope. ... He had become filled with hatred and bitterness and despair, and vented his hatred on the nearest targets. So, finally, had she. (146)

This recognition leads Anna to a decision similar to Ella's, to divest herself of her past—its anger, bitterness, frustrations, and failures. This decision is symbolized by the sale of her home and all its contents, including her beloved books and her mother's belongings. However, Anna's actions are not based on the simplistic belief that she can forget her past completely; Arno, in fact, interprets her behavior as a sign that she is "brooding" over it. Rather, she asserts, she is "only going through [her past], finally, finally passing through it" (155). Thus, she rejects David's suggestion that she journey to Italy to discover her roots; to Anna " 'it's too soon.... for me to go back would almost be like saying my parents' struggle was for nothing' " (158).

Despite their thirty-year age difference, as well as their ethnic difference, the protagonists of these two novels have much in common, as they represent the struggles and choices women face in negotiating the demands of two cultures. Their transformations suggest an implicit faith on Bryant's part in the individual will to change, and to radicalize the self in the face of seemingly overwhelming cultural and societal obstacles. The female protagonists portrayed in these particular novels reflect what Mary Jo Bona asserts is an essential feature of works by

Italian-American women who "have produced texts that concentrate on being denied access to the resources and prerogatives of the dominant class"; the result, she says, is the creation of "a specific kind of female *bildungsroman*, where the emphasis is not only on gender roles, but on how ethnicity impacts a woman's ability to discover herself" (*Claiming a Tradition* 331).

Recognition of the parallels between the tradition of the immigrant success novel and the feminist consciousness-raising novel offers one explanation of the tensions at work in *Ella Price's Journal*. The question remains, of course, about Bryant's resistance to labels and about her refusal to engage explicitly with her Italian heritage until her third novel. Her persistent resistance to labels may reflect that she, like many other authors (male and female), "equate[s] being ethnic with being disempowered in America" (Bona 331). In addition, her reluctance may also result from her family's discomfort with what they regard as betrayal of family secrets, an obstacle faced by many Italian-American women writers. One such writer, Rosemarie Caruso, reports an exchange with her mother, who advises her against including family material in her writing: " 'It's going to start trouble, then I can't go there next Christmas' " (qtd. in Barolini 17). In the case of *Ella Price's Journal*, it is possible to link Bryant's early anxieties as an author to Ella's: both are concerned with establishing "author"ity for their experience, while at the same time facing tremendous resistance and attempts to mute their voices. Both author and character are engaged in the act of writing, a subversive act in and of itself,[5] which in turn gives voice to subversive thoughts. Though she is clearly and explicitly engaged with her Italian heritage in *Miss Giardino*, Anna's refusal at the end of the novel to return to Italy may be a metaphor for Bryant's uneasiness with the more frank depiction of her family history in the novel.

A second reason may be the realities of publishing during the period during which *Ella Price's Journal* was written. Though Bryant relates frustration in her early attempts to find a publisher for the novel (Personal correspondence), it is also true that by the early seventies the mass popularity of the so-called "housewife" novel far outstripped that of novels about white ethnicity.[6] Thomas Ferraro points out that a common strategy of immigrant/ethnic writers is to "[school] themselves in and [give] allegiance to central forms of twentieth-century American literary creativity at the same time they learned the risks of generic forms and presuppositors firsthand" (8); the apparent distancing from ethnic heritage that novels like *Ella Price's Journal* enact (effected in part, at least, by the choice of a "generic," popular form) disguises the "degree of cultural persistence . . . among writers who claim or who have been credited with achieving 'disinterestedness' " (3).

A final consideration is the sociological concept of creative ethnicity, by which a person (or writer) "uses one's ethnic heritage as a starting point upon which to build one's identity in a selective and critical way" (Barolini 14). Thus, Bryant's depictions of Ella and Anna's journeys of transformation link the limitation and oppression of women of both traditional Italian and "American" cultures;

these two novels also link the Italian-American tradition with the larger popular literary tradition through a potentially subversive narrative act. Like many other immigrant/ethnic works, both *Ella Price's Journal* and *Miss Giardino* "[adopt] the paradigm of cultural rebirth—from alien to American—then put it to the test of experience" (Ferraro 1). Both Ella's and Anna's "rebirths" are left incomplete, the novel's endings open; this lack of resolution reflects both the dilemma, and the strategy for working through that dilemma, characteristic of the ethnic writer:

> That is the inheritance, that is the curse, of being born into a world and into a family that wants you to enter another. You say partially goodbye to one, partially hello to another, some of the time you are silent, and if you feel a little bit crazy—and sometimes you do—then you write about it. (DeRosa 39)

Bryant's strategy for closing both of these novels is much like that described by Rachel Blau DuPlessis as "writing beyond the ending." Such open-endedness reflects Ella's, Anna's, and, to a great degree, Bryant's "discovery that [they are] in fact outside the terms of this novel's script, marginal to it" (6). In other words, the narrative strategy of the "open" ending "signals [a novelist's] dissent from social norms as well as narrative forms" (DuPlessis 20), and announces both the feminist and ethnic writer's resolution of tensions "in a personal manner satisfactory to the specific individual" (Ahearn 126).

Ultimately, Bryant's acceptance of or resistance to labels is not as important as her role and position in shaping the literary tradition of Italian-American women. She re-visions the work of predecessors such as Tomasi and Benasutti, questioning the optimism and challenging the sentimentality with which these writers imbue their works. She complements the work of her contemporaries such as Helen Barolini, whose two novels, *Umbertina* and *Love in the Middle Ages*, are examined in the next chapter. In *Umbertina*, we see clear strains of the feminist consciousness-raising strategies employed by Bryant in her novels; additionally, Barolini engages with the effects (and causes) of immigration across four generations. In *Love in the Middle Ages*, Barolini employs the more intimate scale of *Ella Price's Journal* and *Miss Giardino*, focusing on a single female protagonist struggling with her identity in the context of a romantic relationship. Finally, Bryant's work anticipates that of her "descendants" such as Lisa Ruffolo, Mary Caponegro, and Carole Maso; while none of these writers claim a direct influence from Bryant's work, critical examination reveals both stylistic and thematic common ground, especially as all three of these later writers acknowledge a debt to both the feminist theory and feminist fiction that burgeoned during the late 1960s and 1970s.

Chapter Four

CREATING A CONTEXT:
THE FICTION AND CRITICISM
OF HELEN BAROLINI

In *Umbertina* (1979) and *Love in the Middle Ages* (1986), and in her voluminous critical writings, poet, novelist, and critic Helen Barolini examines her explicit concern with the difficulty of securing and maintaining identity for the Italian-American woman; one critic argues that "Barolini's blending of genres and writerly personae articulates the extremity of the Italian/American woman author's exclusion and her willingness, as a result, to explore diverse routes in order to become an author" (Giunta, "Blending 'Literary' Discourses" 2). Barolini's concern has strong autobiographical roots. As demonstrated in Chapter One, the autobiographical is an important aspect of the Italian-American literary tradition. Such roots, argues Rosalind Coward in her 1980 essay "Are Women's Novels Feminist Novels?", are also a common feature of many novels by women written during the 1970s, such as Marilyn French's *The Women's Room* (1977) and Kate Millett's *Sita* (1977). Barolini's novels are set in the same literary and social contexts as Dorothy Bryant's. Like Bryant, Barolini employs the strategies of the feminist consciousness-raising novel; unlike Bryant, she has asserted in interviews that she sees her fiction more in the context of feminist, rather than ethnic, literature. Nonetheless, she engages with her *italianità* in a more detailed and encompassing manner than does Bryant, suggesting that both aspects are equally important in the formation of her identity and authority. Both *Umbertina* and *Love in the Middle Ages* have these dual strands of identity woven throughout their narratives; Barolini's novels reveal her interest in addressing the problem stated by Sandra Mortola Gilbert: " 'I am always struck by how few people have written about what it means to be *us*!' " (Barolini, *Dream Book* x). What it means to Barolini to be "us"—that is, to be Italian-American women—in the worlds she creates in her novels is to struggle against and triumph over sexual and ethnic prejudices imposed by both traditional Italian and mainstream American cultures.

In "Becoming a Literary Person Out of Context," Barolini reflects on her often difficult passage to becoming a writer. Lack of models ("[My ancestors] had only the spoken words and stories of the illiterate" (263)) and lack of validation and support from parents whose culture taught them that women's destiny lay in "self-giving in the service of others" made her pursuit of authorship (and authority) a "circling [of] an elusive identity that . . . was completely out of context with my

Italian-American background" (262–263). Thus, Barolini's experience as an Italian American and as a woman informs her perception of herself as an artist, and the thematic concerns of her fiction.

Primary among these themes is, of course, the family. Mary Jo Bona writes, "Instead of perceiving the family and home to be a reflection of the larger world, however, the Italian-American woman has used the family setting as the starting point for her exploration of the self" ("Broken Images, Broken Lives" 88). Barolini reports in some detail the conflicting ways in which her family ties shaped her aspirations. Her father, whose lifetime of hard work and success despite "morale-depleting setbacks and disasters" ("Becoming a Literary Person" 264), taught her "tenaciousness and how to be on my own" (264). Her mother's influence was more ambivalent; she "aspired to the finer things in life" (264), owned an unread leather-bound set of Dickens, and provided Barolini with her first diary, telling her " 'It's to write in' " (264). She saw in these things, Barolini writes, "something beyond her reach which was valuable and good" (264). She encouraged Barolini to embark on a variety of lessons (ballet, piano, swimming), and to go to college. Yet, Barolini says, "even as she intuited the things of the spirit, some atavistic residue in her also distrusted them" (264).

Barolini's experience with education likewise reflects a sense of ambivalence. Many second-generation parents such as hers simultaneously valued higher education and mistrusted it. For them, education, particularly college, was important (especially for daughters) "not as an intellectual but as an 'American' experience"; at college, connections, such as marriage, could be made that would "complet[e] the forward march of assimilation" (264). Working against such a belief was "the old peasant culture that taught one to stay safe in one's place ... not to make your children better than you" (264). Complicating this particular tension is the engagement of writers with the ideology(ies) of feminism; feminism's challenges to social patriarchy, and, more importantly, familial patriarchy, rocked the very foundations of traditional Italian culture. Certainly, earlier Italian-American women writers maintained an awareness of gender oppression and discrimination. However, the women's movements, as well as the various ethnic reclamation movements of the 1960s and 1970s, and the expansion of feminist philosophy and scholarship crystallized the awareness of writers such as Barolini and Bryant, and have given them additional language to describe and fictionalize their struggles as women, as well as their struggles as members of a non-Anglo group.

Umbertina, Barolini's first novel, traces the lives of four generations of Italian-American women, from the immigrant experience of the title character to the late twentieth-century life of her great-granddaughter. This novel, like many others in the Italian-American tradition, is strongly autobiographical, inspired by Barolini's discovery of a tin heart that belonged to her great-grandmother (this heart becomes an important symbol in *Umbertina,* and even inspires the cover art for the novel). Barolini's decision to depict the immigrant experience and legacy as transmitted through female generations, as well as the generation of feminism in her contemporary characters, clearly reflects the development of her own feminism and authority, as well as emphasizing the departure from the traditional "up-from-the-immigrant-colony" novel discussed in the previous chapter. Interestingly, unlike Bryant, Barolini foregrounds her ethnicity in this novel, yet insists on labelling it a "feminist" novel; she in fact sees it as a feminist work rather than as an Italian-American (or "ethnic") novel. She says, "It happens to be women working through an Italian-American background, but the universal theme is women" (von Huene Greenberg 93). The novel begins by relating Umbertina's early life as a goat girl in the southern region of Calabria. Her life is bound to the land, to the flock in her care, and, above all, to her family. However, Barolini presents in Umbertina a woman who co-exists somewhat uneasily with the demands made upon her by her culture; she expresses, much more explicitly than does Maria Dalli, Petra Dalli, or Rosemary, her resentment of the family structures and gender roles that circumscribe her life.

Umbertina knows that the male—brother or father—has the final word in any matter (this is particularly true in her case, because her mother is dead), but she find herself resenting and resisting their power. For example, she dares to contradict Beppino, her brother, openly during a transaction in the marketplace, because she feels he is making a bad bargain. In doing so, she violates two dicta—first, that a woman's opinions and skills are valued only in the domestic sphere, and, second, that male authority is absolute and beyond question or reproach. When Beppino scolds her, Umbertina "looked at him with the scorn she never concealed from him. She infuriated Beppino by being more clever than he was. And she didn't care" (30).

However, Umbertina also realizes that there is little she can do to remedy the injustice of a society that values a foolish man over an intelligent woman. Her greatest aspiration must be to the position of women like Cristina Muzzi, who, "though not beautiful or clever . . . wore the sign of being taken [she is married and pregnant with her first child] and this was her rank over the virgins" (32). When Umbertina's time comes for marriage, she bows to her father's will, accepting the offer Serafino Longobardi, an "Americano" (an immigrant returned from America) who, by the village standards, is a wealthy man. Her refusal of Giosué, to whom she is attracted but who is poor and is soon to be drafted into the national army, is based on her realization that "her wishes counted not at all . . . she was bound by men's notions of what women must be. . . . In her world . . . a woman could not afford the displeasure of any man—even the sneaky and insignificant Beppino" (34). Her decision to "not think further of Giosué" (35) is confirmed by what she reads as a sign from God, a powerful thunderstorm that causes her to fall down the mountainside. Thus, the final word is that of the ultimate patriarch, whose work, in Umbertina's world, is to to "mete out . . . misfortunes" (35).

Serafino's return to Calabria represents Barolini's recognition of the phenomenon portrayed by Benasutti in *No Steadyjob for Papa* and Bryant in *Miss Giardino*. Like many immigrants disillusioned by the hardships and prejudice of life in

America, Serafino returns with his meager savings to buy land (a mark of tremendous status in a country where land belonged only to the very rich, or to the Church). However, he is quickly reminded of the very conditions that inspired him to leave: barren, wasted land, poor equipment, and the unjust system of exorbitant taxation. He is reminded that Italy " 'pretends to give us land in exchange for our money and work, then takes it back with taxes and interest while the rich are exempt' " (47). His loss of confidence and his acquiescence, ironically, become an opportunity for Umbertina, allowing her to assume the role of family leader and to make the decision to move to America permanently. There is a hint of *destino* mingled with Umbertina's strong-willed character in this decision: "It had been decided in her long before, at the time she had agreed to be his wife" (48). Within this portrayal, then, is a suggested explanation for the mass immigration that contradicts the strong family culture (and the resistance to change) of Italian tradition. While many immigrants returned to Italy, sent for other family members as the necessary money accumulated, or, at least, sent money back home, many completely severed all ties with the "Old Country," leaving behind parents, siblings, and other relatives forever. Clearly, then, the intertwining strains of economic, political, and social injustice (inflamed, no doubt, by the failed promise of reform raised by Garibaldi's rebellion) had finally accumulated enough force to disrupt these century-old ties and traditions.

However, the promise for improvement held out by America is equally contradictory, and Barolini's portrayal of late nineteenth-century tenement life reveals hardships not unlike those in Italy. Witnessing the consequences of the *padrone's* (boss) power over the "greenhorns," she realizes that success in America rests on "the need to be *her* own boss" (my emphasis) (65). However, she finds in America the same injustices she resented in Italy; doubly discriminated against because of her gender as well as her ethnicity, Umbertina realizes that " 'It takes a woman three days in a sweatshop—if she's lucky and not fined—to get what a man does in one day' " (65).

Umbertina learns another harsh lesson as she and Serafino struggle to save enough money to leave New York City, and purchase a farm upstate. Her interaction with Anna Giordani reveals the intraethnic tensions and prejudice many southern Italian immigrants faced. Anna, of northern Italian origin, has converted to Protestantism (shorthand for "American" in the eyes of most Italian immigrants) and embraced assimilationist attitudes with a vengeance:

> "You people are impossible. It is you, from the South, who have given us Italians in this city a bad name. You live where the Germans and Irish and Jews, no matter how poor, won't live. You break the picket lines . . . and when you are robbed and even murdered you won't go to the police—you want to take care of it among yourselves in your disgusting little vendettas." (74)

Umbertina, for her part, "wondered why this woman, who felt so superior because she was English-speaking and Protestant, still bothered to call herself Italian"

(74). Nonetheless, she respects Anna, for she realizes that "no one else . . . had taught [her] the real facts of American life . . . and stimulated her desire to overcome her disadvantages and make good . . ." (74). Her desire to "make good" impels her to sell her *coperta* (wedding quilt), the only artifact of her past, besides the tin heart Giosué gave her, she has brought from Castegna. Later, when she tries to buy it back and is refused, she reflects bitterly,

> It seemed . . . worse than the greed of Baron Mancuso . . . worse than the indifference of Don Antonio and the bishop. For they had taken the work and obedience of the poor but never the things from a poor man's home. What were Americans . . . that they had so few feelings. . . . "This is a country without heart. . . . Only buying and selling is understood here." (76, 78)

Despite her bitterness, however, Umbertina recognizes the need to do away with sentiment and longing for the old ways, in order to survive the harsh energy of America. In contrast, Barolini portrays Cristina Muzzi, whom Umbertina scornfully dismisses as "always crying for the past" (76). Umbertina's acceptance of this bargain is reflected in her exchange with Sister Carmela, a teacher at her children's school. When the nun suggests that Umbertina's children ought to learn proper Italian at school, as opposed to the dialect they speak at home (" 'It's the cultural heritage of these children to know their mother tongue' " 93), Umbertina is alarmed:

> "Oh, no, Sister, not Italian! It is American our children need. They have to go and earn their living in America and they have to read and write for us who have no learning. Leave the Italian to us at home, and teach them the language of how to do business in this country. . . . The culture will come after we make a living, God willing." (93)

"Culture" was a luxury in which immigrants could not afford to indulge; economic security for the family was their primary goal and driving force. The negative consequences of this bargain are portrayed by Barolini in Umbertina's descendants—particularly in her female descendants.

Barolini makes clear the ironies of Umbertina's efforts to ensure her family's survival in America. It is her ingenuity and business sense that catalyze their financial success. More than that, however, she enables them to "make America"—that peculiar Italian expression that encapsulates a host of attitudes toward immigrant success. It means not only to "make it," in the sense of bare survival, nor only in the sense of achieving financial success. It also means to create America, to make it part of their own, and to succeed on America's own terms. Several commentators have pointed out that many Italian immigrants did literally "make" America by being a crucial part of the labor force that built the subways, railroads, bridges, and buildings that exploded across America in the late-nineteenth and early-twentieth centuries.

Rose Basile Green notes that "to make America" was a term of both derision and envy for Italian-American immigrants (720); while it denoted the economic success immigrants desired, it also carried with it the sense that "the alien's struggle in America has little to do with his former position or virtue" and "suggests that success is the reward of aggression, sometimes even dubious means, and even of violence" (*The Italian American Novel* 72). Such suspicion may find its roots in the Italian peasant's experience that the wealthy violate and take advantage of the poor. This suspicion of those who "made America" is reflected in the character of Domenico Saccà, who remarks to Umbertina,

> "You call this success, Tinuzza, but in Italy there's a different *benessere* and the word is more gracious, not so materialistic. Well-being of the total person—not just money, but spirit, too. How crude is the success of money compared with real *benessere*." (145)

While this declaration may be read as sentimental amnesia about the realities of life in Italy, or, perhaps, the "sour grapes" of one who failed, it does illustrate the sense of loss and compromise many immigrants felt in their efforts to succeed. I would argue, too, that for a woman the derisive connotations behind "making America" are multiplied; for a woman to usurp the authority of her husband and to gain material success where he failed was to usurp to the right order of the world. Nevertheless, despite Saccà's nagging, and her own occasional doubts ("only buying and selling is understood here"), Umbertina is proud of what she has achieved. Remarkably, Serafino voices no objections to her power, as one might expect, "somewhat because he was an easygoing fellow, somewhat because she would have done what she wanted anyway" (97). Besides, "she was more intelligent than he; he had always said so" (97).

Nonetheless, the empire she builds bears Serafino's name and leaves no doubt as to who will inherit her power. She and Serafino have four daughters, but "Umbertina, who had become a strong woman, did not ever consider that her daughters should be so; the future of the name and business was in her sons" (100). She acts not out of spite, but out of the traditional belief that "family property should stay with the family name, and that the husbands of her daughters should be expected to provide for them. . . . That was the way things were done in a right and ordered world" (133). Umbertina's belief may also be rooted in the conviction that her daughters will never be faced with economic struggle in America, a stance which ignores their need (and forgets her own need) for emotional and psychological strength and independence. Most important, however, is the recognition by Barolini (and the reader) that although Umbertina has frequently defied the conventions of a "right and ordered world," she is unable to reject them outright—a lesson she has carried with her, perhaps, from her fall down the mountain.

The irony and the consequences of Umbertina's failure to instill in her daughters the same strength, inventiveness, and independence she possesses, and to will to them a means for economic independence become obvious when Barolini relates the stories of Carla, Umbertina's daughter; Marguerite, Carla's daughter; and Umbertina (Tina), Marguerite's daughter. Additionally, it is clear in these subsequent stories the consequences of the suppression of cultural heritage made necessary by the demands of assimilation. When coupled with restrictions imposed by gender, made all the more dangerous by their presentation as natural and benign, such suppression has devastating results, particularly for Marguerite.

However, Umbertina is not entirely immune to these effects, despite her economic success; it becomes clear that her power is confined, and, in many respects, illusory. When Serafino dies, she loses her status because her sons take over the business, as she intended. Relegated to the role of the stereotypical Italian grandmother, sitting in a rocking chair or stirring pots of tomato sauce, she has become an anachronism to her Americanized grandchildren, to whom she is a largely irrelevant and vaguely frightening presence, "the old lady in black who sat under a tree and was served food all day and given babies to kiss" (140). She is baffled by her sudden loss of power and status, for though she has always accepted the notion that "it was a man's world" (134), its truth was not evident "when she was actually in command and wielding her own will" (134). She has masqueraded her own role in the family's success so well that newspaper accounts of Serafino's death "As was customary . . . credited him with the business success and his wife only with having been his working companion" (128). Condolences are directed toward his sons, "who have so worthily followed the paternal example" (128).

Barolini devotes small space to the story of Umbertina's youngest daughter, Carla,[1] but in her story we see the results of Umbertina's failure to follow through on the feminist promise of her own life. Carla is portrayed as living in a "dream world," full of notions of romantic love that baffle her practical and straightforward mother. She harbors early ambitions of finishing high school and going on to college, but is forced to leave school to work in the family business—and it is Umbertina's word that makes this decision final:

> "You help your brothers. . . . we're living in Jake's house and he's head of the family now. And don't talk foolishness about college. No daughter of mine is going off to sleep out of town under strange roofs. Girls should be married." (135)

Carla's easy acceptance of these commands reveal the degree to which Umbertina's strength has been arrested; in fact, she is deterred from these goals (vague though they may be) by promises of new clothes and charge accounts in any stores she wishes. She becomes preoccupied with two suitors (a convention Barolini employs for each of the four major female characters in the novel, as a means of demonstrating the choices available to a woman at different times, as well as to illustrate each woman's character). Carla's rejection of an ambitious law student, who "encourag[ed] her self-education," (137) in favor of Sam Scalzo, who "was quiet and undemanding" (137), ends her vague sense of expectations for the future; she "*as a woman* . . . learned that there was an end to expectations, to going forward, to always succeeding and wrestling destiny to the ground" (my emphasis) (140).

The novel's shift to Marguerite's story reveals the true emphasis in Barolini's novel. Though Umbertina gives the novel its name, and the novel begins and ends with the stories of the two Umbertinas, it is Marguerite who is literally and figuratively the center of the novel,[2] and it is Marguerite's section that is most in the tradition of the feminist consciousness-raising novel. Though she is born to the economic security for which Umbertina had to struggle, she is far from satisfied with the life to which her family has aspired. To her, the sterility of their existence is embodied in their surroundings:

> It was a home in which they never lit fires in the fireplaces. It began to strike Marguerite that in her family all of them, including herself, were as unlit and unnatural as the clean white birch logs neatly arranged on the brass andirons of fireplaces that served no purpose. (153)

The "real *benessere*" of which Domenico spoke to Umbertina is truly gone from their lives. Nor is Marguerite encouraged in this sterile atmosphere to aspire to more than marriage and motherhood when she grows up—showing that not much has changed since Umbertina's time, except for the outward trappings of status and material success. Marguerite's frustrations and anger are reflected in a diary entry from her college years:

> "All these snooty, shining girls! They know who they are and where they're going. One of them is descended from Thomas Edison. I'm the only Italian name here. They're all saying they're going to be writers or doctors or go into the Foreign Service. Whoever told me I could do any of that?" (310)

Ironically, Barolini is suggesting both that Marguerite's identity as an Italian limits her, and that the repression of her Italian heritage contributes to Marguerite's feelings of unnaturalness, of lifelessness, of being an outsider. Her parents, born of Italians, have internalized the hated stereotypes of Italians in America; Marguerite learns early on

> that it was not nice to look too Italian and to speak bad English the way Uncle Nunzio did. Italians were not a serious people, her father would say. . . . Italians were buffoons, anarchists, and womanizers. "What are we, Dad, aren't we Italian?" she would ask. "We're Americans," he'd say firmly, making her wonder about all the people in the shadows who came before him. (150)

Nonetheless, Marguerite finds herself inevitably drawn to Uncle Nunzio's example—his garden, where he tends such exotica as fig trees and grapevines, his cellar where he makes wine—all the time sensing "how un-American it was and how her parents disapproved" (151). Their disapproval of and discomfort with their Italian heritage is remedied by embracing with particular fervor the American work ethic and material success as the defining force in their lives.

Thus, Barolini takes Benasutti's acknowledgement of the relationship between family and capitalism into the next generation. Thomas Ferraro observes of Mario Puzo's *The Godfather* that that particular novel "takes the fusion of kinship and capitalist enterprise seriously" (20). Barolini, too, is concerned with this "fusion." In her portrayal, the concept of what it means to be "American," inextricably linked in the immigrant mind to economic success, has altered the Italian ideal of family; though still at the center of one's life, "family" and the ideal of filial obedience take on a decidedly capitalist spirit. Umbertina's bitter observation that "only buying and selling is understood [in America]" is literalized in her descendants:

> [F]amily talk was always in words of commercial transaction. Children *owed* parents respect; children *paid back* what was done for them by studying hard and leading good lives; children had to *capitalize* on their talents; doing so bore *dividends* in life; you didn't go around with certain people because there was no *profit* in it. The family motto could have been "Money Talks." (154)

Marguerite's various rebellions against her upbringing fail to remedy the deep divisions she feels between her American and Italian heritages, or her frustrations at the limitations both cultures impose on her gender.[3] The dismissive label of "Mad Marguerite," imposed on her by the girls at school, reflects a convention of many feminist consciousness-raising novels, that of the heroine's sense that she is "crazy" for failing to feel comfortable with the demands of society.[4] Likewise, her runaway marriage with Lennart, her affair with Gillo, and, finally, her marriage to Alberto are similar to Ella's attempts to find emotional, intellectual, and spiritual fulfillment through men.

When Marguerite turns to Alberto, she hopes that he can lead her to some resolution of her questions: Who am I? Where do I belong? Though Marguerite, like Umbertina before her, resents the idea that her life be defined in traditional terms—marriage and motherhood—she is unable to break free from the very terms she seeks to defy. Her ethnic confusion leads her to mistake the arrogant and banal pronouncements of Alberto's friends for depth and brilliance, simply because they are Italian, and to covet the role of *Lesbia Purissima*, the poet's wife, as a means of compensating for "the pains of her unhappy past" (175). Alberto, in turn, promises her "I will make a real human being out of you. We will live a life of art together" (177). The implication of this arrogant pronouncement is, of course, that Marguerite, because she is neither Italian nor American, but more particularly because she is a woman, is somehow less than human. Alberto plays Prospero to her Caliban, rescuing her from instability, uncertainty, and incomplete humanity.

Her drive to improve herself reveals her inability to free herself from the

American heritage she feels is sterile and spiritless. Despite her disdain for the Protestant work ethic (which for her is embodied in *The Little Engine That Could,* "that chugging, struggling little prig of an engine full of dutiful fortitude and New World optimism" (151)), she searches for a work identity that will fulfill her emotional needs. Most of her attempts, Barolini implies, are dilettantish, lacking serious commitment. Her moves back and forth between Italy and the States literalize her restless shifts between her Italian and American identities, and the losses and damage to her possessions during these moves suggest the emotional and spiritual losses and damage that Marguerite sustains in her restless struggle to define herself. This theme of displacement, in fact, is central to much of Barolini's criticism and fiction; her earliest literary productions were about "displaced Americans in Rome" ("Becoming a Literary Person" 269). Edvige Giunta points out that

> The immigrant is an outcast in more ways than one: s/he is cut off from the culture of consent and from the culture of descent, which is reduced to a ghost culture within the new country; but s/he also occupied a marginal position within the culture of origins prior to emigration. In other words, the sense of loss and separation pre-exists emigration, and immigration, rather than healing the fracture between self and culture, re-enacts endlessly the drama of separation and subsequent marginalization. ("Narratives of Loss" 165)

Thus, Marguerite's inability to settle in one physical space literalizes and emphasizes her sense of psychological and spiritual displacement. Marguerite "cared enormously for place" and strove "to make beautiful" (305) every place they lived. However, as Anthony Tamburri argues, she cannot stay "placed" because "she focuses her intellectual energy on her husband's professional and personal success" ("Gender/Ethics" 33). The irony of her successful translations of her husband's poetry into English, which secures for him an audience in the States and, in turn, enhances his reputation in Italy is not lost on Marguerite; her success is to her a "sick joke," because "She could do for Alberto what she could not do for herself" (181). However, what she fails to recognize is Alberto's dependence on her—her skill in rendering the translations is necessary for their (and his) success.[5]

Barolini shows that Marguerite's appeal to psychiatry to resolve her restlessness and the questions about her identity is simply a variation of her other fruitless attempts to find resolution through relationships with men. Additionally, she offers the same critique of psychoanalysis that Bryant (and many other women writing in the tradition of the feminist consciousness-raising novel) serves up in *Ella Price's Journal.* The novel's prologue includes one of Marguerite's sessions with her therapist—the session that launches the search for her grandmother, and leads us into Umbertina's story. Marguerite's dream of being in a classroom, where "I am the only foreign one" (14), lays out many of the symbols and conflicts within all three women's stories. The erasure of the abstractions the teacher writes on the board, and the transmutation of the final abstraction, "grossness," into "grocery" (which Marguerite concludes is the store Umbertina started decades earlier) carries several levels of meaning. In Umbertina's case, there is no use for abstractions when bare economic survival is at stake; the "grocery" becomes the method for ensuring this survival. For Marguerite, for whom economic security is established, abstractions have become her whole life, and she feels lost and unanchored in the material world; the grocery for her means "getting back to the base of everything" (18)—that is, to Umbertina. Tina's life, then, represents a synthesis of the abstract and the material; a synthesis, Barolini suggests, is necessary for rooting in the New World. Thus, Marguerite's therapist encourages her insight: "Start with your grandmother" (19).

I would argue that Barolini's use of female generations to illustrate the generation of feminism, though not an uncommon strategy, is particularly significant in light of her Italian heritage. Like Bryant, Barolini does not make explicit this novel's allegiance to the Women's Liberation Movement (though, as Bryant does through Laura's character in *Ella Price's Journal*, Barolini brings the WLM into the novel tangentially through Weezy, Marguerite's other daughter); Marguerite's struggle and Tina's developing self-awareness are depicted largely as internal, private processes. However, it may be said that the family (specifically, female family members) acts in this novel as a substitute for the larger women's movement; consciousness-raising, as Barolini depicts it, is effected by interaction with female relatives and ancestors (if only on an imaginative level).[6] Thus, the old dicta regarding the importance of family to one's identity and place in the world take on additional meaning for the twentieth-century female.

The promise of the breakthrough of Marguerite's dream interpretation and her therapist's support of this interpretation, unfortunately, is not borne out. Marguerite's mental plea to Umbertina—"Oh, Grandma Longobardi, give me your guts!" (7)—suggests a fundamental misunderstanding of Umbertina's character on Marguerite's part. She asks, "Had Umbertina wondered as she lay in steerage . . . what her life would be like, what its meaning was? Had she wondered how she'd speak? And to whom?" (7). However, as noted, Umbertina's overriding concern with ensuring the family's survival left her no time for mulling over such matters; for Umbertina, " 'The important thing . . . is to find your place. Everything depends on that. You find your place, you work, and like planting seeds, everything grows. But you have to be watchful and stick to it' " (139). Umbertina knows, too, that happiness "could [not] come bound up in any one man. . . . It wasn't a prize you were given and could hold on to, but a feeling of satisfaction that receded or advanced according to each day's design" (139). Nonetheless, Umbertina's essentially conservative nature leads her to answer Carla's question " '[Where is] . . . my place?' " with " 'Where your husband will be' " (140).

Thus, the conflicted messages Marguerite receives about her ethnicity and her gender, at least in part, explain her inability to become rooted, to be satisfied. She can only validate herself in relation to others, particularly in relation to men. The narrator tells us, "always she asked for love . . . when she asked the shoemaker if the heels on her shoes could be fixed for tomorrow . . . the flower man how long the anemones would last . . . Tina's boyfriends to return the books of hers they borrowed" (7–8). The sexist assumptions upon which her Jungian psychiatrist's method rests reinforce Marguerite's sense of weakness and ineffectualness. Dr. Verdile's dismissal of her quandary (much like Dan's dismissal of Ella's reading of Tolstoy, Dreiser, and Flaubert) leaves her feeling "stupid and defeated": " 'There's a typical female wile for that. You can get [Alberto] to sign [divorce papers] and then go to bed. . . . It's something women have always been able to do. It's a classic stratagem, no?' " (5).

Her affair with Massimo, a final attempt to find satisfaction through love, simply forces her to recapitulate the role she played with Alberto: she translates Massimo's work and promotes him for the Strega literary prize. Her pregnancy and subsequent car accident/suicide (Barolini deliberately leaves the interpretation of Marguerite's death obscure) are the inevitable literalizations of her life's dilemmas—her giving of life to another can have no other result than her death. Edvige Giunta argues, in fact, that "Marguerite's tragic death captures Barolini's perception of the fragility of her position as an aspiring writer. By killing Marguerite, Barolini gives voice to her own self-doubt" ("Blending 'Literary' Discourses" 4). Thus, Marguerite's story, unlike Ella's, may be read in light of the convention of eighteenth-century novels, for which closure relied on two options: the heroine's marriage, or her death. We cannot "write beyond the ending" for Marguerite; Barolini defers the open ending to Tina's story.

The story of Tina, Marguerite's elder daughter, is Barolini's hopeful resolution to Marguerite's story. Tina embodies Fred L. Gardaphé's description of third-generation Italian-American fiction writers: "assimilation has created a shift in the focus. . . . their [work] is less a means of presenting what it means to be Italian in America and more of what it means to carry the cultural trappings of *italianità* into their everyday American lives" ("Italian-American Fiction" 71–72). Her removal from the immigrant experience allows her in the course of her story to resolve questions about her gendered and ethnic identities; ultimately, Tina is the fictional representation of what one third-generation Italian-American writer, Tina DeRosa, articulates as the basis for her fiction:

> Our grandparents and parents were bound to survival; we, on the other hand, have become freer to use our talents and to rescue the talents of those who came before us. Because we have passed through more time, we have a perspective that gives us the ability to look back and to judge their experiences as treasures we cannot throw out. (Gardaphé "An Interview with Tina DeRosa" 23)

Tina very seriously pursues her role as "rescuer" in the novel. Her scholarship puzzles her practical, assimilated grandparents; when Tina informs Sam, her grandfather, of her plans to pursue a Ph.D. in Italian and classical scholarship, he asks, " 'But why Italian. . . . What will that fit you for? . . . I don't understand this infatuation with Italy! . . . Where will that get you? Italy has no future. What has Italy ever done for the world?' " (397). Tina, for her part, wonders, "What was wrong with the immigrants' children that left them so distrustful of their *italianità?*" (397). Yet she (and Barolini) is "torn between compassion and indignation" (398). She recognizes the costs that immigration and assimilation have exacted upon this generation, while wondering "She understood him, why couldn't he understand her?" (398).

Yet Tina's own history reveals tremendous uncertainty about her identity; like Marguerite, she experiences an internal tug-of-war between her Italian and American selves. Like Marguerite, she literally and figuratively moves back and forth between the States and Italy. However, she pushes Marguerite's shifts one step further by taking on distinct physical and mental characteristics in each location, revealing that she, too, has not yet learned the real lesson Umbertina has to teach: the necessity of finding and accepting one's place. She confesses to an American friend:

> "I've never understood where I belong. It tears my whole life apart each time—I mean I go through this absolute trauma of trying to decide here or there.... Part of me loves this natural, human life over here and the other part sees that it won't get me anyplace and that I've got to go back and plug into the system over there. God, Missy, it drives me up the wall!" (298)

Nonetheless, even as Barolini depicts Tina's uncertainty, she also makes clear that Tina has learned from Marguerite's example; Marguerite has passed on to Tina, and her sister, Weezy, the message that they must seek strength and security for themselves before becoming committed to marriage and children—and the cruel irony of Marguerite's success is that she does not live to witness it. Marguerite's cultivation of oleander (a variation on the symbolism of the rosemary that Umbertina plants and nurtures as a symbol of women's strength) underscores this theme: " 'There's a Spanish proverb . . . that in the house where the oleander blooms, the girls of the house don't marry. I have two daughters and I can never tell whether to get rid of the oleander or the daughters' " (301). Tina wonders, "Did it mean in the kind of house Marguerite Morosini set up, her daughters were deliberately warned against marriage?" (301).

Clearly, Tina and Weezy have choices available to them that Marguerite did not—choices that arose, in large part, out of the sexual revolution of the 1960s and the so-called "Second Wave" of feminism. Barolini traces this theme of (r)evolution in several ways. First, she shows how Tina's opportunity for college education helped eliminate the restless searching that drove Marguerite throughout her life; furthermore, Tina is taught to see college as an opportunity to pursue meaningful work, rather than simply as an opportunity to expand social connections or to find a husband. Thus, Tina succeeds in ways that Umbertina could never have imagined for herself, and in which Marguerite could never hope to participate. It is significant to note the movement that Tina's story makes, as she stakes out a career for herself, in contrast to Marguerite's efforts. Marguerite could only translate her husband's work; she could never imagine engaging with it in a scholarly or critical way. Tina, however, can make the leap to critic and scholar, and establish for herself a reputation separate from the poets she studies. Though Alberto encourages her to stay in Italy, translating his work ("You could . . . get a credit that would help you in your own career" 332), Tina knows that "the trouble with Rome . . . [is that] her part in it was too perfect, too easy. All she had to do was . . . simply be her father's daughter and everything would be accessible and easy and she would only have to let things happen" (314). Tina, however, is not naive about her prospects for success in academia; she loves her scholarship but recognizes, as did Umbertina, that it is a man's world:

> "Of course it pisses me off that I have to sell myself to the Department as a good investment before they'll give me a fellowship! They hesitate with a woman 'cause they're scared we'll quit and get married, as if a woman's education didn't become an integral part of her life as a man's . . . as if a woman couldn't marry and have a career, too! That's the unfair part—but that's real and I've got to live with it and live around it and not let it get me down or take my sights away from what's really important." (320)

It is significant, of course, to consider the subject of Tina's academic pursuits. The fact that she chooses Dante, a traditional subject, rather than engaging with emergent feminist studies, suggests again Barolini's emphasis on her ethnicity, and the necessity for reclaiming it.

Tina's occasional uneasiness with her decision to become a scholar, fueled by her grandparents' practical objections and her worries about acceptance by academia's male-dominated hierarchy, is compounded by her conflict with her younger sister, Weezy. Weezy embraces radical feminism, claiming that she is "into real life . . . she gloried in real work, sweat, the hard edges of existence, survival" (308). Interestingly, this was precisely Umbertina's struggle—but Weezy has had the luxury of an economically secure background. Nonetheless, she criticizes Tina for having a "life centered around this awful contrived thing called getting ahead" (310). Though Tina rebukes her—"Right now all you're really into is yourself"—Tina feels uncomfortable in the "recognition that she was not socially committed" (310).

Tina and Weezy's conflict points to the general upheaval in women's roles, but also recapitulates aspects of Marguerite's struggle. While women of Tina's generation were faced not so much with the question of whether or not they could live outside the traditional scope of women's roles, they still had to struggle with the "meaning" of whatever activity they chose. Is Tina breaking more barriers by entering into a male-dominated profession, or is Weezy's commitment to social change through protest and social activism more valuable in securing sexual equality? Barolini suggests that such comparisons are counterproductive; what matters is that both Tina and Weezy are able to choose freely the role that best fulfills their needs. Nonetheless, the fact that Tina's choice is foregrounded, rather than Weezy's, suggests Barolini's discomfort with an explicit commitment to radical feminism and to the Women's Liberation Movement.[7] Tina's rise to consciousness is depicted as private, inspired by her observations of her mother's struggles and mistakes, rather than as the result of engagement with a larger social and political movement.

Tina's life is linked to those of her female predecessors in one other important way—sex and reproduction. Umbertina endures almost constant pregnancy during the early years of her marriage; she bears nine children, two of whom die, and experiences several miscarriages. Weezy and Tina's discovery of the anguished final entry in Marguerite's diary reveals that little has changed:

> "Is this the bill for happiness? Is this paying the goddam fiddler.... who else but me is going to pay? Now what? Ask him to leave his wife.... A backroom abortion ...And where would the money come from? What could I tell A.? What do women do in Italy ... or anyplace?...." (312)

Though we never know for certain what happens between Marguerite and Massimo, Weezy and Tina fashion for themselves a final scenario: " 'You can just bet he must have rejected her—in some nice, smooth, Italian-men's-style way, but rejection all the same' "(312). Ironically, Weezy reflects, " 'She should have told me; I'd have helped her' " (312)—that is, helped her obtain a safe abortion. The irony of Tina and Weezy's discovery is compounded when Tina acknowledges her own pregnancy by Duke.

That Tina can decide to have an abortion, and is able to act on that decision, marks an important departure from Marguerite's story. Nonetheless, similarities persist; Tina does indeed pay the fiddler, literally—the abortion costs 250,000 lire, the money obtained, ironically, through the sale of Marguerite's jewelry. She pays figuratively, as well; Barolini describes the humiliation (Angela, the friend of Marguerite's who arranges the abortion, takes Tina to the doctor with a date in tow) and pain of the abortion in harrowing detail. Despite Angela's cavalier attitude — " 'An abortion is no more than going to the hairdresser's these days' " (339) — Tina's experience is anything but trifling. The doctor, though well-bred and cordial, makes her feel like "one of those carcasses hanging in all the meat markets in Rome" (343)—a description that echoes Ella Price's sense of being "a plucked chicken about to be gutted" (Bryant 227).

Clearly, through Marguerite's and Tina's stories, Barolini is commenting on the sexist bias of a medical establishment dominated by men, whether they are treating a woman's mind (e.g., through psychiatry) or her body. In *Gyn/Ecology: The Metaethics of Radical Feminism*, feminist theologian and philosopher Mary Daly argues that women's oppression is the result of male desire to control both women's minds and bodies; she uses the term "mind gynecolgy" to emphasize the link between these practices. Nonetheless, Tina reflects to Weezy, " 'I'm one of the lucky ones who had the money. The women who get it done on a kitchen table with knitting needles aren't so lucky' " (347).

Tina's relationships with men (with, of course, the additional link of her pregnancy and abortion) recapitulate Marguerite's, but, Barolini suggests, also resolve them precisely because of Tina's more highly developed awareness. Again, Barolini employs the convention of the two-suitor plot to explore Tina's options. We are presented first with Duke, Tina's college lover, who represents the paradox of the American dream. "[A] poor white from Tennessee who got a scholarship from Harvard" (293), Duke subsequently drops out of school, unable (or unwilling) to accept its demands for success. Initially, Tina is attracted to his intelligence and sensitivity; she romanticizes his decision by seeing him as a "literary Huck Finn" (293), and admires his courage for leaving "the system." Eventually, however, she realizes that his lack of ambition is draining her own determination; her decision to break off their relationship (even though she suspects that she is pregnant) coincides with the news of Marguerite's death and Tina's return to Italy. The abortion, then, is Tina's literal and figurative rejection of confinement to traditional roles. She refuses to tell either Duke or her father about her pregnancy, the former because he would insist on marrying her, the latter because he would pressure Tina to keep the baby and remain in Italy to raise it. Either option, she realizes, would result in the abortion of her own goals, a result no less (and perhaps more) painful than the physical operation.

Tina's second "suitor," Jason, captures another dimension of sexual politics in the novel. Tina envies Jason's secure sense of his place in the world, his personal history, and the assurance with which he pursues his professional goals. Barolini suggests, of course, that this ease is rooted in Jason's masculinity; however, emphasizing the intertwining nature of gender and ethnicity, she also makes clear that Jason's assurance is due equally to his Puritan heritage, his thorough sense of himself as "American." Tina's decision to include Jason in her trip to Castegna is based on her belief that there is an essential connection between them, as Jason relates the story of a ship, the *Castegna*, in his own family history.

This journey literalizes Marguerite's earlier attempt to "start with your grandmother." The trip has overtones of a healing pilgrimage, for Tina needs to recover from the dual blows of her mother's death and the abortion. However, Barolini shows that Tina's search for her roots is, at best, misguided, and is destined to disappoint her. She soon recognizes her mistake in including Jason, and leaves him midway through the journey, realizing that she must reject "the model of the heterosexual couple as a means to self-definition" (Felski 132). In the tradition of many female novels of self-discovery, Barolini portrays "The symbiosis of the couple . . . as inimical to and destructive of the heroine's struggle for identity. . . . Erotic passion, by its very intensity, can sabotage the protagonist's struggle to strengthen an often precarious sense of independent identity" (Felski 131). Instead, such novels portray the importance of relationships with women as the best means to self-discovery, because "Knowledge, rather than desire, is emphasized as the key to the relationships between women" (131). Tina's turn to her mother, and then to her great-grandmother as the source for this knowledge, seems a positive step, for, as Felski argues, "the other woman provides a mirror in which the protagonist discovers herself, finding her own female identity reflected" (131–132).

A typical strategy in the female novel of self-discovery is the portrayal of "Nature . . . as an extension of some kind of 'feminine' principle. . . . Both nature and community are perceived to complement and extend the protagonist's sense of self rather than to threaten it by absolute otherness . . ." (132). However, instead of connecting with her past through nature, Tina discovers a burnt, despoiled, and desolate land[8] whose inhabitants reject any connection with her. Tina's excitement at the village priest's recognition of her great-grandmother's name is dispelled when he adds "[The immigrants] never come back. They left because of *misèria* and they forget the others still here in *misèria*" (386). Tina is dismayed when her romantic conception of the "natural" life of Castegna as one removed from the ill effects of industrialization and capitalism are destroyed. She remarks, " '[I]t's too bad they are losing some of the *natural* [my emphasis] ways of doing things. Sometimes . . . I think it's too bad [immigrants] left at all' " (382).[9] However, Ferruccio rebukes her:

> "Yes, *that's* the really hard nut to crack. . . . You could never have come back to show off your superior taste if they hadn't gotten out in the first place. And they got out to better themselves and use plastic if they want to. But when you come back, you're sorry they're still not what they used to be. . . . They advanced you to the middle-class—but you want them to stay peasants." (382)

Tina has not yet learned the real lesson Umbertina has to teach her—the need to let go of sentimental yearnings for a false past, to find her place and sink her roots. Thus, Tina leaves Castegna knowing "that though she has physically located the where of Umbertina, the secret of why she was lost and Umbertina . . . still eluded her" (387).

Ironically, the moment that Tina discovers the "secret of Umbertina" she is unaware that Umbertina is speaking to her. However, Barolini's placement of this moment brings together important themes in the novel, and emphasizes Tina's role both as rescuer (including her earlier appropriation of Umbertina's tin heart as a talisman for her journey) and her story as resolution of the struggles of her female predecessors. When Tina sees Umbertina's *coperta* displayed at the Museum of Immigration, it seems to "[speak] to her of Italy and the past and keeping it all together for the future. It was as if . . . the Umbertina she had fruitlessly sought in Castegna, had suddenly become manifest in the New World and spoken to her" (408). The significance of the *coperta* of course, is that its sale represents the moment that Umbertina recognized the importance of not sentimentalizing the past for its own sake, and for commiting oneself to a place in the world, despite sacrifices and pain—a lesson Tina has finally accepted. Thus, Barolini's depiction of Tina's "discovery of [herself] can best be described as a process of awakening rather than learning, a recovery of what has always been present but suppressed" (Felski 143).

Tina's reward for learning this lesson structures the ending of the novel. The earlier pain of sacrificing her relationship with Jason has been ameliorated by her successful completion of her doctorate; it is eliminated when they reunite and decide to marry. In a clear break from most consciousness-raising novels, Tina gets to have both a rewarding professional life and a fulfilling romantic and sexual relationship; significantly, this relationship takes the form of traditional, heterosexual marriage. While Barolini alludes to Tina's struggles to succeed in male-dominated academia, she chooses not to depict these interactions, opting instead simply to assure us of Tina's personal and professional success. However, Mary Jo Bona argues that precisely because familial and communal identity are so crucial for Italian-American women's writing, that these writers do not see a portrayal such as this one as inconsistent or as a "cop-out" to convention; in *Claiming a Tradition*, Bona writes, "While community and marriage mean sacrificing selfhood and work to the Anglo woman novelist, they are not necessarily interpreted the same way in the ethnic woman's tradition. . . . There is no dialectic set up in these novels between love . . . and work . . . (336). Thus, Tina willingly embraces Jason's ancestral home on Cape Cod as her own, and consecrates her place in it by planting rosemary: "Her place was marked; all the positioning to come, between her and Jason, would have this as focus" (424). Thus, Barolini's portrayal of Tina's rise to awareness reveals a "focus upon the process of psychological transformation rather than upon a detailed exploration of its social implications. . . . the heroine's new self-knowledge [also] creates a basis for future negotiation between the subject and society, the outcome of which is projected beyond the bounds of the text" (Felski 133).

Barolini's second novel, *Love in the Middle Ages* (1986), is similar to *Umbertina* in its use of the conventions of realism and of the feminist self-discovery novel, and continues the theme of displacement seen in *Umbertina*. However, Barolini's focus in this novel is not on the physical displacement of the immigrant; rather, she continues to explore the consequences of emotional and psychological displacement that dominate Marguerite's story. The novel's protagonist, Donna Scortese, embodies the divided sense of self that Barolini associates with ethnic women. Her fragile sense of self, both as a woman and as an Italian American, is reflected in her attempts to shape not only her own identity, but those whom she loves. Donna's fear of displacement is constant, pervasive; early in the novel she reflects, "she was . . . an emotional scrounger on her children and friends. . . . all the time she was afraid of becoming marginal. . . . Perhaps she was now considered marginal because she was husbandless. Maybe that was like homeless" (24).

At the center of Donna's story is her love affair with Murray Buddenberg, a Jewish divorcé. Barolini deliberately constructs this relationship to explore the dynamics of ethnic difference, as well as the pernicious effects of ethnic stereotypes. She exploits the didactic nature of the self-discovery novel in order to reverse stereotypes (as well as to express her personal irritation with stereotypes of Italians as unintellectual, tacky, loud, and overly emotional); implicit in this strategy is Barolini's faith in the power of fiction to explore and effect social change. Finally, she questions the melting pot romance of novelists like Mari Tomasi, by presenting the romantic convention of opposites attracting, and then subverting that convention by showing how those oppositions, which she explicitly links to ethnicity, cause the relationship to fail.

The title of the novel is important on several levels. At its most rudimentary, it refers, of course, to the fact that the lovers in the novel are middle-aged. On a symbolic level, "middle-age" carries with it connotations of stability, economic security, and comfort. However, for Bud and Donna, this conventional depiction has been turned upside down. Bud, having raised two children and seen them safely into independent adulthood, and having established a comfortable and economically secure life, is suddenly faced with divorce. Donna, though widowed seven years and with one of her three children still at home, still experiences panic attacks when problems arise that her husband used to handle. When confronted with a summons for failing to clear snow from her sidewalk, "she felt the same panic as when a light fuse blew or the car wouldn't start. She felt bereft, persecuted, angry, and sad" (12). Her sense of displacement is exacerbated by her changing role as a mother: she is experiencing the physical discomfort of menopause, and the emotional pain of her youngest child's increasing independence and rejection of her protection.

That Barolini intends Donna to be representative of the state of contemporary Italian-American women is emphasized by her name: Donna means "woman" in Italian, and thus takes on a generic quality.[10] It is clear, too, that Donna's story has roots in Barolini's own experience. Growing up, Donna was confronted with two models for behavior that reinscribe and reemphasize the autobiographical elements of Barolini's work. In those moments when Donna feels panicked, she reminds herself that "She wasn't ... Tony Flamingo's daughter for nothing" (12), learning from her father, as Barolini did from hers, the need for "tenaciousness and how to be on [her] own" ("Becoming a Literary Person" 264). Thus, the typically masculine attributes of strength and independence deeply influence Donna's character.

Barolini suggests, too, that Donna's father keeps her anchored to her ethnic identity as well. However, this link is uncomfortable and ambiguous for Donna; respect for her *italianità* is coupled with a deep distaste for the excessive qualities associated with it. Her discomfort is reflected in her hatred for her maiden name, Flamingo, given to her Sicilian grandfather by an uncomprehending and unsympathetic immigration officer. Thus, the immigrant's sense of belonging neither to the culture he has left behind, nor to the new one, is symbolized by an imposed name, a violation of identity. On their first date, the joke Bud tells Donna about flamingoes putting Italians out as lawn decorations is a double signifier for Donna's uneasiness with her ethnicity. First, it plays on her hated surname; second, the humor of the joke depends on the audience's recognition of the stereotype underlying it: Italian-Americans are fond of tacky, tawdry material displays.

Her mother offers a somewhat different model; again, in keeping with the tradition of the female novel of self-discovery, Donna turns to another woman as a "mirror" for her identity. Like the traditional Italian mother portrayed by Tomasi, she sees her role as one of inculcating certain values in her children, and shaping their lives. However, Donna's mother, Fenora, exerts her efforts toward inculcating an "American" identity and values in Donna. She enrolls Donna in a variety of lessons—ballet, piano, tennis, horseback riding—all of which Donna endured rather than enjoyed. Like Carla, Marguerite's mother, Fenora is interested in imitating the values of WASP America, in the hopes of making Donna's assimilation and upward mobility more secure.

Thus, while Donna recognizes the value of identifying with her father, as a woman she sees her only locus of power in replicating the role her mother played. In Donna's relationship with Fenora, as well as in her relationship with her own children, we see a conflation of Italian and American impulses. That is, we see the powerful shaping role of the mother coupled with the feeling expressed by Marguerite in *Umbertina*, her sense of what is the essence of "Americanness"; Marguerite feels that she must constantly be "laboring at something that should only have been accepted, without that uptight compulsion to better things . . ." (199). Later, as Donna examines the roots of this impulse in both herself and her mother, she recognizes the double message she was sent as a child:

> One said "Be somebody! Be polished and smooth and able to fit into American life as an accomplished person." The other said, "You are a girl, which means that all you're expected to do is marry, have children. . . . It's even a waste of time to send you to college—a little learning is a dangerous thing." (198)

This last lesson is one that many women have learned (e.g., Ella Price). Learning in and of itself is not dangerous; rather, its threat lies in the ways in which it challenges and undermines tradition, and its ability to radicalize thinking and behavior. Donna is also aware of Fenora's own thwarted ambitions to finish high school and attend Vassar: "in an Italian family that just wasn't possible—no girl from a good family would be allowed to sleep away from home at a college . . . even high school was too much of a luxury" (198).

As a result, Donna's attitudes toward change are very conflicted—a conflict that is typical of immigrant cultures. While her Italian heritage values steadiness and relies on the cyclical nature of life, her American life urges change, improvement, movement. Donna values change and its challenges on an intellectual level, and is relieved by the knowledge that "she could relinquish the search for any absolute and know that once and for all life is chancey" (180). Yet she is constantly unsettled by change: the onset of menopause, her developing relationship with Bud, Laddie's increasing independence.

Barolini portrays Donna's divided sense of self and her feelings of displacement by exploring Donna's aesthetic ideals. She values beauty, of course, but rejects the baroque, the opulent, and the ornate in favor of utter simplicity; in other words, she rejects what is identified as "Italian."[11] In the introduction to *The Dream Book*, Barolini writes:

> Italian American homes, gardens, names, churches were embarrassing—too ornate, too foreign. It was the pristine, classic simplicity of the white New England church steeple on the village green to which we conformed our taste, not to the rococo excesses of Catholic sanctuaries. ... (19–20)

In *The Puritan Conscience and Modern Sexuality* (1986), Edmund Leites argues that what he calls the "ethic of constancy," a willful exercise of self-control over all areas of one's life, was an emotional and moral imperative which "extended outward toward all classes of [Puritan] society" (1). Leites argues against the perceptions of Puritans as emotional "cold fish," such as that set forth by Max Weber; instead, he asserts, the rejection of emotional display was rooted in "the Puritan['s desire for] a culture which would encourage an even temperament, steadiness, and reliability" (6). The moral and emotional aspects of this ethic found a corresponding outlet in the rejection of material excess; simplicity and restraint were the guiding principles in dress and material possessions. This Puritan ethic of restraint was transmuted into "Americanness," and immigrants who did not adhere to it were viewed with suspicion and distaste. The love of Italian immigrants for "pagan" Catholicism, excessive in both its material and emotional manifestations (statuary, ornately embellished altar linens, *festas*) was regarded with horror by Anglo Protestants and ascetic Irish Catholics alike; as James Olson argues in *Catholic Immigrants in America* (1987), "For the Irish, the Italian *festa* was the perfect symbol of all that was wrong with Italian piety" (140). Thus, Donna's emotional and material restraint is the result of receiving the same message that Marguerite learned as a child—that it is not "nice" to appear "too Italian."

Certainly, the theme of muting, disguising, or rejecting one's ethnicity is not unique to Italian-American experience or literature. The tradition of the "passing" novel in African-American literature, for example, explores the emotional and psychological costs of denying one's African-American heritage in order to gain acceptance into the white mainstream. In *Love in the Middle Ages*, Barolini links this strategy of "passing" to gender, through her portrayal of Joan Beaverly, Donna's friend and business partner. I would argue that Joan functions as another "mirror" in this novel of self-discovery, as Donna works through her ideas about gender and ethnic difference. Though Jewish, Joan has cultivated the appearance of the quintessential WASP; in Donna's eyes, Joan represents "[a]n incredible act of mimesis" (58–59). Thus, Joan literalizes physically the transformation that Fenora urged Donna to enact psychically. What is even more significant about her transformation, however, is that she attributes it to marriage; she tells Donna, " '[Y]ou start becoming your partner' "(59).

For Donna, this statement has frightening implications. Her relationship with

Bud, based on the principle of opposites attracting, becomes a threat to her identity—will she become Bud? Though she willingly acknowledges the physical similarities between Italians and Jews (she remarks, for example, that Bud has "Italian hair"), she rejects vehemently the ways in which Bud reminds her of what she dislikes most about her *italianità*. She asks him, for example, to stop wearing his diamond pinkie ring, a family heirloom, because it makes him look "[l]ike one of the mob" (29). She is dismayed by his fondness for synthetic fiber, showy furniture, and ostentatious jewelry. She is irritated by his lack of interest in books, art, and music; he can parody a Tosca aria but does not recognize or appreciate the original. Donna reflects,

> After all the stereotypes of the intellectual Jew and the dum-dum Italian, here was a switch.... It wasn't just life Buddenberg had to be taught about, it was art and poetry... and everything else." (73–74)

Donna's sense that Bud is displacing her in her own home also fuels her irritation with him; his moving in and "taking over" her physical space is a metaphor for his attempted appropriation of her emotional and spiritual being. Significantly, the home Donna lives in, a small Victorian on the WASPy Collins Place, is the first she has owned and maintained entirely on her own; originally displaced from the large (and somewhat isolated) home she and her husband shared in the country after his death, she embraces both the feelings of independence and community that Collins Place gives her. However, when Bud moves in, bringing with him prodigious amounts of things accumulated during his married life, Donna feels her independence and identity being overwhelmed; her own bedroom ("just right for one" 133) becomes an unfamiliar space:

> Buddenberg's presence wiped out hers in the little room.... Everywhere she looked, he was there.
> Truthfully, she hated to give up her private sanctuary, the private space that was her definition of herself as a person. She dreaded the future of her two tiny closets jammed with the excesses of [his] clothing. All his feelings had gone into his Countess Mara ties and drip-dry shirts, and soon all that stuff would be taking over her room. (138)

Donna's determination to seize control of the transformation process is significant on several levels; it is a power struggle that has both gender and ethnic dimensions. One character remarks,

> "[Jewish men are] the worst, my dear. Jewish men are ridden with tribal guilt induced by their women—their mothers start it, the wives feed it, and the daughters get it as their dowry. The Jewish male has to appear perfect and impeccable to his women; he gives them everything and is adored in return. But God forbid they find

a crack in his armor and discover he's human." (193)

In this commentary, rife with stereotypes of Jewish men and women, Barolini shows how norms of ethnic and gender identity are intertwined and internalized. Bud's insistence upon caring for and protecting Donna, in exchange for her dependence and admiration, fuels their conflicts, and is thematized in Bud's use of money; he "love[s] acquisitions" (145) and uses his greater economic power to control their relationship. Donna reflects, "[T]here was something very aggressive about Bud and his money. He used it as a power tool, and she didn't want him to have power over her" (146). She resents his buying what represents to her the worst of kitschy, conspicuous consumption (e.g., a Mr. Coffee). Her weapon of choice to restore the balance of power, then, is to reach back to the traditional role her own ethnic background demands of women: to force him to conform to her ideals and values.

Barolini sympathetically portrays Bud's own crisis of identity; what Donna views as a stubborn refusal to embrace change actually disguises his own questions about his life. He is convinced that his roles as a faithful husband, a responsible father, and a hard worker have given his life meaning; however, this conviction is shaken when Bud is confronted by his son's decision to divorce after less than a year of marriage:

> Just like that, David was going to walk out of his commitment, justifying it by saying he had a right to live his own life and not waste it on something that turned out to be wrong. Would David have been born if he, Murray Buddenberg, had been made of the same flimsy stuff? But the pain was the pain of revelation: David made Buddenberg see his own life not as a jewel of duty and solidness, but as a wasteland. (168)

Bud's revelation bears remarkable similarity to the journal entry in which Ella Price wonders what would happen if "one day, [a person] wakes up and . . . says, 'My whole life has been a mistake' "(Bryant 36). Thus, Barolini constructs a dual novel of self-discovery, and ties Bud's self-discovery to the emotional burdens imposed by culturally constructed masculine gender roles. In "Mantraps: Men at Work in Pietro di Donato's *Christ in Concrete* and Thomas Bell's *Out of This Furnace*," Nicholas Coles observes that in immigrant novels such as di Donato's and Bell's, "the ideal of man as provider . . . is one of the strands that binds him to his exploitation" (25). Bud is just now, in middle age, beginning to recognize this truth, but is unable to relinquish his traditional role entirely; to his mind, he is behaving unselfishly by sharing his money with Donna and is upholding the right order of the world. His sense of displacement in Donna's world is captured in their differing responses to a block party on Donna's street. While Donna enjoys the elegant food and "the intricacies of real conversation" (172), Bud "[is] honed for action — for aggressive salesmanship, for fencing the demands made on him, for bearing the responsibilities laid on him, for squirreling away a safe repertoire of cracks or restatements of acceptable ideas" (173). In his experience, "the *men* barbequed thick steaks and the *girls* [my emphases] talked shopping on such a summer evening" (173).

Certainly, the power struggle in this relationship is meant to echo the nature of immigrants' relationship to the "culture of consent" which they seek to enter; to become "American" means to relinquish aspects of identity that do not conform to the ideal. Interestingly, in the same party scene cited above, a discussion arises about the notion of intellectual rebirth; one of the party guests comments that "Rebellion is all about rebirth. The first birth is only the physical one" (173). Bud is unable to accept this statement; in his experience, "neither I nor my sisters ever did anything against our parents . . . nor did I ever have any trouble with my own children" (173). Donna realizes at this moment that "Bud had never developed. He had never had the intellectual rebirth that evolved out of loosening primal ties. He had accepted everything he had been taught" (173). Thus, she is determined to get to Bud's "hidden spirit"; she wants "to crank up the gears and expose him to life" (175)—that is, to midwife his "rebirth."

As Werner Sollors points out in *Beyond Ethnicity*, the concept of rebirth is of "central importance" to most religions (85); additionally, Sollors notes, the metaphor of rebirth is commonly invoked by ethnic American writers, whether in the conversion narrative of Malcolm X, or in the opening of Mary Antin's *The Promised Land* (1921). Here, Barolini invokes this metaphor on several levels; obviously it recalls her own grandparents' "rebirth" as Americans, as well as her invention of herself as a writer. In the context of the novel, the metaphor recalls the changing of Donna's grandfather's name upon his arrival, thus literalizing his new identity. It also brings together Donna's role as a literal mother, and her desire to reshape Bud's identity, to teach him about "life . . . and everything else" (73-74).

Perhaps Donna and Bud's conflict is best summed up in Donna's frustrated lament after their affair ends: "If only people wouldn't persist in being themselves once it was pointed out to them they should be someone else" (192). Ironically, this is precisely the attitude against which immigrants had to struggle; while most recognized and accepted the necessity to "be someone else" (that is, to become "American"), the psychological and emotional cost, as shown, could be tremendous. Donna's refusal to accept Bud "as is" fuels his uncertainty and confusion in leaving behind the careful, responsible life he has led for the last thirty years—a life that, although unsatisfying, was at least familiar and safe. Additionally, Donna is shocked to learn from Laddie, her youngest child, that none of her children were certain of her love while growing up, so determined was Donna to mold them into her ideal of perfection. Donna insists on the removal of a wart from Laddie's cheek "because it is ugly," despite Laddie's attitude that "Life is life. . . . You can't help what is ugly" (14). Thus, Donna's perception of herself as an ideal mother, and her efforts to fulfill this role, ironically, only cause her children to doubt her love for them.

The ways in which the novel invokes ethnic and cultural stereotypes create interesting paradoxes. Clearly, one irony lies in the lack of self-perception that easily allows Donna to accept stereotypes without any reflection or sense of hypocrisy; her lack of self-awareness emphasizes the irony, for this lack is the very quality for which she faults Bud. While Donna is angered by stereotypes of Italians as stupid, overly emotional, and tacky, she continues to see others in terms of mean-spirited and sometimes racist stereotypes. For example, through Donna's eyes we see a woman in her exercise class as "look[ing] like a squaw, very ugly" (31). Her mental picture of Bud's ex-wife, Lillian, invokes every aspect of the Jewish American Princess stereotype. She sees one of her neighbors, Clem Moore, as "an interesting case of arrested sociocultural development" (19–20), a "hippie," a "drifter," and a "scrounger" who cannot hold a "real" job; however, she sees her son Johnny, who travels around the world and writes home periodically for more money, as simply trying to "discover himself": "She knew that Johnny's restless walking the earth was for some larger insight and goal that he would bring to his life and enrich it" (88).

Nonetheless, it is sometimes unclear how ironically Barolini intends these stereotypes to be taken. For example, stereotypes of Jews, such as the one cited above about the "tribal guilt" of the Jewish male, are invoked frequently in the novel, not just by Donna, but by several other characters as well. A friend of Donna's explains,

> "Of course [Bud] didn't play around while he was married even though his wife gave him nothing.... He probably forgot all about sex he was so busy consummating deals.... Then there's Jewish male guilt! For years they've neglected their wives for their business. Then they have to atone ... for it in shopping sprees. You've heard of Jewish American Princesses?—who makes them JAPs if not their husbands and fathers?" (56)

The image of the Jewish wife as sexually cold and materially demanding, and the husband as obsessed with making money, are unreflectively accepted by Donna as explanation for Bud's behavior. That these images are peculiarly Jewish, I would argue, is emphasized by the choice of the word "atone," which recalls the Jewish high holiday of Yom Kippur—Day of Atonement. In this context, "atone" simultaneously reinscribes the stereotype of the deeply guilt-ridden Jew, and trivializes the psychological effects of such guilt.

The novel's ending is quite different from that of *Umbertina*. Like Tina, Donna arrives at a crucial piece of self-knowledge, but this time Barolini does not allow her protagonist to have both love and work; Bud's resentment of her desire to start her own business and be independent of his money is one major cause of the failure of their relationship. Barolini thus reverses the quality that Mary Jo Bona sees as characteristic of Italian-American women's fiction; it is as if Barolini accepts the dialectic between love and work that Bona argues is more typical of Anglo women's writing. Despite Joan's flagging interest, Donna gains the confidence to propel their fledgling tour business on her own. Significantly, her first tour is a group of feminist scholars attending a conference at the local college; Donna's admiration of their freedom and openness is reciprocated: " ' This is a great thing you're doing. . . . More women should get out on their own and start their own businesses' " (223). This exchange recalls the Tina-Weezy dynamic in *Umbertina*; it also echoes the theme seen in much Italian-American women's literature—the need for a woman to be economically independent, to "be her own boss."

More significantly, Donna recognizes the harm her obsession with reshaping others has inflicted. She reflects,

> This must be the original sin . . . trying to take over someone's life. Parents do it to children, friends to friends, lovers to lovers. But who sins the most—the doer, or the one who lets it be done? (258)

Donna realizes that her need to reshape others is based on her own fears of being alone, of being "marginal." The phrase "original sin" is significant, for it recalls the Judeo-Christian tradition underlying the novel; it also suggests the generational (and, therefore, perhaps unstoppable) nature of this dynamic. Interestingly, while this passage suggests the genderless and universal quality of this struggle, Barolini's depiction of it is clearly gendered. Will Donna's daughters continue this legacy? Her elder daughter, Eleanor, frequently remonstrates with Donna, pointing out that she is "wasting her life" working in a library, and eyes her "thickening middle" with a critical eye. On a larger scale, Donna's struggle mirrors those of the history of immigration, of people being forced to change, to reconform their tastes, to reshape their identities, and to sacrifice much of what they value in order to gain acceptance. Thus, Barolini reminds us again that the personal is political—that the smaller power struggles that shape relationships among individuals replicate and reflect larger cultural and social struggles.

Finally, the novel's ending re-emphasizes the irony of its title (which I see as a parody of a Harlequin romance, and Barolini posits as a parody of large-scale academic treatises); the "lesson" Donna learns is a reversal of what Rosalind Coward sees as the conventional, sentimental lesson of romance novels: "knowledge or understanding for women is produced . . . across sexual experience. . . . understanding is finding the proper mate" (234). The final line of the novel reinvokes the open-endedness of the novel of self-discovery, with Donna's inner acknowledgment that "She still had everything to learn" (259).

The ways in which Barolini creates context and authority for herself and for her fictional characters form the core of her critical and fictional work. Donna's fear of being marginal on a personal level reiterates Barolini's own sense of herself (and of Italian-American women writers in general) as marginal to American literature, its canon and its traditions.[12] In the "Preface" to the *Dream Book* anthology, Barolini reports feeling at something of a loss when asked to speak about Italian-American women writers at a 1982 conference; she writes,

> I knew ... not enough [names] to wipe out the prevailing notion that there are no Italian-American women writers as there are, so notably, Black women writers, Jewish, Asian. In histories, sociological tracts, bibliographies, learned conferences—the names mentioned as Italian-American writers are those of male authors, just as the achievers in other areas are also male; it is a totality of male presence that effectively undercuts the importance and witness of women in the Italian-American experience. (ix)

Like many of the writers examined in this study, Barolini uses conventional forms (realism, the novel of self-discovery, the "recovery" anthology) to call attention to and explore the experience of those who have been marginalized. Like Toni Morrison, who is alleged to have commented once that she writes the kinds of books she wants to read, Barolini announces that "If books did not tell me who I was, I would write those that did" ("Becoming a Literary Person" 265); she extends her "authorial persona" to include that of critic, to create a context in which not only can Italian-American literature be written, but in which it can be legitimized in the traditionally accepted language of academia. As Edvige Giunta argues, that "while the terrain remains still largely uncharted, Barolini's ... subversive strategies forge alternative territories that have begun to legitimize Italian/American women's voices" ("Blending 'Literary' Discourses" 6). In the next chapter, we see the ways in which younger contemporary writers have continued to "forge [such] alternative territories" and have expanded the terrain of Italian-American women's literature.

Chapter Five

"SOLVING THE MYSTERY":
THE THIRD-GENERATION NARRATIVES OF
LISA RUFFOLO, MARY CAPONEGRO,
AND CAROLE MASO

Recent developments in Italian-American fiction point to an important shift in this literary tradition. As previous chapters demonstrate, most works written prior to 1980 are explicitly concerned with articulating and validating the immigrant experience and perspective. Several of these works demonstrate various degrees of engagement with feminist thought, an important philosophical and epistemological departure from early Italian-American fiction. However, for the most part it seems that in these earlier works, in Helen Barolini's words, "as though style and linguistic daring [was] still being sacrificed to the white heat of telling our story" (qtd. in Gardaphé, "Italian-American Fiction" 71); authors' interests have lain primarily with remaining faithful to the historical facts of immigrant history in the content of their narratives. The writers examined in this chapter, Lisa Ruffolo, Mary Caponegro, and Carole Maso, have been able to "transcend history in order to present a story" (71); these authors

> have met that challenge to experiment with technique and style.... the immigrant past is recreated, not through self-reflection, but through a more distant historical perspective, a perspective gained by removal from the ethnic experience.... and assimilat[ion] via educational institutions, intermarriages, and exodus from "Little Italy" ghettos.... [by which] they have gained greater political, social, and economic control over their lives. (Gardaphé 71)

These developments are closely tied to recent reconceptualizations of what it means to be an "ethnic" writer, and what constitutes "ethnic" literature, such as those put forth by Werner Sollors in *Beyond Ethnicity: Consent and Descent in American Culture* (1986) and William Boelhower in *Through a Glass Darkly: Ethnic Semiosis in American Literature* (1987). Such reformulations of the concept of "ethnicity" emphasize self-determination—that is, a writer's identity as "ethnic" is no longer necessarily determined by an externally imposed definition. Thus, these writers' incorporation of their *italianità* into their art is inextricable from their engagement with modernist and postmodernist developments in literature. Additionally, it is possible to identify clear stylistic and thematic links between the works of these Italian-American women and writers working out of other ethnic traditions: Jewish-American, Asian-American, Chicana, and African-American.

Most important, however, for the writers studied here are feminist/postmodernist theories of subjectivity, voice, and identity construction. Though their responses to these issues are complex and varied, all have at their core a concern with articulating and validating female experience and point of view. However, their work departs from earlier feminist works like Dorothy Bryant's *Ella Price's Journal*, whose explicit engagement with the feminist consciousness-raising genre closely resembles the immigrant novel stereotype associated with ethnic writers. Rather, these writers engage with feminism and issues of gender and sexuality in a more oblique manner that parallels Gardaphé's sense of third-generation Italian-American writers' engagement with their ethnic heritage.

Lisa Ruffolo: Rediscovering Realism

Lisa Ruffolo was born in September, 1956, in Milwaukee, Wisconsin. Like all of the writers in this study, she has a close connection to immigrant experience and history; both her maternal and paternal grandparents left Italy sometime in the 1910s, her mother's parents from northern Italy, her father's from Calabria. Ruffolo received a B.A. in English from the University of Wisconsin–Madison, and an M.F.A. from Johns Hopkins University; in 1991 she received the Paulette Chandler Award in Fiction. Currently, she teaches fiction writing courses at Madison, and works at Software Associates. She has also taught in Florence, and has recently completed a collection of stories about Americans living in Italy, one of which, "Southern Italy," is included in the recent *The Voices We Carry: Recent Italian/American Women's Fiction* edited by Mary Jo Bona.

Ruffolo, whose first collection of stories, *Holidays*, was published in 1987, may be considered a "bridge" figure in this study. On the one hand, she writes in the realistic mode; her use of character, plot, language, and point of view have more in common with works studied in previous chapters, than with the works of Mary Caponegro and Carole Maso, who are experimental in technique and language.[1] Conversely, her deceptively simple stories explore issues of identity, subjectivity, and language in ways that align her closely with more obviously experimental postmodernist writers such as Caponegro and Maso. Here, I will the discuss the collection generally, and then focus on a few stories that seem representative of Ruffolo's technique of blending postmodern content with more conventional, realistic form. In a sense, Ruffolo's artistic dilemma may be summed up in the words of one of her characters, a first-year English teacher at a private prep school:

> "It's not that I don't like what I'm teaching. Hawthorne, Melville, good, evil, fidelity, honor. I love those old words." My cheeks and hands are flushed—I think I have come upon a fundamental truth about myself.... "What am I going to do

when we come to the moderns, where everyone's neurotic and forgivable?" (18)

In other words, how does one (or, indeed, can one) use old forms effectively to express new ideas? How does one negotiate issues of instability and uncertainty using forms and techniques that have, at their core, an essential faith in linearity, in the knowability of origins, in the ability to organize and make sense of experience? Ruffolo says that in the course of her graduate work at Johns Hopkins, she "did experimental," but already sensed that this movement was on the wane. Nonetheless, during this period she found herself more interested in the "surfaces" of stories—form and structure. She remembers reading a Raymond Carver short story and feeling that it was "too minimalist, too spare." She subsequently became interested more in characters, and found traditional narrative techniques more conducive to exploring this interest (Telephone interview). Thus, in many ways, Ruffolo's position as artist recapitulates that of the immigrant: how to reconcile the old, familiar ways with the new.

Generally, several themes emerge from the stories in *Holidays*. The title of the collection (and the last story) connotes celebration; it also carries the meaning of "holiday" in the sense of "vacation," as time away from everyday life and responsibilities. Finally, "holidays" also suggests associations of tradition and of family—important issues in most Italian-American fiction. In these stories, characters grapple with moments of transformation, of revelation and negotiate relationships with lovers, spouses, friends, and family. The first two stories, "Halloween" and "You'll Lose Them Before Thanksgiving," have as their narrators/protagonists young women in their first year of teaching high school English courses, reconciling a new identity as an authority without being fully convinced that they have earned it (or even want it).

In both stories, Ruffolo emphasizes the relationship between the outward physical signs of authority and the psychological acceptance of oneself as an authority figure (on the part of both the protagonists themselves and those around them: students, other teachers, parents). For example, both Francie ("Halloween") and Marie ("You'll Lose Them . . .") are mistaken for students in several instances—a fact that is attributed to their youth and inexperience (or, to think of it another way, their projection and sense of themselves as inexperienced). Francie's moment of flux is captured in the following passage:

> Two professors from Boston University . . . explain that by emphasizing certain activities, drawing for example, formerly weak students can be transformed into strong, confident ones. After the presentation, we all attend a party the head of the upper school traditionally hosts. . . . At the first party in September, a middle school teacher mistook me for a senior, and asked me to bring her clean silverware. This time, one of the Boston University professors joins me on the couch and asks me what I teach. He *assumes* I'm not a student. (10)

This passage emphasizes several transformations: that of weak students into strong, confident students, and that of Francie from a weak teacher into a strong, confident one. Also within this passage is the transformation of others' perceptions of her, from one of the "[m]ature seniors" who "hang coats and serve food" (10) at faculty parties to that of professional colleague. Implicit, too, is another sort of transformation, that of Francie from her recent student status to that of teacher. She notes, "As an intern/teacher, I am really once removed from being a student, and once removed from being a teacher. . . . I can, on any given weekend, be invited to party at a student's house . . . or be asked to chaperone the Freshman dance" (12). Later, one of her students confides that Francie had earned the nickname "Space Cadet" from her classes, but that "now I seem to know what's going on" (13).

Accompanying this sense of transformation for Francie is a kind of playacting on her part; the instability of her current status leads her to assume another persona: "I think of myself as a World War II widow. There is even an ornate gas heater in my apartment" (10). Similarly, at a dance where she is a chaperone, Marie thinks, "I could be Katherine Hepburn. . . . Or Amelia Earhardt. Or Annie Oakley. . . . I swing my feet, wishing I had braids. Or an aviator's scarf. Or high cheekbones and trousers" (21). Clearly, Ruffolo is also concerned with the idea of how clothing functions as a semiotic, affecting both one's self-perception and perceptions of others. Francie reflects, "At the beginning of the year, I wore my old college clothes: denim skirts and crew-neck sweaters. Now I am ready to buy something *more professional:* blazers and blouses" (12–13) (my emphasis); at the beginning of "You'll Lose Them By Thanksgiving," Marie is uncomfortable because she has nothing appropriate to wear to the first faculty party: "[M]y closet is filled with faded Indian-print wrap-around skirts, but no pumps, no plaid dresses" (14). In both cases, the protagonist's awareness of the relationship between her manner of dress and how others will respond to her causes psychological discomfort.

However, I would argue that the relationship between dress and authority is particularly complex for women. In *Three Guineas,* Virginia Woolf, speaking to educated men of power (political, social, economic) of her culture, notes:

> For dress, as [women] use it, is comparatively simple. Besides the prime function of covering the body, it has two other offices—that it creates beauty for the eye, and that it attracts the admiration of your sex. . . . But your dress in its immense elaboration has obviously another function. It not only covers nakedness, gratifies vanity, and creates pleasure for the eye, but it serves to advertise the social, professional, or intellectual standing of the wearer. . . . it says, "This man is a clever man—he is Master of Arts; this man is a very clever man—he is Doctor of Letters; this man is a most clever man—he is a Member of the Order of Merit." (20)

Thus, Francie's and Marie's awareness that their manner of dress does not correspond to their positions as "authorities," has a dual effect: it influences others' perceptions of them, and in turn, fuels their own uncertainties about the strength (and desirability) of their positions. Marie reflects, " 'I'm just not cut out to be a Ms. Delancy. . . . Just what do I want from these kids anyway? For them to remember their notebooks and sit quietly in class everyday?' " (18).

The themes of playacting, clothing, and self-perception become connected in "Halloween"; Halloween is, of course, the holiday that relies on costume, disguise, and mask in its celebration (and the mask theme reappears in Carole Maso's work, discussed later in the chapter). Francie attends a "Sublimated Desires" costume party; her costume choice is "a Miss Jean Brodie kind of cape" (13), signifying her desire to transform and present herself not only as a teacher, but as literature's premier teacher (except, perhaps, for Mr. Chips). Part of her transformation into this role depends, of course, on a transformation of her students—both in terms of real change, and of her perceptions of them. She feels she is "making progress" with her students. Two of her "most incorrigible students" finally react positively to a reading assignment; one of them tells her, " 'My mother can't stand it. I'm *becoming* Holden Caulfield' " (11) (my emphasis).

The theme of transformation is repeated with other characters in the story as well; Francie tells of the Spanish teacher, a former nun from Costa Rica, now married, raising a family, and known for her red shoes and cigar-smoking. Francie wonders:

> What happened? Did she walk out of the convent and into a Costa Rican tobacco shop? Or did the changes metamorphosize when she moved to America? Did she, for example, wear red shoes with conservative black skirts, or smoke cigars and go to Mass every morning—part dull caterpillar, part gaudy butterfly? (11)

Francie's questions, of course, apply to her own situation: "What does a real teacher do?" (10); implicit in this question is "How does one become a *real* teacher?" and "What is a *real* teacher, anyway?" Francie's initial reticence to assert her identity as an adult and as an authority is pushed aside; in a significant scene, she uses her face to express her newfound confidence. When a bartender asks to see proof of age before serving her a beer, "I stare at him as severely as I've stared at Oswald Dow, and he popped open two bottles of beer. They were cold and delicious" (13). The significance of Francie's use of facial expression to communicate her status is reflected in Gloria Anzaldùa's exploration of the meanings of "mask" and "making faces" in "Haciendo caras, una entrada," the introduction to *Making Face, Making Soul/Haciendo Caras: Creative and Critical Perspectives by Women of Color* (1990):

> Among Chicanas/*mexicanas, haciendo caras*, "making faces," means to put on a face, express feelings by distorting the face—frowning, grimacing, looking sad, glum or disapproving. For me, *haciendo caras* has the added connotation of making *gestos subversivos*, political subversive gestures, the piercing look that questions or challenges, the look that says, "Don't walk all over me," the one that says, "Get out of my face." "Face" is the surface of the body that is most noticeably inscribed by social structures, marked with instructions on how to be *mujer, macho*, working class, Chicana.... To become less vulnerable to all these oppressors, we

have had to "change" faces.... Some of us are forced to acquire the ability, like a chameleon, to change color when the dangers are many and the options are few.... The masks, *las mascaras*, we are compelled to wear, drive a wedge between our intersubjective personhood and the *persona* we present to the world. (xv)

Though Anzaldùa's sense of "wearing masks" has negative as well as positive connotations, in Francie's case this strategy brings desirable results. Though on the surface it is a rather insignificant "victory"—she gets her beer without having to provide legal proof of her age—this moment carries greater significance than first appears. This particular scene also recalls the image of *malocchio*, or the "evil eye," that is pervasive in traditional southern Italian culture. According to custom, trying to see too much, trying to make oneself distinct from the group, is destined to attract undesirable (and perhaps unwarranted) attention, particularly for women. However, many contemporary Italian-American women writers have adopted this image, and, in the feminist tradition of reclaiming and redefining negative images associated with women, embraced it as a means of power and control. Thus, Francie affirms her identity as an adult/authority and convinces society, represented by the bartender, that she has earned the right to be taken seriously without external validation or "proof": her authority simply *is*.

Both stories end with their respective protagonists affirming and accepting their new lives and roles. Examining her reflection in the classroom window, Francie sees "A smiling woman in a blue blazer ... floating among the November clouds.... [Now], I thought, I am a teacher" (13). Her sense of her reflection here as something separate from and other than herself becomes transformed by her first person affirmation—"*I* am a teacher." Similarly, Marie must reject the emotional pull of a failing relationship in order to accept her new life. In her case, it is the boyfriend from whom she is separating who forces her to realize that she is doing what she must: " 'Face it ... You're a teacher now. You've been teaching since you were in kindergarten.' I hate it that he is right" (21). The decision to let go of her "old life" is signified by "a flurry of activity" around her apartment of cleaning and arranging: " 'This is where I live.... Right here. Right here where I am' " (22). In contrast to the previous story, in which Ruffolo emphasizes the relationship between one's psychological and physical constructions, here she highlights the relationship of one's place to one's identity. Gloria Anzaldùa writes in *Borderlands/La Frontera*, "I had to leave home so I could find myself, find my own intrinsic nature buried under the personality that had been imposed on me" (16).

Two stories in the collection, "Independence Day" and "Holidays," are linked in their treatment of the ambivalence many women feel toward heterosexual romantic relationships. In "Independence Day," Margie, the story's narrator and protagonist, is preparing to move to California from a small town in Wisconsin with her husband Kenny and brother-in-law Lou. For Margie, the move means the start of a new life: " 'I just want to get on the road and let it take me somewhere.... I'll be glad when I see this town in my rear view mirror' " (24).

Margie's dreams of escape, however, are not merely those of the immigrant fleeing limited economic options or the escape from the intellectual/emotional narrowness of small-town life. We quickly come to understand that Margie's hope is for a transformation of her weak and irresponsible husband, and of their relationship.

Kenny is portrayed as immature and barely able to handle the demands of marriage and fatherhood. When we first see him, he is "weaving down the street on his skateboard . . . red, white and blue streamers attached to his elbows and knees" (25), having left the chore of cleaning out the garage and loading the truck to Margie and Lou. They learn that Kenny has reneged on the deal to sell their house and plans to stay in Wisconsin. Hearing rumors of new highway construction with an "exit ramp right at our doorstep" (29), he decides they should start a roadside restaurant, reasoning "Why move to California to get rich . . . (29). Margie is stunned and angry because, for her, the move to California represents "more than money" (29) ; however, she is all too aware of the familiarity of the scene: "He had it all planned, staged even. I stepped into his blocked-out scenes, as I had before, because this was our dance; he was the con and I was the sucker"(30). Thus, though Kenny is initially seen as the child in the relationship, it is clear that he controls Margie in important ways—and that Margie herself somehow feels unable to break the circle. Thus, Kenny's "weakness" is a monumental strength, one which Margie is unable to resist. Margie's decision to leave with Lou seems to be a victory, but Kenny has the final word. Ironically, though Kenny "warns" her not to leave, his threat is not directed toward her. A self-inflicted hatchet injury emphasizes the complexity of their relationship. By behaving like a child he controls and manipulates his wife: "But when I wiped the blood away and saw a flap of skin, I realized his drama was a sign: he'd never let me go"(33). Margie is reduced to accepting her relationship with Kenny as is, and ends up "toast[ing] Independence Day with a fresh can of beer" (33).

The final story in the collection, "Holidays," is similar in its theme but reversing the terms of "Independence Day," embraces the familiarity and stability of family and tradition. The story's protagonist and narrator, Merle, returns to her parents' home after a long-time relationship breaks up. Her lover, Duncan, is fond of changing his appearance so frequently that, as he tells Merle, "You can fall in love with a new man every week" (102). Though early in their relationship she "appreciated his unpredictability and spontaneity, qualities I hoped would rub off on me" (102), she eventually comes to feel "off-balance, dizzy" from his kaleidoscope persona.

Merle explains the breakup to her sisters by saying simply, " 'We just couldn't make it through the holidays' " (104). Duncan's discomfort with and rejection of her desire to become rooted, symbolized by her desire to establish holiday traditions, reflects an essential difference in their natures. Duncan feels that, by living together, they are already "married," and that "the wedding would be a mere formality" (99), while Merle "didn't think I could feel married to Duncan until years after some kind of ceremony" (100). His decision to leave her is a need, he says, "to be irresponsible awhile" (101). Thus, Merle's return to her childhood home is a logical response to Duncan; in a sense, it is her own opportunity to be irresponsible for a while through a metaphorical return to the womb. She asks her mother " 'Can I come home for awhile?' " and envisions her childhood room, "dark and cool [where] I want to sleep as I haven't in weeks" (100). Her return home is an immersion in family, traditions, and memories; in some respects, too, there is an ambivalent reversion to parent-child roles. She will not smoke in front of her father, for example, a remnant from a high-school incident; her mother comes into her room after her first night home, forcing her to get up, even though Merle insists " 'I need the sleep' " (101). However, Merle's return is meant to be interpreted positively, as a healing process and reclamation of her past. When Duncan shows up, trying to persuade her to return, they are in the midst of celebrating her father's birthday, another occasion of carefully preserved rituals: "We have been polishing the napkin rings and setting out the water goblets on birthdays for at least fifteen years" (104). Though Duncan scorns the stasis represented by such traditions (" 'You'll rot' " 105), Merle tells him " 'I *like* birthday cake and all that' " (106).

Though at first glance this story seems to be a simplistic sentimentalization of family and holiday traditions, Ruffolo's choice to end the collection with this particular story, I think, is significant.[2] Though Merle's return home may be read as a regression of sorts, when compared to Margie's helpless resignation at the conclusion of "Independence Day," it is actually an affirmation of her nature that has more in common with the protagonists of "Halloween" and "You'll Lose Them By Thanksgiving." Reconnecting with her family and her heritage (though not in an explicitly ethnic way) restores Merle's sense of balance. She finds her intrinsic nature by returning to her home, and rejects Duncan's identity rollercoaster.

The complexity of the collection lies not so much in individual stories but in the interweaving of the stories on various thematic levels. For example, the questions raised about independence and choices link "Independence Day" with "Holidays," and with "Halloween" and "You'll Lose Them by Thanksgiving" as well. "Holidays" is also linked thematically with "Birthday" and "Commercials," as the latter stories are concerned with the dynamics of family relationships ("Birthday" and "Commercials" share a woman's discovery of her husband's infidelity). "Commercials," in particular, offers a pointed contrast to "Holidays." The O'Connor family, like Merle's, has three daughters, all living at home (though in a reversal of "Holidays," the eldest, Miriam, leaves to move in with her boyfriend, and, it is suggested, to escape the fragmentation of her family). Unlike Merle's family, however, this family is linked not by tradition, but by television. Its ubiquitous presence suggests an artificial life; the family's togetherness before it in the story's opening scene suggests an artificial unity. When Margaret calls Miriam to invite her home for Thanksgiving dinner she hears the same commercial playing in the background that is on her own TV, and "[s]he imagines all the people in her family, in her neighborhood, in the country, linked by common televised images" (55).

The themes of reconnection with one's heritage, and the relationships among clothing, face, and identity construction, find their most complex expression in "My Grandfather's Suit," a story not contained in this collection. In addition, this story is most explicitly engaged with Ruffolo's Italian heritage. This story is in fact Ruffolo's first "Italian" story; her discovery, she says, of the family as fitting and fruitful subject for her fiction led her to "a deeper and more interesting theme." At around the time of writing this story she also read Helen Barolini's *Dream Book*, and recognized in it a profound influence on her own writing—not so much in the work of any particular writer, but in the idea that women writers of Italian-American descent exist and have an identifiable literary tradition and connection (Telephone interview).

The story is a kind of *bildungsroman* in miniature, a quest for self-discovery and identity. Its narrator and protagonist, seventeen-year-old Anna, tells us that physically she resembles no one in her family; more significantly, she has no specific psychological identity: "Except for me, everyone in my family plays a distinct role in the family drama.... But I am simply Anna.... I've tried for a role of my own, jockeying for the Smart One or the Talented One. Then I flunk a quiz or get kicked out of choir, and I'm back to simply Anna" (75–76).

Anna's transformation begins innocuously enough when her father, seeing her studying herself in the mirror, remarks, " 'Now I know who you look like.... There's a picture of my father with that same expression on his face' " (75). Anna digs up a photo of her grandfather, the first she's ever seen:

> My grandfather looks composed, dapper, but though I see the shadow of my father's lips and hairline, he also looks undeniably foreign, fresh from Italy. The expression on his face is fierce—not quite a scowl, but tougher than a frown. Seventeen and not pretty at all, I practice that expression in front of the bathroom mirror, flexing my jaw, flaring my nostrils, trying to look like him. (75)

Anna's quest for resemblance (and, therefore, an identity) goes beyond the physical. She "imagine[s] that [her] grandfather had talents" (76) and tries to display those same qualities. Like many of her generation, Anna has a connection to some of her history and customs, but this connection primarily relates to food. She does not know Italian, a loss she does not feel until now. She dreams of her grandfather, sitting in his chair, "look[ing] stern" (76) until he sees Anna; he touches her face, kisses her, and "the Italian rolled out of me like a song, and my skin grew dark, my eyes dreamy" (76). The significance of this dream recalls Helen Barolini's description of the dream book, a guide for dream interpretation used by immigrant Italian women, which "gave them explication for the strangeness around them and a clue to their *destino*" (xii).

Anna's imaginative reconstruction of her grandfather, however, fails to satisfy her, and she turns to her family to make the man in the photograph come more fully alive. She learns that her grandfather was a great singer, wanted to buy stock in

Coca-Cola (but Grandmother wouldn't let him), and once told Al Capone that "living like a king was a state of mind" (78). The answers she gets to her questions, however, also point to the mutability of identity construction. Her father remembers "a rich man, rich for his village" (76), who sacrifices his wealth in order to marry the poor but beautiful woman he loves. Her mother tells a somewhat different story:

> "All I really remember is that your grandmother was often exasperated with him. Everyone said he was a saint.... He was very poor in Italy, and any extra money he made here in America he wanted to give away, send back. Your grandmother took his weekly pay, and she'd dole it out.... Once a month she'd give him a little extra so he could have anisette in his coffee with his friends at the Italian American." (77)

Her aunt and her friends, Mary and Lil, give Anna other pictures. Though Anna's father has told her "that Grampa Cavallo could have been an actor in the movies" (78), Mary asserts that he was far too quiet for that. Lil, however, asserts, " 'He was quite a ladies' man. . . . Your grandmother had her hands full, keeping him happy at home' " (79). Her aunt proclaims, " 'My father was a very pious man. He had no interest in ladies at all, except for my mother, even though she was nothing much to look at . . .' " (79). Though Anna presses for more information, she is dismissed. In an exchange typical of second and third generations, Anna's request for more details of her family history is brushed off: " 'Oh, Anna, that was so long ago. I don't even like to think about these things since my mother died' " (79).

Ironically, Anna's search for identity and for connection with her lost grandfather is fulfilled when her father decides to sell her grandparents' house. Her mother tells them, " 'We're making a clean sweep. . . . The trick is to work fast' " (79). While this remark literally refers to clearing out all the objects and furniture left in the house, it also echoes the immigrant's impulse to assimilate quickly, to relinquish all remnants of the past in order to achieve social and economic success. The price exacted by this pressure is demonstrated, not only in Anna's ethnic confusion and lack of identity, but in her grandfather's constant vacillation between the old world and the new: " 'Did you know that when he was in Calabria, he couldn't wait to come over? And then when he got here, all he wanted to do was return? We'd all be in Italy today if my brother hadn't got the measles that time he wanted us to all go back together' " (79).

Because she has not been in this house for ten years, Anna's own sense of the past is challenged. She feels dizzy, remembering her grandmother's kitchen as enormous but now feeling that "everything is shrunken, almost miniaturized" (79). As she surveys the objects that were part of her childhood, Anna comes to the realization that the past itself is not a static entity; like one's identity, it shifts with perspective, is altered by experience and context. Thus, she rejects the sentimentality of her father, who often sits for hours in a darkened basement, viewing videos and films of his children, forever frozen in time "as we head off to kindergarten or swing at baseballs on the school playground" (76). Now "scrounging for memories" (80), she recognizes and accepts the changes time has wrought in her, and in her perspective.

When Anna finds her grandfather's suit in the closet, her quest is complete, the conflicting images of him reconciled. She dons the suit, "waiting to see the grandfather in me appear." While the suit is too small, and "can't hide my second-generation bones, my American health" (80), Anna "can see that this is not the suit of a ladies' man or a poor man" (80). She tries again, posing in a chair as her grandfather did in the photograph: "I push my brow and cheeks into their practiced scowl. Now the suit settles into place—its blueness and padding make me look darker, smaller, its tailored lines make me elegant . . . I am someone who knows who she is" (80). She begins to sing, making up lyrics to (ironically) "Arrivederci Roma," but then in an instant remembers the Italian, and understands how to sing it properly. Her own identity and the images of her grandfather are crystallized: "And my voice has soul—it is the voice of a rich man, a saint, a quiet man, a singer" (81). Thus, Anna's dream is literalized, her *destino* made clear.

It is, of course, significant that Anna chooses to identify with her grand*father* rather than her grand*mother*. While the initial suggestion for this identification comes simply from her father's recognition of physical resemblance, Ruffolo suggests a deeper significance to Anna's choice. Anna enacts a kind of "double transvestitism," the first being the ethnic crossdressing of which Werner Sollors speaks in *Beyond Ethnicity* (that is, she becomes Italian rather than American), the second one of a gendered nature. Several elements of the story, in fact, suggest that Anna is not willing to embrace or feels uncomfortable with traditional gender roles. Interestingly, both parents' roles in the "family drama" are feminized; her father is the "Sentimental One," an identity Anna rejects by the end of the story. Her mother's role is one of seemingly contradictory images (but both explicitly gendered as feminine); in one scene she is wearing a business suit, but is standing in the kitchen "wiping mustard from her lacquered fingernails" after preparing lunches for her family. She is the "Beautiful One," a fourth-grade teacher and a part-time model; hers is a role for which Anna feels ill-suited. Her earlier observation that she is "seventeen and not pretty at all" reflects, first, her sense of difference from her mother, and, second, her sense that because she is seventeen (and female), she *ought* to be "pretty," and that her lack of conventional prettiness is a "failure" on her part. Anna's younger brothers, on the other hand, have the physically active and more conventionally masculine identities: Mark is The Jock, Michael, The Klutz.

Other incidents confirm this reading of Anna's testing of gender conventions. She purchases a man's fedora, wearing it because "it looks like something my grandfather would wear on an outing" (77). She relates that, when she was younger, she loved being in the kitchen while her mother and her sisters prepared food, although she herself did not participate in this traditionally female ritual, choosing instead to sit apart and simply listen to their family gossip. She attends a wedding shower for a cousin, "slump[ing] down in her chair," as she realizes that her gift of a wedding photo album is somehow "wrong" next to the "five lacy negligees" (78) Giuseppa receives. The romantic elements of this ritual are lost on her; the shower takes place in "a damp basement where pink ribbons have been taped on the painted concrete walls" (78), and her cousin's fiance is simply "a moody guy named Sam" who eats all the leftover food.

Anna's uneasiness with gendered identity parallels her sense of division between her American and Italian selves, and serves to explain her lack of identity. The story's ending is thus a synthesis of all these elements for Anna, and captured in the image of her grandfather's soul in her own being. However, Ruffolo seems to be using this image not only metaphorically, but also literally, since her grandfather dies on the day of Anna's birth. Indeed, Ruffolo's presentation of Anna's "reacculturation" suggests what Carol Bonomo Ahearn sees as the fourth stage of assimilation of the immigrant in America, that of "integrated autonomy, in which all three forces [heritage, personal goals, and new culture] are resolved in a personal manner satisfactory to the specific individual" (126).

Mary Caponegro: "A Later Entry on My Own"

Mary Caponegro was born on November 21, 1956, in Brooklyn, New York, to physician parents. Her mother sacrificed her professional identity to stay home and raise her three children, though Caponegro felt the significance of her mother's rare status as a female who passed through medical school. Interestingly, she adds that watching her parents made her decide very early in life to go into anything but medicine, despite strong familial pressure to do so. Ironically, she learned recently that her father has the desire to write, but was unable to do so under the pressure of supporting his family (Telephone interview).

Caponegro received a double B.A. in Literature and Creative Writing and Music at Bard College; the atmosphere there was very nurturing of the arts, and she felt it a world far removed from her previous twelve years of Catholic education. She later received an M.F.A. at Brown; both at Bard and at Brown she was mentored by writers (Robert Kelly and John Hawks, respectively) who deeply influenced her writing—opportunities which she regards now with tremendous gratitude. Her Italian heritage is paternal, and she was not exposed while growing up to the language, traditions, and culture; her family, she says, showed little interest in preserving tradition. Thus, she says, "I made a later entry on my own into that heritage" when she received a grant to study at the American Academy in Rome in 1991; she sees that grant as "most meaningful" in her reconnection with her Italian roots. Nonetheless, her response to her label as an "Italian-American" writer (and, for that matter, as a postmodern writer) is "complex." Caponegro says that while "One appreciates being read," regardless of the reason, she is sometimes surprised by the labels that are affixed to her work (Telephone interview).

In her first collection of stories, *The Star Café* (1990), Caponegro writes of many of the same issues of identity as Ruffolo. However, in contrast to Ruffolo's use of realism, Caponegro engages with postmodernist practice and philosophy in order to offer profound challenges to conventional notions about the fixed and stable nature of language, sexuality, and knowledge. The collection consists of four stories, the first of which, "Tales from the Next Village," is in turn divided into ten brief tales, all of which have a surreal, fable-like quality, emphasizing their distance and seeming lack of connection to the rest of the collection.[3] The removal suggested by the title—"Tales from the *Next* Village"—emphasizes the distance and removal from the ethnic/immigrant experience that is characteristic of the writers studied in this chapter. However, close examination of the tales reveals some significant thematic ties to the rest of the stories in the collection, as well as to feminist and postmodernist theory. Caponegro sees these ten stories as positive statements about heterosexual love; they are meant to reveal "the poignancy of the failure to achieve idealized love," and to enact the conflict between spiritual and erotic fulfillment. In this way, they set the thematic tone for the stories that follow, all of which chart the failure to connect, whether that connection be sexual, filial, religious, or cultural.

The final story in the collection, "Sebastian," is similarly disconnected from the collection's "center." It is a kind of miniature of Joyce's *Ulysses*, a day in the life of a man in pursuit of very ordinary activities: gassing up the car, picking up a suit at the cleaners, driving to the airport for a business trip. However, through Sebastian's physical and mental wanderings, we are given insight into contemporary issues surrounding linguistic, cultural, ethnic, religious, and sexual difference. Its two major characters—Sebastian, a British Catholic, and Sarah, an American Jew—also reiterate the theme of removal from direct ethnic experience that is common to the entire collection. Though presented primarily through a male perspective, its presentation of sexual politics is clearly framed by a feminist sensibility and epistemology.

For the purposes of my study, I am focusing on the second and third stories of the collection—its center, in a manner of speaking—because these stories speak most directly to both the ethnic and feminist aspects of Caponegro's work. The collection's second story, "The Star Café" relates a surreal sexual encounter between Carol, the story's protagonist, and the unnamed proprietor of the eponymous cafe. The story begins innocuously enough; while preparing for bed, Carol hears a noise outside her apartment she cannot identify. After going downstairs to find the source (a blender of banana daquiris), she meets the owner, goes inside the cafe, and finds herself suddenly in a mysterious bedroom of mirrors. The action of the story is catalyzed by a common—if not clichéd—situation. But on another level, the story's genesis is epistemological—the obsession to know origins. This need to know leads Carol to startling discoveries about her sexuality, about the nature of reality and about the conflict between intuition and judgment.

At its core, this story has much in common with Dorothy Bryant's *Ella Price's Journal*; a central theme in both works is a woman's discovery and validation of her sexuality, and her confrontation with male dominance. The crucial difference is the mode—Bryant's realism versus Caponegro's modernist/postmodernist techniques. Initially, Carol's sexual encounter with the cafe owner, "an extremely handsome man in all the conventional ways: dark and tall, both noble and rugged" (25), is intensely pleasurable and satisfying: "It was if they were lovers reunited after a long separation.... What was passion if not this?" (27). At this point, time seems suspended in the story; Carol sleeps and wakes to find herself surrounded by mirrors. As they make love again, she is subsumed by sexual pleasure—until she looks into the mirrors and can see only herself. Feeling "humiliated, horrified, and guilty" (28), she interprets her situation as "an extreme case of some kind of sexual etiquette" (28). The choice of the word "etiquette" is significant here, for it refers to a socially accepted and codified set of conventions and behaviors that do not necessarily imply moral attitudes or consequences—that is, in its ordinary sense, "etiquette" does not carry connotations of morality. However, it is precisely the effect of connotation that influences our interpretation of Carol's dismay. According to Roland Barthes, connotation "is a determination, a relation, an anaphora, a feature which has the power to relate itself to anterior, ulterior, or exterior mentions, to other sites of the text" (8). Thus, despite her conception of her situation as merely a matter of "etiquette" (and therefore nonmoral), Carol has the sense that she is being punished for "loose" behavior, having sex with a man whose name she does not even know; she thinks of her mother and what she would say about her careless promiscuity.

However, Caponegro translates this dilemma of sexual etiquette (behavior) to one of knowledge and of language: "How could she carry on this charade, when she possessed knowledge that her partner was missing?" (29). "Missing" here may be interpreted to mean "not present," and refer to the fact that from her standpoint her lover is not visible or present. Second, it can mean "failing to understand or perceive"—that is, her partner fails to perceive the fact that she cannot see him. The dual sense of "missing" here points to the instability of language, to the ways in which meaning is not fixed, but rather is determined by the circumstances under which the utterance is made, as well as the perceptions of the sender and the receiver. Caponegro's linguistic play and reliance on linguistic indeterminacy reflect Roland Barthes' argument that "the goal of literary work (of literature as work) is to make the reader no longer a consumer, but a producer of the text" (4); in other words, it may be up to the reader to decide what meaning of "missing" is at work in this passage, and thus produce a meaning for the text.

The mirror, then, becomes the site for multiple levels of meaning and symbol, all of which can be constructed and produced by the reader. First, the obvious question arises: does the man (and therefore the encounter) exist only in Carol's mind? The reader's doubts are underscored by the fact that the cafe owner is unnamed. Additionally, he is the "tall, dark stranger" of romance novel and fortuneteller clichés. Reading/interpreting his character in light of several literary conventions becomes an obvious and appropriate means to answer this question. First, he may be interpreted in the tradition of the demon lover—a tradition that reaches back to ballads of the medieval period of British literature. One version of this story, entitled "The Carpenter's Wife" (of which over 145 versions have been collected), is prefaced as being "A warning for married women" (Trapp 434). In all instances of this convention a female protagonist is borne away by a man who sexually entices and eventually terrorizes her.[4] A second convention is that of the vampire, which echoes the demon lover's characteristics of both sexual attractiveness and terrorism; in both instances the female becomes sexual prey and is, paradoxically, victim of both her own and male desire. The vampire myth also has associated with it the belief that, like Carol's lover, such creatures cannot be reflected in a mirror. Finally, there is the convention of the döppelganger, a ghostly double that haunts the protagonist. This final convention connects to Caponegro's own sense of the relationship between Carol and her lover. The dynamics of their relationship is inspired by the work of German philosopher Rudolf Steiner (1861–1925), who argued that as one is reborn, she re-enacts the thousands of daily interactions experienced during the previous life; however, the person being reborn experiences not her own emotions and physical sensations, but rather those of the other. Thus, Caponegro envisions Carol as a man reborn as a woman, suffering the same sexual insensitivity and abuse of power inflicted in a previous incarnation. Thus, the mirror takes on an additional meaning of "reflecting" the self, of "bouncing back" one's reality in a reversed, distorted manner.

On one level, the relationship between Carol and her lover enacts the classic Jungian concept of *animus,* the masculine personality, and *anima,* the feminine. In Jung's formulation, the female "cannot relate to an erotic other on her own or exercise eroticism for her own sake . . . she *is* the other in a male configuration of selfhood" (Pratt 8). Thus, Carol's initial experience of sexual pleasure becomes transformed into her lover's pleasure alone, even as he disappears from her view, suggesting that she is, as Annis Pratt notes, "either the exterior container for male projections or [a] subordinate element of the male personality" (8). According to such thinking, male sexual arousal depends primarily on visual stimulus and the power of the gaze, while female arousal is effected by more "subtle" stimuli— touch, scent, sound. In other words, the power of the gaze is withheld from women; "normal" females will not (and, indeed, *should not)* be influenced (and perhaps should even be repulsed by) visual representations of sexuality. Thus, Carol experiences tremendous pleasure during the first sexual encounter, until she sees herself in the mirror and realizes that she is alone. Her pleasure vanishes at the moment the male "participant" does, because Carol must, as a woman, reject both the power of the gaze and the power of providing sexual pleasure for herself. However, she attempts to explain the inexplicable, to rationalize the (apparently) irrational:

> Maybe there was a device analagous to a one-way mirror: a half-mirror, in which only one party at a time was visible. Such a thing could exist. So now the big question was, did he see only himself, the same way she saw only herself? How simple it all was . . . she . . . was overjoyed to realize that the sum of their perceptions

would yield a complete love-making couple; she thought she might cry with the relief of it. (30)

It is significant that Carol's pleasure turns not into pain, but into numbness—an absence of feeling that corresponds to the visual absence of her male partner. A reversal occurs; "vision . . . inform[s] her [that he had stopped], because feeling had long since been used up" (31). Watching him dress, she becomes "ashamed at feeling renewed attraction for this man whom she'd minutes ago felt utterly victimized by"(33). There is apparent affirmation of the Jungian archetype; Carol reflects that "She'd never had such a strong sense of being with a man: that she was the feminine to his masculine" (33). Significantly, she admits this "response . . . may be hopelessly bound up in the conditioning of role" (33).

In the subsequent scene, Carol's request for a bathroom results in her being led to a space "she could have sworn had not existed" (35), a room containing "two gleaming urinals, affixed to the wall at waist height" (35), which remind her of baptismal fonts. Like the mirror, these objects enact a synthesis of opposites. As urinals, of course, they are designed to carry away human waste and water; as baptismal fonts they are receptacles for holy water that removes the stain of original sin. Carol recognizes that in order to use them she will have to find "a position that would somehow enable her to put feminine form into masculine function" (36). Her request for assistance in positioning herself is met with a firm but ultimately useless gesture on his part; he stays, to her dismay, with "an expression foreign to his face as she knew it: being *in* the power of something rather than being in power *over* something" (my emphasis) (36).

Carol's perception of her lover's "foreign expression" points to a shift in the balance of power for the rest of the story. French feminist Luce Irigaray conceives of a masculine/feminine opposition similar to Jung's anima/animus archetype. In *This Sex Which is Not One,* she posits the speculum, the instrument used for vaginal examinations, as the image for how men see women: "as reflections, or images and likenesses, of men" (Tong 227). In this masculinist, or "phallic" view, to use Irigaray's term, "feminine" is a concept which "allow[s] oneself to be caught up again in a system of 'masculine' representations, in which women are trapped in a system or meaning which serves the auto-affection of the masculine subject" (Irigaray 32). Thus, Carol's sense of needing to "put feminine form into masculine function" (that is, of redefining the feminine against the masculine as "norm") apparently confirms this masculinist view, and links the symbolisms of the mirror and of the urinal.

Irigaray suggests several strategies for evading this phallic, masculine power. The first is to pay attention to language, to embrace subjectivity (as opposed to the falsely posited "neutrality" valued and validated by phallocentric discourse) and the active, rather than the conventionally "feminine," passive voice. The second is for woman to embrace her multiple sexuality, which Irigaray juxtaposes with the phallus, the singular, linear nature of male sexuality (the image by which

Irigaray defines patriarchy). Thus, by engaging in "lesbian and autoerotic practice ... women will learn to speak words and think thoughts that will blow the phallus over" (Tong 228). The third strategy is for women "to break out of the male imaginary and into a female one" (Tong 229) by "tak[ing] those images [that men have of women] and reflect[ing] them back in magnified proportions" (228).

Carol's final confrontation with her unnamed lover exhibits all these strategies. When she tries to force him to admit whether or not he was present during their encounter, he is evasive, willfully misunderstanding her questions. Carol's " 'Were you ever there?' " is met with an answer referring to a travel poster of Greece hanging in the cafe:

> She resented this glib distortion of her meaning. He had no right to be so evasive. Or had he just misunderstood? He had no right to misunderstand. Anger supplanted her nervousness so that now she had no trouble looking directly at him ... [but] before she could challenge him he was onto ... [a] new topic, as if his little remark had been an adequate response to her searching question, and no more be said about it. (40)

His subsequent dismissal of her as a "silly thing" fuels her anger; though tenderly expressed, it seems "grossly inadequate, even pathetic" in response to "an experience of suffering so vivid that it created a landscape in her mind as powerful as the mythical one in which she had just been lost" (41).

Irigaray's emphasis on and validation of autonomous, autotelic female sexuality is confirmed in the story's final scene. In her second search for a usable bathroom, Carol is successful. The room is lined with mirrors, and Carol sees a "new" reflection of her lower body, which she finds attractive, a "lovely landscape under canopy of skirt" (43). First intrigued and gradually aroused, she begins to dance, enjoying both the sensation of movement and the sight of her body. Interestingly, she separates her own identity from that of her reflection; she, in fact, takes on the male gaze:

> She knew that she often allowed herself to become the victim of her own speculations, reflections. Now it all seemed unimportant compared to the immediacy of the woman in the mirror, the urgency of that woman's sexuality or physicality.... The mirror-woman did a seductive dance.... she wanted to possess this beautiful moving image. (44)

She does indeed take possession of the image—that is, she takes possession of her own sexuality. This scene is significant in terms of Sigmund Freud's narcissistic model of ego formation, which, according to Elizabeth Grosz, "implies that the ego can take itself, its own image, parts of its own body, as an 'object,' and invest in them as if they were external or 'other' " (30). Carol's desire to possess her image corresponds with Jacques Lacan's concept of the mirror stage, developed out of Freud's narcissistic model of ego formation, which "marks the child's first recognition of lack or absence"; the child recognizes the distinction between self and other, and "attempt[s] to fill lack by identifying with [its] own specular image" (Grosz 48). According to Lacan, this specular image is complete and totalized, in contrast to and in conflict with "fragmentary felt reality" (Grosz 48) (represented by the earlier scene in which the lover has apparently disappeared, and Carol's "reality," paradoxically, is "unfelt"). Significantly, Grosz adds, Lacan believes this mirror image to be both literal and ideal, and "positions the child in a . . . spatial field—the body" (48). Carol begins to masturbate; as she climaxes, semen spurts forth.

Though Carol (and the reader) explains this phenomenon *vis à vis* her previous encounter, I would argue that Caponegro employs this image to express Carol's seizing of both "masculine" and "feminine" sexuality—an interpretation underscored by the owner's description of the bathroom as "androgynous" (that is, neither a "men's" nor a "ladies' " room). I would argue, too, that this moment represents Carol's entrance into the symbolic order, which in Lacan's schema is primarily the realm of the male; to his mind, the female's entrance into this order is necessarily incomplete, her position within it "marginal or tenuous" (Grosz 72). Caponegro subverts this phallo(go)centric position; the story concludes emphatically with Carol's new sense of her own power. She leaves the bathroom, drawn to the poster of Greece, uninhibited by her nudity: "she wanted to see every box [on the poster] clearly. . . . He didn't matter so much anymore, she wouldn't let him keep her from exploring" (45). Despite Lacan's assertion that "the phallus is *never* a matter of indifference for women," a feminist reading and Caponegro's vision recognize that such indifference "may be the mark of [a woman's] (sexual) difference, the trace of her location elsewhere" (Grosz 192).

The third story in the collection, "Materia Prima," retains important thematic links to the previous story, though it is quite different in tone and style. Too, it demonstrates a more explicit engagement with Caponegro's *italianità* than any of the other stories in the collection. It is told primarily from the point of view of Clara, who remarks early in the story, "Only one's parents can steal past and present irrevocably in one dismissive blow" (50). This story most clearly arises out of Caponegro's ethnicity; relationships between child and parent (and, more particularly, mother and daughter) dominate the narrator's perceptions of herself and of her world. The story's title, translated from Italian, may be translated as "first matter" or "before matter," and reflects Caponegro's concerns with subjectivity, and the construction of knowledge and of identity, particularly for women. Caponegro's experiments with point of view and language choices underscore this theme. Useful here is a discussion of language theory, particularly those theories articulated by linguist Noam Chomsky and linked to theories of knowledge developed in Jeremy Campbell's *Grammatical Man: Information, Entropy, Language, and Life* (1982).

The story's voice shifts between Clara's as adult and Clara's as child. The adult's voice is sophisticated and philosophical, articulating the frustration of powerlessness experienced by the child: her parents' thoughtless and casual dismissal of her memories ignores the child's need "for confirmation to legitimize what was to me more tangible than the brick and wood of our house. . . . or the flesh and blood we all, at least partly, are" (51). The child's voice is reflected in its very literal logic and imagery; she refers, for example, to the massive mailbox at their apartment building as "the place where our mail lives" (50). This description is at once completely inaccurate and totally apt—pointing to the complex and contradictory natures of language and perception, and the ways in which we process information and construct knowledge. Is the more "sophisticated" language of the adult Clara (and the memories of the adults who deny Clara's own) a more "accurate" depiction of "reality" than the "simple" expression of the child Clara?

Clara's own response to this question, and her parents' refusal to accept and validate her point of view, leads her to study of the natural sciences. She says, "I tried to correct my allegedly invalid perceptions: to redeem them by way of the empirical" (59). Though the child Clara does not recognize this motive, the adult can: "I was too young then to understand the direct correlation that wisdom of maturity now affords me" (55)—though this assertion itself may be ironic. Her choice points to the artificial separation between the subjectivity of human perception, emotion, and memory, and the "objective" nature of scientific knowledge. Clara believes that, by immersing herself in encyclopaedic knowledge of zoology (specifically, ornithology), she can free herself of the "befuddlement and exasperation" of humans. Her research becomes the obsession of her life, the accumulation of books, facts, and knowledge her reason for being, for she recognizes that her parents cannot challenge it. However, it is important to note that Clara not only loves the research and the knowledge she accumulates, she loves the *language* of that research; though "arid, tedious, and too specialized to be within the domain of [her classmates'] youthful comprehension" (59), it has the "advantage and expediency" which Clara feels her own life lacks. That is, to her mind, the language of science is "pure," its meaning unobscured by the subtext of emotion, desire, connotation. Caponegro underscores the contrasts and relationships among these various languages by juxtaposing the narratives of the child and adult Claras with interpolations from *Scientific America, Inc.* and *A New Dictionary of Birds.*

Like the traditional, pre-Chomsky linguists who believed it possible to develop a theory of language free of considerations of meaning and subjectivity, Clara believes that immersion in the language of science will free her from the unknowablility of parental whim and control. Thus, by "advantage and expediency," Clara refers not only to the language of her studies. She is enamored of the details of avian maturation, the "clean break" by which the baby bird is pushed out of the nest, its ties to its biological parents neatly severed:

> Then, when it is on its own, there are no confusions. The break is clean; independence is clarity. . . . the fledgling circumstance is also characterized by . . . a purity,

a precision, that contrasts . . . with the murky set of variables wrought by that complex phenomenon we call personality. (59–60)

Thus, Clara's study of birds becomes linked in important ways to themes and motifs that are part of much of Italian-American women's fiction—her relationship to her family, particularly to her mother, and to her maturation and socialization as a woman in traditional culture. Initially, her parents are pleased with her devotion to this knowledge, and its carryover into success at school. Clara, however, has another interpretation of her mother's acceptance of and pleasure in her studies: "She had no investment in that information; thus it did not constitute a threat" (57). However, the threat eventually becomes apparent in a variety of ways. Clara's accumulation of specialized knowledge, to the exclusion of other activities, alarms her mother and leads her to restrict and control Clara's access to it. Her mother's alarm stems primarily from her recognition of Clara's separation from her, but also from Clara's failure to behave in conventional adolescent female ways. To her parents' minds, her "hobby [had] become something of an obsession. . . . I was not . . . becoming 'socialized'. . . . remaining a very selective bibliophile who spent little time dialoguing with nature 'in vivo' as it were" (63). Clara's refusal to participate in "normal" female adolescent activities—friendships, parties, piano or dance lessons—leads her mother to drastic measures: she confiscates Clara's library and reference books.

This confiscation of knowledge is correlated to another significant event in Clara's life: her mother's restriction on her friendship with her older cousin, Laura. The connection is encouraged until Laura drops hints to Clara regarding her impending physical maturation. She does not reveal to Clara the facts of menstruation; rather, she

> *tells me something happened to make her different. . . . Laura says she's not supposed to tell me but she wants me to be ready because someday I'll be different too and she can't stand to have a secret from me anyway. . . . she says she is not allowed to tell exactly what except that it happens to everyone who is a girl. . . .* (62)

Clara then *"spends weeks imagining what the horrible thing will be"* (62); when she can stand it no longer she asks her mother, who refuses to tell her because *"it is too early to think about things I can't understand yet"* (64). As a result, *"this is the last I see of my cousin for a long time"* (64). These two instances of her mother's withholding/confiscation of knowledge are further linked when Clara gets her first period soon after her books are taken away. Significantly, she remarks, "I was genuinely distraught, felt I no longer had an identity, after such assiduous labor to attain one" (67).

While this remark seems to stem only from Clara's distress at the loss of her books, closer examination reveals her distress is also related to her sexual maturity. Like Benasutti in *No Steady job for Papa*, Caponegro links the milestone of physical maturity, her female protagonist's first period, with a milestone of emotional and intellectual maturation. Earlier, Clara relates an incident from summer camp, when she sees what an older girl's body (i.e., her future body) looks like for the first time. The "things that have happened to it" bring to Clara's mind a startling image: bread and butter, an image of softness and consumability. This moment sparks her recognition (and dread) of her own inevitable maturation: *"Laura is not like that but she will be before I am. I don't want her to be or me to be"* (61). This image of bread and butter is called up again when Laura reveals her "difference," and Clara reflects on *"this horrible thing [that] will make me into bread and butter"* (62-63). Thus, Clara sees the end result of her sexuality as a transformation into something to be consumed or destroyed: *"I dream of birds pecking me apart in the woods or a slow poison from inside my body not caused by any berry"* (63).

The links among Clara's education, her conflicted relationship with her mother, and her sexuality are further developed. After her mother confiscates her research books on birds, Clara discovers a "new" language about them: that of literature and mythology. Her source for this new language is her schoolbooks, and "As my new *passion* was not on the surface, subversive, it was as good as invisible and thus truly inviolate, affording me rebellion in the guise of acquiescence" (67-68) (my emphasis). When she is sent to boarding school as a result of her dedication to her studies, her muted rebellion continues. She rejects socialization, immersing herself in her schoolwork, taking on intellectually difficult projects that set her apart from the other girls. She develops anorexia, and, to her delight, *"the thing stopped way before mama said it would. wait till she hears how lucky I am she will be surprised"* (69). I would argue for another connection to the earlier image of the female body as "bread and butter," which Clara fears and wishes to avoid: butter is fat, and the accumulation of fat (in the breasts, the hips, etc.) is one important sign of female physical maturation; fat is also physiologically necessary for menstruation to occur. Therefore, Clara's reduction (if not elimination) of body fat through anorexia renders her, physically at least, a child again. Ultimately, Clara literalizes the fear of the consequences of education (especially for women) in traditional Italian culture—she becomes emotionally alienated and physically separated from her family (and, more particularly, from her mother), and she ceases to be a "normal" female.

Her alienation is heightened when she goes home and is reunited with Laura. She has already had disturbing hints of change in Laura's letters; Laura's excitement over a new boyfriend, with parties, and other activities for which Clara has no use give Clara a sense of forboding, confirmed when she sees Laura:

> *I hardly recognize her wearing a fancy dress her hair all styled wearing makeup even. . . . you look different I say and she laughs and says she will show me how to look that way too. . . . [she] opens her purse and takes out makeup and puts a creamy stick of color all around her mouth. this is good practice she says and when*

I ask what for she says kissing you dummy of course. (72)

The lipstick has multiple significance; as makeup, it represents masking and disguise, and a conventional part of femininity and female sexuality. It is also a phallic symbol, a sign that Laura has accepted and embraced conventional sexuality; the "creaminess" of the lipstick also reiterates the butter image of earlier passages. These connections are underscored (in the passage immediately following the one quoted above) when Laura asks Clara what she thinks of her boyfriend's picture, only to discover accidentally *"what [Clara] forgot [she] did jerry's head cut from the picture she sent pasted on top of a baboon's body"* (72) in a biology textbook (sic).

Clara's anguish upon seeing Laura's transformation confirms her sense of isolation and alienation from her body and from her family. She is forbidden to return to school; her mother agonizes *"will she ever grow up to be normal"* (73). Clara's "arrested development" is aberration because, as the adult narrator notes, puberty is

> that universal, "natural" rite of passage, characterized exclusively by increases, proliferations.... One speaks of blossomings, sproutings, as if the body were emerging from the ground in its own mimic of springtime.... One kind of growing, in this paradigm, has value or validity, one circumscribed set of changes. (71)

Thus, the irony of Clara's independent stance, of her departure from the "normal," is precisely the value that "American" culture places on individuality and independence—precisely the value which traditional Italian culture fears. Adult Clara reflects "how important for development of one's self is the way we grow away from one another, declare ourselves other, apart, so as to have the means to craft ... our own identity" (71).

At this point, the mode and point of view of the story abruptly shift. Caponegro moves into a dramatic mode, complete with stage directions, and to the mother's perspective. While these shifts may at first seem bizarre (or, at least, unnecessary), they make sense when interpreted according to Campbell's information theory. He writes:

> What memory depends on is context, and contexts change.... Of greater importance is the particular way in which an individual "processes" the information, endows it with syntax and meaning, places it in a personal context.... the brain constructs and reconstructs information, creating a highly personal mental artifact and calling it a memory. (222–223, 228)

Thus, the context changes to allow for a "new" memory: the narrator announces, *"It is time we allowed Clara's mother her own voice"* (75).

The shift is announced by the words ENTER MOTHER, which is a stage directive for the rest of the story's action, but also Caponegro's suggestion that, through her mother, Clara may find "a useful perspective on the separateness she so keenly feels" (75). Her mother believes she has the solution, a solution rooted in traditional feminine roles; significantly, she carries Clara into the kitchen, the center of domesticity, where the rest of the story's action takes place: "we sent you too far away . . . and all the while I could have been showing you so many useful things at home" (76). These "useful things" include cooking, knitting, and sewing; more important, however, "before you know it you'll be all grown up with a husband and you'll want a baby and then your friend [Clara's menstrual periods] will stop for the right reason. Nature will work in you to make a change instead of you tampering with it" (77).

The drama detours into the surrealistic, the absurd. The mother leaves the kitchen momentarily, only to return and find it in flames, Clara nowhere in sight. The flames generate a flock of birds—thus calling up the image of the phoenix so important to Clara's literary exploration of birds—which the mother battles with a succession of ineffectual, domestic weapons, all the while carrying on a monologue directed toward Clara. Finally, her return to find only a soot-covered floor, which she regards with frustration, reflects the dilemma faced by mothers in other novels—she is ineffective, facing new conflicts with old ways, old weapons. Her monologue emphasizes repeatedly the traditional woman's investment in a home-centered life, particularly in her role as mother:

> Growing up is all about that: working hard and being patient. The best example is probably having a baby. For instance, when you weighed me down, loosening my firm tummy, all of me, clamoring to get out . . . that was still a joyous time for me, for all of us. . . . And your Aunt Jean had just given birth to Laura. . . . We dreamed of the big families we would have. One big happy family, all of us. (81)

She calls herself "a tabernacle . . . a house for something sacred" and appeals to Clara to help her "feel that way again" (82). This emphasis on Clara's mother's emotional investment in her role (underscored yet again by the fact that she is never named, and even refers to herself in the third person, as "Mama") is reiterated when she notices the small worm that has emerged from the ash on the floor: "*Neither flying creature nor brutal flame could elicit the terror, the revulsion that this small crawling worm elicits*" (82), for it upsets her sense of herself as a careful housekeeper, one who "always keep[s] a clean house, to set an example for [Clara]" (82). The worm is a kind of snake in her Eden and her fear may reflect a paradoxical embracing and fear of masculine power and phallic sexuality, a message which Clara has obviously internalized.

Finally, though, there is a fleeting connection between mother and daughter, though Clara remains "offstage," invisible, apart from the action. The return of the birds leads Mama to reflect on imagination, though she emphasizes, "Mama is dizzy from not having sleep and all the commotion, and so, Mama *imagines* the birds." Significantly, she adds, "Do you understand the difference? . . . I think that's a very important part of your education" (83)—that is, to mistrust the imagination, to recognize the line between what is "real" and what is not. What is most real to her, ultimately, is motherhood: "Be my burdensome bundle of joy like some special possession that never gets put down, no matter how heavy, because it's so precious" (85).[5]

The story ends with Clara's final transformation; she now knows that "The present and the past, which seem to us vast landscapes . . . have actually no integrity until resolved as trinity, in future" (86). She resolves, too, the earlier, false division between "pure," objective knowledge and language, and emotional expression, between science and art. The connection is brought out by a final quotation from "How Birds Sing," taken from *Scientific American*, which argues for "The idea that birdsong is often an expression of irresponsible joy. . . . [and] that songs of birds can be regarded as the first towards true artistic creation and expression . . . (87). Clara herself becomes the song, and disappears beyond her mother's perception permanently—a disappearance the mother perceives as "annihilation," but which Caponegro suggests is appropriate and necessary.

In her fiction, Caponegro seeks to enact and represent synthesis, a "creative, constructive, and constitutive process of forming identity" (Hogeland, Letter). In "The Star Café" this synthesis is grounded in sexuality; Carol's appropriation of the male gaze and male sexual activity in conjunction with her renewed sense of her femininity suggest an idealized synthesis that grows out of Caponegro's feminist vision. Likewise, "Materia Prima" performs a synthesis grounded in memory, between the adult and child Claras. Caponegro upholds the notion of an ego of fluid and variable boundaries, while asserting an essential faith in one's ability to construct an identity—emphasized by the fact that the ground for synthesis (sexuality, memory) is rooted in the psychology of the stories' protagonists. Thus, she stakes out an entirely postmodernist/feminist notion of subjectivity in her fiction, in a manner echoed in Teresa de Lauretis's description contained in the introduction to *Feminist Studies/Critical Studies*.

Carole Maso: Fiction as Terrible as the World

Carole Maso asserts that her art is informed by and grounded in her upbringing in "a very middle-class family" (Cooley 33). Her mother was an emergency room nurse, her father, a jazz musician and, later, a labor organizer. Her grandfather was a labor leader, and Maso remembers "as a little girl, listening on the phone when these guys would call at five in the morning to get their [work] assignments . . . they sounded . . . so tired, so hopeful, so vulnerable" (33). Her life, she says, is rooted "in the real world, not in the rarified, the precious or elite" (33). Both her maternal and paternal grandparents were immigrants, the former from the south, the latter from the north. Like most third-generation members, Maso did not hear Italian spoken in her home, though she regards Italy as her "cultural home" (Telephone interview).

Maso received a B.A. in English from Vassar; though offered a Helen Deutsch Fellowship to pursue a graduate degree in writing, she refused, feeling that "my talent, or whatever it was, was far too fragile and far too silent to bring it into that kind of situation" (Cooley 32). Despite parental pressure to accept this honor and go to graduate school, she resisted, and, significantly, this moment "was really when I could finally break with my parents' desires for what I should do and how I should do it" (Cooley 32). Still, she says, her parents "loom large" and she remains quite close to them (Telephone interview).

Maso, like Caponegro, is concerned with the construction of memory and identity in her poetry and her fiction. Furthermore, she links her concerns to issues surrounding ethnic and feminist literary traditions. In a recent interview with Nicole Cooley, she says,

> It's such a self-conscious male thing to actually think that you're writing the great American novel. I can't imagine what that might be or what that might look like.... It's so commodity, product, goal driven. But it has also come from a certain male sensibility—I'm going to make it, this is what it's going to be, it's going to be that for all Americans.... And that the self actually exists seems like a fairly naive notion. That the self exists at all and that one could from this coherent self write this coherent great American novel. (32)

Her questions about the coherent self are also linked to authenticity of a novelist's art. Maso's first novel, *Ghost Dance* (1986), constantly interrogates itself. In one scene, the autobiography Vanessa has constructed for a school project is challenged by her teacher: " 'This is good, but it lacks authenticity' " (30). In a later scene, as Vanessa and Fletcher interview two elderly sisters known as "The Relics" about the history of previous occupants of the Turin house, the question of authenticity, and the seductive dangers of the novelist's position, again arise:

> They could no longer react genuinely to their story, but took vicarious pleasure in other people's dismay. In us they had a good and partisan audience.... They were caught up in the bravado of speech, in the storyteller's art, in the desire to move, to impress, but my brother's copious notetaking gave a legitimacy that they were unaccustomed to.... [They] were trying to come up with a version of the past they could agree upon.... [They] were exhausted. They had given up their last story. (55–56)

Ghost Dance has been characterized by reviewers as a "family chronicle" (Review, *VQR* 21) and "an elaborate elegy for a tragic family" (Review, *TNY* 120). In this novel, Maso seizes upon the Italian reverence for the family and mythologizes it; the Turin family, as one critic notes, "has inherited or created the legends they live by" (Broner 13). Like Tina in *Umbertina,* Vanessa Turin, the novel's narrator, takes on the role of third-generation "rescuer," unearthing the treasures that cannot be thrown out, tracing her family's history and identities. What reviewers of the novel have ignored, however, is the impact that Maso's particular ethnic heritage has on this theme of "family." Though E.M. Broner, in "Dance of Life" links Maso to a distinctly female tradition that crosses cultures, comparing her work to family "archeologies" such as Maxine Hong Kingston's *The Woman Warrior*, Broner does not address the specific ways in which Maso's *italianità* shapes the novel.

Early in the novel, the narrator reflects, "This is our fate: to love too much—even the dead, who might not need our love" (6). I would argue that Maso's novel simultaneously upholds and undercuts romance—the sexual kind, but, more importantly, that of the melting pot metaphor, as identified by Werner Sollors in *Beyond Ethnicity*. She links this romance, too, to the romance of the family and the images of motherhood in traditional Italian culture. The link of these romantic myths is established in the novel's opening scene, set in New York's Grand Central station. Vanessa relates a meeting with her mother, renowned poet Christine Wing, returning from one of her mysterious trips to the Maine coast, a meeting described in the language of a lover's tryst:

> There is no place more vital than this one, more exciting, more filled with promise. There is no better place on earth, nowhere else that can fill us with such hope. It will all go on. She is beautiful. People turn to look at her. The poem is complete. I run to her. There has never been a better moment to be alive. I am immensely happy. Love makes it so. We love too much and still. . . . (7)

This scene is reiterated throughout the novel, like a musical theme; however, as in a Beethoven sonata, "When a theme returns in a recapitulation, it is no longer heard as it was in the beginning" (73). Thus, the mythic, romantic image of "The mother," and of Vanessa's mother, specifically, hovers over the novel much like the Topaz Bird, the image used for the artistic gifts and the madness that have graced and haunted her ancestors for hundreds of years. Furthermore, as these images are recapitulated, they are invested with different and sometimes conflicting meanings for Vanessa, and for the reader. As Vanessa unravels and unearths these family legends, she attempts to answer this question: "How do you get a point of view . . . . How do you know something for sure?"(82) Thus, the family is the narrator's means of explaining herself to herself, but also of explaining the world.

In a sense, this question—"How do you get a point of view?"—is the epicenter; the novel's central concern is the need to make meaning and the (sometimes deluded) ways in which we attempt to do so. The postmodern project of critiquing and deconstructing Enlightenment epistemology and challenging its foundations of reason and objectivity is both Maso's content and form. The question of how one gains a point of view is echoed in the novel's structure; it is a quintessentially postmodern text, fragmented, formed by many stories from multiple perspectives, and seeks to explore, as Michael Serres argues, "ways of knowing that negotiate complexity, uncertainty, and disorder" (Paulson 36). While Vanessa turns to the methods of archeology, sifting through the layers of generations to understand herself and the world, the novel seems ultimately to deconstruct the teleological impulses of Western thought, to find definitive origins and explanations. *Ghost Dance*, then, is exemplary of what Hal Foster calls "resistant" postmodernism:

> [It is] concerned with a critical deconstruction of tradition, not an instrumental pastiche of pop- or pseudo-historical forms, with a critique of origins, not a return to them. In short, it seeks to question, rather than exploit cultural codes, to explore rather than conceal social and political affiliations. (xii)

The question of epistemology has been of great concern to feminist scholars of postmodernism. The postmodern project has been to reject the "metanarrative" of a grounding philosophy for social and political thought and practice; legitimacy in and of the so-called postmodern era becomes "plural, local, immanent" (Fraser and Nicholson 23). The problem with this solution to the universalist impulses of philosophy, as noted by feminist theorists such as Nancy Fraser and Linda Nicholson, is that "There is no place . . . for critique of pervasive axes of stratification, for critique of broad-based relations of dominance and subordination along lines like gender, race, and class" (23). Thus, the positive connotations of "resistant" postmodernism can be deconstructed. Denial of the value and viability of seeking one's origins is simply a variation of the pressure on immigrants to assimilate; one's origins are to be criticized, denied, forgotten, destroyed. Thus, the urgency of Vanessa's mission cannot be overestimated. As she and Fletcher, her brother, attempt to elicit family history from their reluctant father, Michael, they urge "[W]e need the truth, Dad . . . or we'll fail" (29). However, working against Vanessa's need for a "metafiction," for a story that will organize and explain her life, is Maso's conviction that "a lot of fiction tries too hard to organize experience, to tame it and to make it comprehensible in ways that it's just not" (Cooley 34).

The variables of one's identity—as well as the variability of identity—are closely examined in the novel. Indeed, the status and situation of the immigrant becomes a case study in identity politics and construction, particularly in the case of Vanessa's paternal grandfather. He rejects his *italianità*, embracing all the externals of an "American identity": " 'I change my own name from Angelo to Andy. . . . The accent must go. . . . We need new clothes for a new country' " (76, 77). In one crucial scene, he violently attacks what he regards as the vestiges of his Italian heritage. The scene is reported by Vanessa, who imaginatively recreates a scene she has not witnessed:

> My grandfather lifts his ax. When it is poised above his head, my father, just a boy, freezes the scene. . . . He rubs his eyes just to be sure and then he sees it: his father is cutting down the beautiful tomato plants, grown from seed, hacking them down to the ground. . . . He hacks down those sweet tomatoes while the small boy looks

on from his bedroom window and the eggplant and the peppers cower in terror. (74)

While this scene emphasizes the violence and determination underlying Grandfather Turin's rejection of his European heritage, one must note that tomatoes were a fruit that originated in the Americas and were carried back to Europe during the fourteenth and fifteenth centuries—thus, the grandfather's destruction of what he feels symbolizes his Italian identity is an ironic commentary on the artificiality of identity construction. He engages in what Werner Sollors terms "ethnic tranvestitism," modeling his "American" identity initially on blacks, whom he considers "the most authentic Americans," primarily because "they were not Europeans" (77).

Ultimately, he embraces what is to him the genuine American identity, that of the Native American.[6] He launches a kind of vision quest, impelled by a dream to leave Pennsylvania and seek knowledge in the Black Hills of the Dakotas. Though mistrustful at first, suspicious that the grandfather's appearance is merely "the white man's trick" (78), Two Bears shares his knowledge with Angelo, and accepts him as part of his tribe. Angelo returns to his family, with yet another name change for himself and for his wife and a new sense of the afterlife that challenges his more practical wife's conception that "the end was the end," despite her Catholic upbringing and "years of Mass" (80). She does, in fact, see herself as "the watchdog of rationality in a largely irrational family" (79). For her, "life is comprehensible . . . the clothes flapping in the wind on the line . . . how the cat bristles when frightened, how steam rises from the kettle" (175). She resents Christine for "ruining" her son's life, for distracting him from the life of achievement she envisioned for him. Vanessa says:

> The dream of my father's greatness was the only dream my pragmatic grandmother had ever cared to keep. After all these years, it still shone in her eyes like a light, but it served no purpose except to make the reality of my father's life unbearable to her. She had wanted to be intimately related to greatness and not just a mother-in-law to it. (174)

Thus, given the practicality of her nature, it seems ironic that she is most upset by the denial of her *italianità*, denial seen by most immigrants (as it is for Barolini's Umbertina) as a price they are willing to pay in exchange for assimilation and success. The toll this denial has taken on her is evident in a touching scene where, confined to a nursing home, she fashions for herself a traditional Italian peasant costume out of odds and ends, and dances the tarantella on the home's lawn in celebration of the Fourth of July. For the first time in her life, Vanessa feels deeply connected to her practical, stern grandmother, for whom the world of imagination inhabited by her son and his family (particularly Christine) is "utter nonsense . . . no way to live" (176). However, on the last day of her life, she connects with her son and grandchildren on an intimate, emotional level. Grandmother Turin laments the lost opportunities to share her native Italy with her son and grandchildren, a lament expressed in homey images of food, in lovely Italian words: ravioli, tortellini, torta, strufoli. In a moment reminiscent of *Like Lesser Gods*, she gestures to the dandelions growing on the lawn around her, remembering the simple meals enjoyed in her childhood: " 'We ate weeds and we were happy' " (224). The dandelions are a metaphor for the immigrant's native culture in America—a weed to be uprooted, dug up, destroyed.[7] Michael breaks down and weeps, and she apologizes for the lost years, the unspoken Italian words, the never-prepared feasts. Grandmother Turin's symbolic return to Italy and her "other self" is prefigured by a similar (though literal, rather than psychic) return by Christine's father, Frank Wing, to his birthplace, Armenia. Like Grandmother Turin, he is frustrated by what America has taken away from him, and his daughter's rejection of his ambitions for her. He re-adopts his "real name," Sarkis Wingarian, and re-embraces his Old World values upon his return:

> "In America they will laugh at me, they will call me a fat man, but here my weight is cause for respect. Here I am worth my weight in gold. In America I would look like an old man, but here old men are respected. Old age means wisdom." (212)

The family, particularly the mother, formerly portrayed in much Italian-American fiction as the institution of loyalty, security, and stability, has thus been transformed. It is useful here to consider Elsbeth Probyn's notion of "locale," which she defines as "a place that is the setting for a particular event" (178). In Probyn's formulation, the family is both place and event, a private and idealized locale which can never be reached or realized. As many feminist theorists have noted, the family is also a "locale" of contradictions; while an oppressive structure, it also offers pleasures sufficient to secure our investment in it. The question is, why does this investment occur? The ideal of family contained within *italianità* and Vanessa's attempts to "locate" herself through it, then, seem deluded and destined to fail. Though Vanessa's father Michael is portrayed as an intelligent and loving man, he is anything but the traditional Italian model of paternal authority and strength. He distances himself from his children, losing himself in quiet adoration of his beautiful wife and resigned toleration of her eccentricities and frequent mysterious absences from home (which, we eventually learn, are lengthy trysts with her female lover at a coastal home in Maine). He escapes to the movies or to his private, soundproofed study, where he listens for hours to classical music. A carefully hidden notebook, recording his research on the so-called Golden Rectangle, the form of perfection that will order reality, becomes Vanessa's philosopher's stone; for her, "to understand this one notebook . . . would be to understand everything: my father, my mother, the world, all that would happen" (71). Michael's obsession with the Golden Rectangle, as well as Vanessa's obsession with decoding her father's work, is, as Linda Nicholson writes, "an attempt to reveal general, all-encompassing principles which can lay bare the basic features of natural and social reality" (2)—for the postmodernist, an attempt destined to fail.

For her mother, coping is even more difficult:

> Her mind could not be trusted completely. It stopped, it skipped, it added, it forgot. It changed things. . . . If she allowed herself to see and hear everything, she would not have survived, for everything to her was a challenge, imperfect, asking to be transformed, rearranged, made over. (37)

In one sense, everything "asking to be transformed, rearranged, made over" is the immigrant, and is personified in her grandfather's attempts to refashion his identity. But this observation carries other meanings as well, for it does represent the traditional Italian-American mother's need to shape and manipulate those around her (as seen, for example, in Tomasi's *Like Lesser Gods* and Barolini's *Love in the Middle Ages*). For Christine Wing, this role is taken to its logical extreme, resulting in complete helplessness before the demands of daily life. In one sad and frenetic scene, she gathers the family on her four-poster bed, encircling it with layers of twine to keep them together and "safe." In another, she gets drunk as the family eats dinner at an expensive restaurant before she is to give a reading of her poetry at the Guggenheim; in full view of her husband and children, she then makes explicit sexual advances to a stranger at the bar.

Thus, through her construction of the mother figure in this novel, Maso both reinvents and challenges the traditional Italian mother/Madonna icon. Christine Wing is construed, at least physically, as the ideal Madonna figure—blonde, beautiful, almost beatific. However, her Madonna-like qualities—she wants to keep her family intact and safe from danger—are balanced by those of the whore—she gets drunk and makes sexual advances to strangers. She is a living myth in the lives of her husband and children; she is both presence and absence. She is worshipped and adored, the center of their universe. However, her role as center is made ironic (in fact, is made possible) by her distance and her absence. Indeed, its ironies extend even further. Her apparent weakness and helplessness become a subversive strength: she is freed of the responsibilities and burdens imposed by the traditional maternal role. Furthermore, she is unfaithful to her husband, not with another man, but with a woman—a subversion of her sexual and romantic roles. Finally, she is a *puttana* (whore) as De Salvo defines it—she not only does things without her husband, she maintains a professional, public identity that is completely separate from his. As a world-renowned poet, she is Christine *Wing*— a name that carries connotations of both the Topaz Bird (the image of insanity and of artistic gifts), and of freedom and flight.

Her ethereality, her apparent lack of connection to the earth, is underscored by her inability to deal with fundamental material reality. She is frequently dressed inappropriately; unable to interpret the weather, she swelters in wool in August heat, shivers in cotton in December. In the Grand Central Station scene cited earlier, Vanessa tells us that her mother is swathed in layers of clothing, makeup, and jewelry; she wears rings on every finger, and "hundreds of tiny gold chains encircle her ankles" (9), a literal and metaphorical attempt to anchor herself to the world. Vanessa, in fact, remarks that "There was an urgency about her dressing.... to keep one ... foot in the material world" (40). Her frequent absences are always preceded by what to her is the impossible task of packing; Vanessa, in these moments, faced by her mother's "multitude of clothes," finds "it easy to imagine that she would never come back again" (41). These images of the mother are, at least on the surface, conventional associations with femininity—expression of the self, construction of one's gender through clothes, jewelry, and makeup. However, one is also reminded of construction of makeup as "mask," or "masquerade," and of Gloria Anzaldùa's exploration of the meanings of "face" and "mask," cited earlier, and the relationship of these words to issues of identity construction. Though Anzaldùa does not explicitly tie these ideas to wearing makeup, I would argue that they are nonetheless present, for example, in the common expression "to put on my face." Christine's attempts to construct a public persona that she believes will make her look "normal" are destined to fail, because of the ways in which her own "intersubjective personhood" and the world's construction of femininity, of femaleness, of motherhood are so at odds with one another.

This theme is reiterated when we learn that, when Christine was a child, her father sought to make her over in the image of the blonde Hollywood starlet, to exploit her beauty to ensure his own economic and parental success in America. Just as Michael Turin disappointed his mother, failing to fulfill her expectations of greatness for him (and, thus, her own success as a mother and as an American), so Christine refuses to submit to her father's attempts to mold her to his own needs and expectations. She cultivates an oppositional, intellectual persona, wearing cheap eyeglasses purchased from Woolworth, reading poetry. The theme of mask is repeated in a minor variation, in a scene from Vanessa's childhood, in which Christine puts a mud mask on Vanessa's face, but dismisses her before explaining its purpose. Vanessa wanders off to her friend Sonia's, who, like Vanessa, suffers the small (and seemingly strange) tyrannies of a strong-willed and demanding mother. Though astonished by Vanessa's appearance ("Dirt was to be washed off the face, not put on in thick layers"—84), she is intrigued enough to want a mask as well. They walk through town, ignoring the whispers and stares:

> Perhaps we shut them out on purpose; too fragile to hear what they really said, perhaps we magnified the sounds of the wind in the trees and the birds and the lake and the cars. If we did in fact do that, it was a good idea, and Sonia and I were far smarter than I ever thought. I have seen so many people hurt by the close-mindedness of others that I know now it is best not to take too seriously the opinions of those you do not love or cannot ever imagine loving—finally, a point of view of my own. (85)

Later, after washing off the mud, they are transformed: "We are so beautiful." "[T]ransfixed by [their] dazzling images" (85) in the lake, they celebrate their difference in childish innocence (or, perhaps, ignorance). Thus, "mask" is a means of transformation from the ordinary to the extraordinary, a means of leaping beyond the petty, the average, the everyday.

This theme is repeated in a third variation later, between Vanessa and Marta, her college lover. Vanessa says, "Everything in the world bruises us" (226), so she turns to "the magic of plants" to heal them both, mixing henna paste and applying it to Marta's hair. Again, the transformative nature of "mask" is echoed. Vanessa wonders "how [Marta] will look as a redhead" and enjoys the rare feeling of tranquility this moment provides: "We are so at ease with each other at this moment, so happy, so much ourselves here, green everywhere, so natural, that we almost forget that this all must be strictly timed, that we must watch the clock, that it cannot go on forever" (227). Vanessa's assertion that she and Marta are "so much ourselves here" points to the fact that "mask" may actually uncover rather than conceal the truth, "unmasking" one's real self. However, the childish ignorance that characterized the earlier mask scene with Sonia is gone; Vanessa recognizes that such revelation is fleeting and temporary. This recognition is emphasized when Marta abruptly and violently seizes Vanessa, begging her, " 'Don't make me love you' " (227).

Clearly, a link exists between the images of makeup, mask, femininity, and identity construction and another central exploration and critique of the novel: the nature of sexuality. Indeed, the whole notion of "family," as it has been traditionally defined, takes for granted the notion of heterosexual relationships at its foundation. The fantasy of this notion is captured in the parallels drawn between the marriage of Prince Ranier and Grace Kelly and the beginning of the courtship between Vanessa's parents. The former event brings together the private and the public; ritualized heterosexuality becomes a worldwide media event. It also embodies (and unites two bodies through) the melting pot romance of America. Exogamy, a crucial factor in the mingling and muting of ethnicity, is both reality and romantic myth. The location of sexuality in the body is also of explicit concern to Maso; in an interview she speaks of being unable to "keep the body out of [her] writing, how the body keeps entering language" (Cooley 33). She remarks, "Even in *Ghost Dance*, I was investigating different ways the body might be translated into the work. It's a very sensual book, and uses the sensuality of language as a salvation" (33). In a similar vein, in her essay "For the Etruscans," Rachel Blau du Plessis asserts that Monique Wittig's writing is "a form of sexuality" (278). Finally, there is a clear link between Maso's implied critique of the insistence upon the self-contained and symmetrical unit known as the "nuclear family" (father, mother, and, ideally, one child of each sex) and traditional notions of artistic beauty: "The [Western] concept of beauty involves proportion between various elements and a relation between parts and whole—a reproduction of macrocosm in microcosm" (Maso 73). Thus, Maso explores the cracks and disturbances behind the facade of perfect proportion and beauty that the Turin family enacts.

The themes of epistemology and the acquisition of knowledge, and the location of identity (ethnic and sexual) in a physical body, are clearly linked most particularly through the character of Vanessa. As Linda Nicholson points out, location in the body, which, by definition, is finite and limited, becomes a metaphor for cognitive location through theory—just as the body has definable limits, so the mind has limits of perception and understanding. Indeed, Christine realizes that "there are limits, places the architecture of your brain will not permit you to stay, to experience" (98). Vanessa's attempts to "get a point of view," to construct a story and an identity for herself, are body-centered. Her affair with Jack is one of these "body-centered" attempts to make meaning in her life. His first command to her is "Invent me" (51). This command, along with descriptions of Jack's enormous size (he even makes Vanessa's refrigerator seem tiny), has led some reviewers and readers to speculate that Jack is an invention of Vanessa's psyche (much like the unnamed lover in Caponegro's "Star Café"). This reading is underscored by the fact that Jack reveals little about himself—his history, his family, his work. Instead, Vanessa "invents" scenarios from his childhood, imagining a kind of parallel life for him, in which his German heritage is denied him in the same way her history and ethnic heritage are denied. When she asks him about his origins, he tells her he is from Detroit but asks, " 'Does that help you at all? Does that change anything that will happen here? . . . . Oh, love . . . it won't help us' " (187).

The frequent references to his enormous physical stature may be metaphors for Vanessa's own sense of the enormity of the past, of her family, of her responsibilities for protecting her mother and making her happy. However, Maso does intend Jack to be a literal presence in the novel (Telephone interview), and he performs an important function for Vanessa's development. In one scene he takes on the role of teacher to her student, wanting to give her the gift of discipline. Vanessa reflects, "What he is teaching me is that what we must do will not be easy, and we will have to work hard to get there" (68). "What we must do" is take responsibility, ironic because Vanessa seemingly takes responsibility for everyone in her family (particularly her mother). What Jack means, possibly, is that Vanessa must take responsibility for herself, relinquish her own dependence on her mother for her own happiness and cease to be " 'a poor innocent victim of circumstances' " (189). Their sexual encounters are fiercely intense, bordering on the violent; in one horrifying scene, Jack ties her up and beats her with a leather belt, telling her that only she can stop it by commanding him to stop. He urges her, " 'Fight back. Save yourself. . . . You've suffered enough. . . . It's not your fault that your whole family is gone' " (190–191). But Vanessa remains silent, unable to resist the impulse to suffer for her "sins."

Silence is also a significant theme, unifying several events and other, minor themes in the novel. It is represented most forcefully (and in its most negative aspects) by Michael Turin, whose silence masks an inability to connect with and nurture those he loves:

> My father was comfortable in the quiet. It made the silence in him seem not so

strange. People thought he had cultivated it, worked on it, restrained himself because it was so necessary for my mother. But that was not the case. Had loquaciousness and vivacity been demanded for my mother to write, my father could not have done it.... his silence had been legitimized by my mother's art. (109)

Thus, Maso's novel investigates a phenomenon noted by Helen Barolini as characteristic of many ethnic/women writers: "For that old sanction of *omertà* [silence] both defies creativity and instigates it" (27); Maso's own sense is that "Silence causes a lot of grief and sadness [in this novel], but is also a means to recreate the self" (Telephone interview). Maso links Michael Turin's silence with other forms of "silencing" in the novel as well—for example, in Grandfather Turin's enforced muting of Grandmother Turin's *italianità*, in Grandfather Wingarian's refusal to communicate with his daughters after he returns to Armenia, and, later, in Fletcher's abandonment of his political activism and in his retreat into silence, literalized by his sending blank postcards to Vanessa as he travels the United States.

The theme of silence also connects in important ways to the presentation of female sexuality in *Ghost Dance*. Additionally, Vanessa's affair with Marta at Vassar develops and repeats several of the novel's important themes and images, particularly that of "mother." In her depiction of Vanessa's love for her mother, Maso offers a variation of traditional presentations of female experience of the Oedipal complex. In the conventional description, girls experience a split; men become erotic objects, while women become emotional objects. For Vanessa, Christine is both an erotic and emotional object, introducing the theme of a distinctly lesbian sexuality—a reading underscored by the novel's opening scene in Grand Central Station. In "Zero Degree Deviancy," Catherine Stimpson asserts that

> A mother waits at the heart... of some lesbian texts. There she unites past, present and future. Finding her, in herself and through a surrogate, the lesbian reenacts a daughter's desire for the woman to whom she was once so linked, from whom she was then so severed. Because the mother was once a daughter, a woman approaching her can serve as the mother's mother even as she plays out the drama of a daughter. (310)

Thus, Christine's affair with Sabine may be linked to the loss of her own mother, Alice, who died when Christine was still a child. Vanessa's affair with Marta, in turn, reiterates Christine's with Sabine. First, their relationship directly parallels that between Christine and Sabine (who met at Vassar); Vanessa and her mother are blond, Marta and Sabine dark and foreign (Marta is Venezuelan, Sabine is French). In another instance of the novel's use of deferral and substitution, Vanessa takes the place of Marta's previous lover, Natalie, a beautiful blond who committed suicide (and, ironically, Vanessa meets Marta only because Marta's roommate wanted to meet "Christine Wing's daughter"). Marta and Vanessa's intensive drug and alcohol use is a substitution for feeling; the frequent references to the whiteness of the cocaine and heroin they imbibe echo other images of white (and ghosts), which, Christine informs Vanessa, is the color of mourning in China. Ultimately, Vanessa's inability to "save" Marta (who attempts to commit suicide through drug overdose) echoes her "failure" to save Christine from her own demons, though Maso seems to suggest that the role of savior is not Vanessa's responsibility. This theme is brought to its logical conclusion in the novel when Sabine and Vanessa, grieving in the aftermath of Christine's death, make love, trying to recapture her presence. Their bodies are merely conduits for each woman's last attempt to connect with Christine: "For a moment she was with us, in me, or I in her, in the center of that darkness where she was still alive, and we talked to her" (253).

Maso's presentation of these lesbian relationships constitutes another important theme in the novel. In *Beyond Feminist Aesthetics*, Rita Felski argues that the "transference of allegiance from heterosexuality to intimacy between women involves overcoming the negative value which women have been conditioned to place upon their own sex; the recognition of the other woman serves a symbolic function as an affirmation of self, of gendered identity" (138). Felski goes on to point out that the positive presence of female community and female lovers in many women's narratives, such as Alice Walker's *The Color Purple*, inspires activism which "serves to attenuate the clash between individual ideals and oppressive social forces.... and makes it possible to project a visionary hope of future change . . ." (139). Maso, however, challenges this feminist utopian ideal through her portrayal of the Natalie/Marta/Vanessa triad. Marta is yet another "station" which Vanessa must pass through, a level of suffering she must endure; she enacts another sort of tyranny over Vanessa, disguised as love. Vanessa's passive acceptance of Marta's domination of her body (including the drugs, which Marta always provides and whose use she initiates) echoes the bondage scene with Jack described earlier, and indicates a more sinister aspect and more ambivalent approach to such woman-centered relationships.[8]

Implicit in the presentation of all of these women-centered relationships is Maso's critique of Catholicism (already established by Grandfather's Turin's rejection of Catholicism in favor of Native American religious practice), particularly of its imposition of suffering as the means to happiness, and the feminization of such suffering. Vanessa becomes a sort of modern day Angel in the House, for whom the burden of saving her family becomes paramount, regardless of its cost to her. Her obsession with saving her mother is paralleled by endless speculation upon and recreation of Natalie's death, in finding a moment when it could have been prevented. Finally, Maso calls up the image of Christ, "the man on the cross dying for love" (234), who must, by order of a Church that puts "simple feelings in His complex heart" (234), reject many of those whom Vanessa has loved: "The church has Him turn His face away from Natalie. The church has Him disown Marta. The church makes Him say He cannot love Florence or Bethany; he cannot love Sabine—ever" (234). Interestingly, though the Catholic Church clearly rejects the lesbian and the notion of erotic love between women, statements of

Church doctrine rarely contain more than a brief mention of such relationships. In *Eunuchs for the Kingdom of Heaven: Women, Sexuality, and the Catholic Church* (1988), Uta Ranke-Heinemann documents and discusses the extensive writings by men of the Church on female sexuality; however, there are few specific mentions of lesbianism. Rather, statements on (and, obviously, against) homosexuality are focused primarily on *male* relationships. This "silence" may be explained, in part, by traditional attitudes of male clerics toward women. Ranke-Heinemann cites, for example, an entry from the "spiritual diary" of Pope John XXIII, in which he reflects on several conversations held with a fellow cleric:

> About the persons in the Vatican, from the Holy Father downwards, there was never an expression that was not respectful. . . . But as for women or their shape or what concerned them, no word was ever spoken. *It was as if there were no women in the world* [my emphasis]. This absolute silence, this lack of any familiarity with regard to the other sex, was one of the most powerful and profound lessons of my young life as a priest, and even today I thankfully keep the excellent and beneficial memory of that man who raised me in this discipline. (324)

Maso's critique of the power of the Catholic Church is complemented by her critiques of America's racist social structure and of the power of its capitalist economic structure. These critiques are brought together most forcefully in the "World's Fair" section of the novel, with its theme of "The World of Tomorrow," and meant, ironically to celebrate diversity. Amidst the celebration of and tribute to human ingenuity and cultural diversity is a civil rights sit-in, which Grandfather Turin joins, five-year-old Fletcher in tow. Juxtaposed with Ford's Progressland is a crowd of whites hurling invectives at the black protestors. Surveying the technological wonders which surround him, Grandfather Turin reflects, "along with the the beautiful lights and the sports cars and the stairs that moved and the fusion display, we had invented a system of hatred and fear so elaborate and so subtle and efficient—in short, so perfect—that it would be nearly impossible to crack" (129). The critique is echoed throughout the novel, in Fletcher's environmental activism, which he eventually gives up in frustration over his inability to "crack the system"; in a litany of capitalist offenses; and, most forcefully, in Christine Wing's death in a fiery rear end collision of the Pinto in which she is riding.

In the face of this litany of hatred, destruction, and deception, it would seem that Maso is painting a bleak and hopeless vision. Ultimately, of all the ways of seeing, of coping, of making meaning in the world, Maso's faith seems to rest with art, particularly in the art of storytelling. As Rita Felski argues in *Beyond Feminist Aesthetics*, "Narrative constitutes one of the most deeply embedded and culturally significant forms of the symbolic production of meaning . . ." (127). However, it is important to remember that for Maso, and in this novel, there is no one single story, no metafiction that explains everything. Rather, it is the interweaving of many stories, of many points of view, some of which challenge and contradict one another, which makes meaning of experience and of the world. Art, particularly that of the narrating imagination, is fraught with both glory and danger, beauty and insanity. Over and over, Maso presents us with characters for whom the role of artist is both blessing and curse; more significantly, she links this theme to that of family and history. Vanessa relates, for instance, the story of Eva Hauser, a nineteenth-century ancestor of Christine's, whose *bricolage* technique prefigures modernist art, but also earns her the label of "crazy," because her work lacks convention and exhibits "audacity" (15).

The question arises, then: is the artist necessarily crazy, her artistic vision a burden from which "There is no rest" (49), as Christine tells Vanessa? The Topaz Bird, the symbolic representation of artistic vision, takes on various interpretations through history (just like art itself); at various times it is " 'The Bird of Truth and Light'.... 'the Bird of Supreme Sacrifice'.... the 'Bird of Insight'.... the 'Bird of Ultimate Pleasure' " (15). Maso is suggesting that all of these conceptions of the bird (and of the role of art) are naive and inaccurate at best, dangerous at worst. Christine assures Vanessa that the Topaz Bird "means us no harm," but still, "You must not look away.... There is no way to stay safe" (69). Thus, Maso seems to suggest, the role of the artist is one of taking on the responsibility of showing a culture its faults as well as its beauties, even at tremendous emotional risk. As noted, an important aspect of Vanessa's development in the novel is her willingness to take on such responsibility.

Vanessa's role as artist/storyteller is central to the novel and to her attempts to create meaning in and of her life. She creates "intricate scenarios" that are centered in the house, and bring together a series of images taken from her family's (his)stories:

> In my house.... I have seen a beautiful bride whispering her marriage vows in the white curtains that flutter in the wind.... In my house there are racehorses and flowers and satin and my mother is a little girl there, drifting off to sleep.... In my house the sun constructs perfect golden rectangles on the ceiling; they clang together, making lovely music.... In my house there is order. In my house there is sense. In my house the father who is so remote smiles finally.... Everything has an explanation, a reason.... In my house I can hear my grandfather two states away walking on the crackling earth, listening for water.... In my house, which is vibrant and alive, my Grandma Alice does not die before I am born. (17)

This section links two important locales in the novel: the house and the family. The anaphora, "In my house," of course, refers to the literal house inhabited by the Turin family. However, through the narrative impulse, the house is transformed; Vanessa's use of "my," rather than "our," imposes a metaphorical meaning on "house," a physical space that becomes memory, a psychological space. This transformation allows Vanessa to order her experiences, to make the move from chaos to order, from obscurity to clarity. Most importantly, however, these psychic operations bring Vanessa closer to the center, to her mother: "In my house there are love and violence and wonder. . . . In my house she is always there, next to me" (17).

As noted, she and Fletcher labor to unearth the history of their family; one summer they turn, at their mother's directive, to discovering the history of their house, of its previous occupants, in order to see the "ghosts" which inhabit it. Their mission becomes a kind of Grail quest — the Grail being, of course, their mother:

> And so for a few weeks one summer we threw ourselves into the project with a sort of reckless zeal. . . . We did not hesitate, we had waited our whole lives for the chance, and we grew giddy at the thought of pleasing her. The danger, of course, was all too clear. . . . it might not work; our best efforts, our purest love might not begin to bridge the distance that separated our lives from hers. But . . . nothing could stop us. We were captives of her vision. . . . we had little choice but to follow. . . . What we could not do without was her. (53–54)

Their search leads them to "The Relics," two elderly sisters who know the history of the Osbournes, previous occupants of the Turin home. Their memories, the narrator implies, are faulty, inaccurate—but "truth" is not what draws the children to them, for well they know that "the truth was useless, if it did not make Mother happy" (57).

Though Vanessa presents her need for her mother as a child's natural need, Maso is presenting a far more complex relationship. Christine takes on the role of the male lover presented in so many of what Rita Felski calls "novels of discovery."[9] In the stereotypical heterosexual relationships in these novels, female identity is presented as lack; female characters are "lock[ed] . . . into a relationship of psychological or economic dependence upon a lover who is unable to acknowledge women other than in relation to his own emotional and sexual interests" (129). Christine wields a similar power over her children; the tyranny of her psychological, spiritual, and emotional demands confirms and underscores Vanessa's sense of herself as an absence. Vanessa's identity at Vassar (where her mother studied) is that of "Christine Wing's daughter"; she spends hours in the library, staring at the photographs on her mother's book jackets, trying to attain an essential understanding of her mother, but "She will not hold still for me" (110). Interestingly, she envisions herself as part of a distant, anonymous mass audience of her mother's work: "We can't know what she's thinking. We look harder. . . . We pursue her and she eludes us" (110).

A resolution to all of these silences, and, most particularly, to the mother's absence, is enacted by the novel's ending. Vanessa's healing, in part, has already begun with her encounter with Sabine; it is furthered by Jack, who takes her out into the snow (another image of whiteness that figures prominently in the novel) and forces her to recreate imaginatively her mother's fiery death. Though she initially resists, she decides finally to reject her silent suffering, speaking now not only for herself but for all who have suffered racial, political, social, or economic injustice. Her healing is completed in the novel's final scene. She and Fletcher, reunited for the first time in several years, enact a Native American ceremony for the dead that their grandfather told them about on his deathbed. They meet Christine, who leads them through a series of vignettes, encounters with ghosts of their family history. When the moment for the final, complete separation comes, Fletcher offers Vanessa one last chance: " 'We could go with her' " (275). However, Vanessa rejects annihilation for herself and accepts what she has not been able to throughout the novel—the loss of her mother: " 'We can't come yet, Mommy. . . . We must live' " (275).

The necessity for Vanessa and Fletcher to remain a part of the material world reflects Maso's sense of herself as artist, particularly in her persona as a postmodern, experimental writer. In a recent interview, she emphasizes her desire to walk the difficult line between narrative experimentation and accessibility:

> Experimental writing has become much too precious, much too rarified, much too much about itself. . . . I come from a very middle-class family. . . . It was a life that was grounded in the real world, not in the rarified, the precious or the elite. . . . To a lot of people, "accessible" is a dirty word, as if it means imitating television or commercial fiction. But I think it means simply something everyone can have access to. . . . A lot of writing has become simply elitist and game-playing for its own sake. . . . [It] has lost any real passion and love of the world. And love of the world is really my main love, this table, this piece of bread, this hand. This afternoon light. The sound of your voice. (Cooley 33)

This passage points to a central tension in *Ghost Dance*. On the one hand, Maso identifies with Christine Wing: "She was my stand-in, in a way. Her struggles with language were mine, are mine" (Cooley 34). However, Maso's assertion of her love for and essential faith in concrete reality ("this table, this piece of bread, this hand") echoes Vanessa's description of her rational, practical grandmother, for whom life is "the clothes flapping in the wind on the line" (175). Thus, in this novel Maso achieves a synthesis similar to what Caponegro portrays in her stories.

Though the three writers studied in this chapter are very different, they demonstrate Carole Maso's observation that "narrative can of course be many things" (Cooley 32). All three of these writers demonstrate new possibilities for exploring both gender and ethnicity in contemporary American fiction; furthermore, they point to ways in which critical responses to Italian-American fiction may be expanded. In the critical responses that these writers generate, we see a radical departure from Rose Basile Green's assertion, cited in Chapter One, that the "veracity" of Italian-American novels must bear up under comparison to "the personal oral accounts" of Italian immigrants. Instead, these writers, in their treatment of topics such as immigration, generational conflict, sexual and emotional maturation, and the sense of displacement imposed by a dual heritage, demonstrate what Mary Jo Bona observes about Tina DeRosa's 1980 novel *Paper Fish*:

Analyzing how these topics are aesthetically transformed . . . will suggest something unique about the work, for it does not reflect the by-now conventional struggle to become American, but rather, it "solves the mystery" of ethnicity advanced in its epigraph: "Our images and our memories/face each other,/bewildered,/in a mirror./ Who is to solve the mystery?" The image the reader sees in the mirror, by submitting imaginatively to the work, is the ethnic experience, not as it is defined by the hegemonic society, but as it is created by an Italian-American woman who has found her voice. ("Broken Images, Broken Lives" 95)

Conclusion

Italian-American literature, and particularly the writers studied in this book, may be looked upon as a case study in how a group writes itself into America's literary tradition. In a very real sense, Italian-American literature, scholarship, and criticism grew out of one essential need: that of a people to read about and analyze itself. Recognition of this need at the root of Italian-American literature becomes all the more astonishing when one considers the relatively recent state of illiteracy dominating Italian immigrant experience; yet, as Walter Ong argues, "Orality is destined to produce writing" (*Orality and Literacy* 15). Immigrants (and, more frequently, the children of immigrants) recognized the importance of achieving literacy for successful assimilation; however, achieving literacy was often an emotionally risky venture. A primarily oral immigrant's process of transformation from the old culture to the new (that is, from orality to literacy) involves more than learning a new language, new customs, new ideals; it involves a radical psychological transformation. Ong writes, "More than any single invention, writing has transformed human consciousness" (78).

Thus, as Fred L. Gardaphé argues, "More than shedding light on social problems, a culture's writers, especially its early writers, can tell us much about a storytelling tradition once a culture shifts its emphasis from oral to written channels of communication" ("From Oral Tradition" 294). The life story of Rosa Cassetteri clearly demonstrates this shift, as orature becomes literature, as Italian becomes American. However, I would argue that even this formula is too simple: Rosa's orature (including her orally-transmitted life story) does not simply become literature, and she does not transform herself from wholly Italian into wholly American. Rather, her story is representative of the hybrid nature of immigrant experience and literature—not simply one or the other, nor simply a "half-and-half" joining, but, rather, a complex interweaving. Traces of Rosa's orality can be identified in all of the novels studied here; however, these novels also demonstrate the conscious stamp of literacy, so that each writer's work is "a charged imagining rather than a history, not a record but self-consciously a myth" (Viscusi 276).

As Nina Baym points out in "Melodramas of Beset Manhood: How Theories of American Fiction Exclude Women Authors," the decision to enter authorship has always carried with it a certain degree of alienation. Nonetheless, much in the way the male autobiographical subject is both alienated from and embraced by the dominant culture, those (male) American authors long considered "major" writers are "permitted . . . to belong, and yet not belong, to the so-called 'mainstream' " (69), simply by force of "their membership in the dominant middle-class white Anglo-Saxon group" (69). For the Italian-American writer, alienation from *both* the ethnic and mainstream cultures was usually the dominant result.

Ironically, Baym also notes the insistence of critics such as Lionel Trilling on the necessity of the struggle for "integrity and . . . livelihoods" (qtd. in Baym 69) for (male) writers to earn the label of "our best fictionists" (qtd. in Baym 69). If struggle and alienation alone defined an author as a "major, American" writer, then Italian-Americans, with their immediate history of social, political, and economic struggle ought also to have had a quick acceptance into American literary tradition. However, such acceptance clearly has not been the case; as Nina Baym notes, according to many (male) critics, "only a handful of American works are really American" (67). Thus, what defines a writer as "American" must entail something else. Baym explains:

> Despite the theoretical room for an infinite number of definitions of Americanness, critics have generally agreed on it. . . . First, America as a nation must be the ultimate subject of the work. The author must be writing about aspects of experience and character that are American only, setting Americans off from other people and the country from other nations. The author must be writing his story specifically to display these aspects, to meditate on them, and to derive from them some generalizations and conclusions about "the" American experience. . . . Such content excludes, at one extreme, stories about universals. . . . But at the other extreme, the call for an overview of America means that detailed, circumstantial portrayals of some aspects of American life are also, peculiarly, inappropriate: stories of of wealthy New Yorkers, Yugoslavian immigrants, Southern rustics. (67)

Thus, an Italian-American writer, removed from immigration (and from Italy) by only a generation or two, faces the difficult task of walking the lines between the universal and the specific, American and Italian.

Poets and fiction writers of Italian-American heritage have repeatedly emphasized the void and the conflict they experienced during childhood engagements with literature. On the one hand, exposure to literature opened up new possibilities for their lives, possibilities that liberated them from the confines of the family, from limited (or, at least, limiting) job prospects, and from exclusion from mainstream culture; for the children of Italian immigrants, "literacy became synonymous with 'going American' " (Gardaphé, "From Oral Tradition" 300). On the other hand, many of these writers realized early on that the world of literature contained within public libraries and schools, while open and available to them, did not *include* them. Thus, we frequently see characters portrayed by women writers experiencing this same void and conflict. Marion Benasutti's Rosemary, for example, ultimately rejects the blonde, blue-eyed angel, Rose Marion, as her literary model; Dorothy Bryant's Anna Giardino escapes her father's brutality through books, but must finally reconcile herself to him and to her *italianità* in order to feel whole (and, it may be argued, this novel imitates what Bryant herself is doing—reconciling her authorship with her Italian heritage).

The writers studied here truly have much in common with women writing out of other marginalized, ethnic traditions. They are, in large part, doing what Alice

Walker insists African-American women do within their tradition: writing the missing parts to one another's stories. There does, however, seem to be an essential (and ironic) difference; Italian-American women writers have frequently asserted a feeling of isolation in their "author"ity, while the literary traditions of African-American, Native American, and Chicana women have been steeped, from their inceptions, in a strong sense of community. It may be that because women of Italian heritage have more easily "passed" into mainstream America that their sense of connection to one another as writers has been tenuous. The lack of community may also explain why so few earlier works survive. Novels such as Antonia Pola's *Who Can Buy the Stars?* (1957) and collections such as Alma Vanek's *True Life Stories* (1978) are all but impossible to find today; even relatively recent, critically acclaimed works, such as Tina DeRosa's *Paper Fish* (1980), which was nominated for the Carl Sandburg Award, quickly went out of print. Too, as Helen Barolini has observed, "Few of us are self-consciously writing 'ethnic'; we are American writers, writing in the fullness of our exposure to, and experience of, American literature" (*Dream Book* 55); many writers identified by critics today as "Italian-American" are surprised by that label (and some even resist it).

Several commentators have discussed in some detail the relationship that Italian-American literature bears to the larger American literary tradition. Many critics note that a hallmark of American literature is the loner, the independent, unconventional hero pitted against the strictures of society—Natty Bumppo, Rip van Winkle, Huck Finn—who willingly separates himself physically from that society and embraces the freedom that this separation bestows. However, the recently arrived immigrant already has the status of "outsider," and, having physically separated himself from one culture, eagerly embraces the new, even though that new culture is usually not so eager to return the embrace. Thus, as Mary Jo Bona notes, "the Italian American writer confers ordinary status [rather than heroic status, as Cooper, Irving, and Twain do] on the outsider figure, pondering instead the effects of immigration on a group of people with a radically different cultural ethos" (*Claiming a Tradition* 340).

However, this is not to say that only immigrant fiction can claim this distinction. In the introduction to *The Voyage In: Fictions of Female Development* (1983), Elizabeth Abel argues that novels of development by women emphasize connection, rather than separation and independence; similarly, in "Melodramas of Beset Manhood," Nina Baym argues that a peculiarly male version of what it means to be "American" has worked against the inclusion of women's narratives in the canon of American literature. Nonetheless, even within the tradition of the female *bildungsroman* in Anglo-American fiction (Bona cites as examples Chopin's *The Awakening* and Woolf's *Mrs. Dalloway*), while there is an "insistence on relationship" (Abel 10), the focus remains, nonetheless, on the individual female protagonist. Frequently, in Italian-American women's fiction a twist on that traditional theme occurs. Mary Jo Bona notes the common strategy of Italian-American women (like many women writers of any cultural tradition) using the conventions of the *bildungsroman* "to trace the maturation of their female characters . . . invest[ing] that form with an awareness of ethnic values such as group affiliation, family cohesion, security, affection, and an abiding sense of relatedness" (*Claiming a Tradition* 332). Thus, says Bona, these writers have created a "new" form, "a specific kind of female *bildungsroman*, where the emphasis is not only on gender roles, but on how ethnicity impacts a woman's ability to discover herself" (332). Although such fiction frequently focuses on the voice or point of view of a single, female protagonist (such as Benasutti's Rosemary, Ruffolo's Anna, or Maso's Vanessa), the real protagonist of these narratives is the family itself—its development, its survival, its viability as a cultural institution—even as these protagonists struggle to find their own voices. This conflict may be the key to defining the literature studied in this dissertation as "Italian-American women's fiction"; women are preserving their old roles as keepers and transmitters of traditional culture, but in a different guise (as writers) and through a new medium (the written word).

Thus, the autobiographical foundations of Italian-American fiction are crucial; the conflict between an Italian-American woman's connection to and identification with *la famiglia* (both her own individual family and the cultural ideal of *the* family), and the "American" quest for autonomy and selfhood, ironically, creates the very conditions necessary for authorship. However, various writers respond to this conflict differently. Some writers, such as Tina DeRosa, have expressed a conviction that alienation from both the ethnic culture and the mainstream is the inevitable consequence of an Italian-American woman's decision to write.[1] In contrast, Tomasi's and Benasutti's novels both express a strong faith in the possibility to integrate (and be integrated within) the ethnic and mainstream cultures. Tomasi's depiction of Petra's exogamous marriage and Benasutti's depiction of familial (and, more particularly, maternal) support for Rosemary's authorship display a conviction that reconciliation of contradictory cultural demands is indeed possible. Others, such as Bryant, work through the process of alienation from their *italianità*, and then end by embracing it; and in Maso we see a longing for the family (and, implicitly, for traditional culture) as an anchor in a decentered, fragmented world.

While acknowledgement and analysis of Italian-American fiction is the primary goal of this study, I also want to comment on the state of Italian-American literary criticism at this point. Interestingly, the impetus for the creation of a literary tradition also fuels the creation of a critical tradition. Henry Louis Gates, Jr., in his essay "Criticism in the Jungle," notes that

> In a 1925 review of James Weldon Johnson's *The Book of American Negro Spirituals*, W.E.B. DuBois argued that evidence of critical activity is a sign of a tradition's sophistication, since criticism implies an awareness of the process of art itself and is a second-order reflection upon those primary texts that define a tradition and its canon. Insofar as we, critics of the black tradition, master our craft, we serve both to preserve our own traditions and to shape their direction. All great writers demand

great critics. The imperatives of our task are clear. (8)

I would argue that a similar urgency underlies the relatively recent explosion of criticism of Italian-American literature. In many ways, the development of an Italian-American critical tradition has the same autobiographical roots as the literature it examines. In an essay entitled "The Italian-American Writer," Fred L. Gardaphé, one of the foremost current critics of Italian-American literature, writes of his discovery of his literary heritage when, as a youngster, he was handed a copy of Mario Puzo's *The Godfather* (though, he admits, he had no desire "to read about a group with which I no longer wished to be associated" until he learned that the novel had "an excellent sex scene on page 26"); the novel's power lay in "Puzo's use of Italian sensibilities, [which] made me realize literature could be made out of my own experiences" (10). As Gardaphé progressed through high school, college, and graduate school, he also realized that

> very few [members of the Italian-American cultural community]... knew anything about Italian-American literature. Most of the books were out of print. Writers were dying with little or no public records of their existence.... I decided that what these writers needed was an advocate, and that I would become that advocate.... I had always wanted to be a lawyer, but not having the means to make it into and through law school, I could turn those yearnings into literary advocacy. (16)

The critical writings of Helen Barolini, Mary Jo Bona, and Edvige Giunta, to name just a few of those working on articulation of Italian-American women's literary tradition, have similar, autobiographical origins. The excitement of discovering one's self and one's cultural experience in literature is transformed into a desire to analyze the ways in which that self and that experience are represented. Thus, criticism asks the question raised by Robert Viscusi: "What does Italian American literature think it is?" (265).

I would argue that until recently, criticism of Italian-American literature has been dominated by an apologetic (in the sense of an *apologia* as a defense) tone; like early literature that sought to justify the Italian immigrant's presence in America and to plead for acceptance by the mainstream, works such as Rose Basile Green's study of the Italian-American novel sought to call attention to and defend the existence of Italian-American literature. Even more recent works such as Helen Barolini's introduction to *The Dream Book* tend to emphasize recognition and acceptance of an Italian-American literary tradition. However, the trend in this criticism has shifted; critics are increasingly employing methods for examining Italian-American literature that borrow from various critical traditions while assuming its existence and value as a given; thus, questions such as Gay Talese's "Where Are the Italian American Novelists?" are rendered moot. Much in the way African American and feminist critics are interrogating the usefulness of "mainstream" literary theory for analysis of African American and women's literature, so are critics of Italian-American fiction increasingly interested in finding alternative ways of thinking about such fiction and its production. Inevitably, a variety of societies and journals, such as *Voices in Italian Americana*, dedicated to fostering critical and scholarly investigation of Italian-American experience (including, but not limited to, literature) have grown in recent years.

This is not to say that the "recovery" movement in Italian-American fiction has ceased. Out-of-print works are constantly being revived, often prefaced by new critical introductions. Two prominent examples are the 1992 reprint of Pietro di Donato's *Christ in Concrete*, with Fred L. Gardaphé's critical introduction and Studs Terkel's preface, and Tina DeRosa's *Paper Fish*, a 1996 reprint with a critical afterword by Edvige Giunta. The recent anthology *The Voices We Carry: Recent Italian/American Women's Fiction* (1994), edited and introduced by Mary Jo Bona, gathers short stories and novel excerpts by fourteen writers, past and present, who "are digging up their cultural origins in order to 'rediscover place' and carry their unique voices into the future" (Bona 25). In addition, the works of writers such as Don DeLillo, not considered conventionally as "Italian-American," are being reevaluated in light of the growing interest in acknowledging, defining, and articulating this tradition.

Thus, this study is part of an ongoing conversation, in which notions of ethnicity, gender, culture, literary tradition, and critical perspective are hotly debated. If American literature is not, properly speaking, a "melting pot," at the very least it is the responsibility of critics to recognize and articulate as many of the threads that constitute that tradition as possible. The exclusiveness that has until recently characterized the "canon" and literary studies is unquestionably decreasing (if not being eliminated entirely). I paraphrase Elaine Showalter's unequivocal assertion about feminist criticism in "Towards a Feminist Poetics": "One thing is certain: [Italian-American] criticism is not visiting. It is here to stay, and we must make it a permanent home" (142).

Bibliography

Ahearn, Carol Bonomo. "Definitions of Womanhood: Class, Acculturation, and Feminism." *The Dream Book: An Anthology of Writings by Italian American Women.* Ed. Helen Barolini. New York: Schocken, 1979: 126–139.

Allen, Paula Gunn. *The Sacred Hoop: Recovering the Feminine in American Indian Tradition.* Boston: Beacon, 1986.

Antin, Mary. *The Promised Land.* New York: Houghton Mifflin, 1912.

Anzaldùa, Gloria. "Haciendo caras, una entrada." *Making Face, Making Soul/ Haciendo Caras.* Ed. Gloria Anzaldùa. San Francisco: Aunt Lute, 1990: xv–xxviii.

———. *Borderlands/La Frontera: The New Mestiza.* San Francisco: Aunt Lute, 1987.

Barnes, Djuna. *Nightwood.* Intro. T.S. Eliot. New York: Harcourt, 1937.

Barolini, Helen. *Love in the Middle Ages.* New York: William Morrow, 1986.

———. "Becoming a Literary Person Out of Context." *The Massachussetts Review* 27 (1986): 262–274.

———. Introduction. *The Dream Book: An Anthology of Writings by Italian American Women.* Ed. Helen Barolini. New York: Schocken: 3–56.

———. *Umbertina.* New York: Seaview Books, 1979.

Bauer, Dale. "Gender in Bakhtin's Carnival." Warhol and Herndl 671–684.

Baym, Nina. "Melodramas of Beset Manhood: How Theories of Fiction Exclude Women Authors." Showalter 63–80.

Bell, Michael Davitt. *The Problem of America Realism.* Chicago: U of Chicago P, 1993.

Benasutti, Marion. *No Steadyjob for Papa.* New York: Vanguard P, 1966.

Birnbaum, Lucia Chiavola. "red, a little white, alot of green, on a field of pink: a controversial design for an Italian component of a multicultural canon for the United States." Tamburri et al. 282–293.

Bodenheimer, Rosemarie. *The Politics of Story in Victorian Fiction.* Ithaca: Cornell UP, 1988.

Boelhower, William. *Through a Glass Darkly: Ethnic Semiosis in American Literature.* New York: Oxford UP, 1987.

———. *Autobiography in the United States: Four Versions of the Italian American Self.* Verona, Italy: Essedue Edizoni, 1982.

Bona, Mary Jo, ed. *The Voices We Carry: Recent Italian/American Women's Fiction.* Montreal: Guernica, 1994—. "Claiming a Tradition: Italian American Women Writers." Diss. U of Wisconsin—Madison, 1989.

———. "Broken Images, Broken Lives: Carmolina's Journey in Tina DeRosa's *Paper Fish*." *MELUS.* 14:3–4 (1987): 87–106.

Broner, E. M. "Dance of Life." *Women's Review of Books.* 3 (1986): 13.

Bryant, Dorothy. Letter to the author. 20 September 1992.
———. *Miss Giardino*. Berkeley: Ata, 1978.
———. *Ella Price's Journal*. New York: J.B. Lippincott, 1972.
Cahan, Abraham. *The Rise of David Levinsky*. New York: Harper, 1917.
Campbell, Jeremy. *Grammatical Man: Information, Entropy, and Language*. New York: Simon, 1982.
Caponegro, Mary. Telephone interview. 7 April 1995.
———. *The Star Café*. New York: Norton, 1990.
Capozzoli, Mary Jane. *Three Generations of Italian American Women in Nassau County, 1925–1981*. New York: Garland, 1990.
Chodorow, Nancy. *The Reproduction of Mothering: Psychoanalysis and the Sociology of Gender*. Berkeley: U of California P, 1978.
Claro, Fran. "South Brooklyn, 1947." Barolini, *The Dream Book* : 77–83.
Coles, Nicholas. "Mantraps: Men at Work in Pietro Di Donato's *Christ in Concrete* and Thomas Bell's *Out of the Furnace*." *MELUS*. 14:3–4 (1987): 23–32.
Cooley, Nicole. "Carole Maso: An Interview by Nicole Cooley." *The American Poetry Review*. March/April (1995): 32–35.
Coward, Rosalind. "Are Women's Novels Feminist Novels?" *Feminist Criticism*. Ed. Elaine Showalter. New York: Pantheon, 1985: 225–239.
Crenshaw, Kimberlé. "Whose Story Is It, Anyway? Feminist and Antiracist Appropriations of Anita Hill." *Race-ing Justice, En-gendering Power*. Ed. Toni Morrison. New York: Pantheon, 1992: 402–440.
Daly, Mary. *Gyn/Ecology: The Metaethics of Radical Feminism*. Boston: Beacon P, 1978.
Davies, Carol Boyce. "Collaboration and the Ordering Imperative in Life Story Productions." *De/Colonizing the Subject: The Politics of Gender in Women's Autobiography*. Eds. Sidonie Smith and Julia Watson. Minneapolis: U of Minnesota P, 1992: 3–19.
Dearborn, Mary. *Pocahontas' Daughters*. New York: Oxford UP, 1986.
DeConde, Alexander. *Half Bitter, Half Sweet: An Excursion into Italian-American History*. New York: Scribner, 1971.
de Lauretis, Teresa. "Feminist Studies/Critical Studies: Issues, Terms, and Contexts. *Feminist Studies, Critical Studies*. Ed. Teresa de Lauretis. Bloomington, IN: Indiana UP, 1986: 1–19.
DeRosa, Tina. "An Italian American Speaks Out." *Attenzione*. May 1980: 38–39.
DeSalvo, Louise A. "From *A Portrait of the Puttana as a Middle-Aged Woolf Scholar*." Barolini, *The Dream Book*: 93–99.
di Donato, Pietro. *Christ in Concrete*. 1939. Preface Studs L. Terkel. Intro. Fred L. Gardaphé. New York: Penguin, 1993.
Dinnerstein, Dorothy. *The Mermaid and the Minotaur: Sexual Arrangements and Human Malaise*. New York: Harper, 1978.
DuPlessis, Rachel Blau. *Writing Beyond the Ending: Narrative Strategies of*

Twentieth-Century Women Writers. Bloomington, IN: Indiana UP, 1985.
Eisenstein, Zillah R. *The Radical Future of Liberal Feminism.* New York: Longman, 1981.
Ets, Marie Hall, ed. *Rosa: The Life of an Italian Immigrant.* Minneapolis: U of Minnesota P, 1970.
Fauset, Jessie Redmon. *Plum Bun.* 1929. Intro. Deborah E. McDowell. Boston: Pandora, 1985.
Felski, Rita. *Beyond Feminist Aesthetics: Feminist Literature and Social Change.* Cambridge, MA: Harvard UP, 1989.
Ferraro, Thomas. *Ethnic Passages: Literary Immigrants in Twentieth-Century America.* Chicago: U of Chicago P, 1993.
Flax, Jane. *Thinking Fragments: Psychoanalysis, Feminism, and Postmodernism in the Contemporary West.* Berkeley: U of California P, 1990.
Foster, Hal, ed. *The Anti-Aesthetic: Essays on Post-Modern Culture.* Port Townsend, WA: Bay, 1983.
Fraser, Nancy and Linda Nicholson. "Social Criticism without Philosophy: An Encounter between Feminism and Postmodernism." Nicholson. 19–38.
Gallo, Patrick J. *Old Bread, New Wine: A Portrait of the Italian-Americans.* Chicago: Nelson-Hall, 1981.
Gambino, Richard. *Blood of My Blood: The Dilemma of the Italian-Americans.* Garden City, NY: Doubleday, 1974.
Gardaphé, Fred L. "The Italian-American Writer." Spencertown, NY: Forkroads, 1995.
———. Introduction. *Christ in Concrete.* By Pietro di Donato. 1939. New York: Penguin, 1993.
———. "From Oral Tradition to Written Word: Toward an Ethnographically Based Literary Criticism." Tamburri et al. 294–306.
———. "Italian-American Fiction: A Third Generation Renaissance." *MELUS.* 14:3–4 (1987): 69–85.
Gates, Henry Louis, Jr. "Criticism in the Jungle." *Black Literature and Literary Theory.* Ed. Henry Louis Gates, Jr. New York: Methuen, 1984: 1–24.
Rev. of *Ghost Dance* by Carole Maso. *The New Yorker.* 15 September, 1986: 120.
Rev. of *Ghost Dance* by Carole Maso. *Virginia Quarterly Review* 63 (1987): 21.
Gilbert, Sandra M. and Susan Gubar. *The Madwoman in the Attic: The Woman Writer and the Nineteenth-Century Literary Imagination.* New Haven: Yale UP, 1979.
Giunta, Edvige. "Crossing Critical Boundaries in Italian/American Women's Studies." *ItalianAmerican Review* 5.2 (1996-97): 79–94.
———. "Blending 'Literary' Discourses: Helen Barolini's Italian/American Narratives." *Romance Languages Annual.* 6 (1995): 261–266.
———. "Narratives of Loss: Voices of Ethnicity in Agnes Rossi and Nancy Savoca." *Canadian Journal of Italian Studies.* 19:53 (1996): 164–183.
Green, Rose Basile. *The Italian American Novel: A Document of the Interaction of Two Cultures.* Madison, NJ: Fairleigh Dickinson UP, 1974.

Grosz, Elizabeth. *Jacques Lacan: A Feminist Introduction.* New York: Routledge, 1990.
Harper, Frances Ellen Watkins. *Iola Leroy: Or, Shadows Uplifted.* 1892. College Park, MD: McGrath, 1969.
Heilman, Carolyn. *Writing a Woman's Life.* New York: Norton, 1988.
Hogeland, Lisa Maria. "Re-Visionary Heteroglossia: Two Studies in Women Writers and the Politics of Referentiality." Diss. Stanford U, 1992.
———. Letter to author. 6 December 1995.
Holly, Carol T. "*Black Elk Speaks* and the Making of Indian Autobiography." *Genre* XII (1979): 117–136.
hooks, bell. *Ain't I A Woman: Black Women and Feminism.* Boston: South End P, 1981.
Iorizzo, Luciano J. and Salvatore Mondello. *The Italian-Americans.* New York: Twayne, 1971.
Kaplan, Amy. *The Social Construction of American Realism.* Chicago: U of Chicago P, 1988.
Larsen, Nella. *Passing.* 1929. New York: Negro Universities P, 1969.
Larsen, Simeon and Bruce Nissen, eds. *Theories of the Labor Movement.* Detroit: Wayne State UP, 1987.
La Sorte, Michael. *La Merica: Images of the Italian Greenhorn Experience.* Philadelphia: Temple UP, 1985.
Leites, Edmund. *The Puritan Conscience and Modern Sexuality.* New Haven: Yale UP, 1986.
Madden, David, ed. *Proletarian Writers of the Thirties.* Carbondale: Southern Illinois UP, 1968.
Maglione, Catherine A. and Carmen Anthony Fiore. *Voices of the Daughters.* Princeton, NJ: Townhouse, 1989.
Malpezzi, Frances M. and William M. Clements. *Italian-American Folklore.* Little Rock: August House, 1992.
Mangione, Jerre and Ben Morreales. *La Storia.* New York: HarperCollins, 1992.
Marshall, Paule. *Brown Girl, Brownstones.* New York: Feminist P, 1981.
Maso, Carole. Telephone interview. 8 April 1995.
———. *Ghost Dance.* San Francisco: North Point P, 1986.
McGovern, Arthur F. *Marxism: An American Christian Perspective.* Maryknoll, NY: Orbis Books, 1981.
Moraga, Cherrie and Gloria Anzaldùa, eds. *This Bridge Called My Back: Writings by Radical Women of Color.* 2nd ed. New York: Kitchen Table Women of Color P, 1983.
Morgan, Robin, ed. *Sisterhood is Powerful: An Anthology of Writings from the Women's Liberation Movement.* New York: Random House, 1970.
Morrison, Toni, ed. Introduction. *Race-ing Justice, En-gendering Power: Essays on Anita Hill, Clarence Thomas, and the Construction of Social Reality.* New York: Pantheon, 1992.
———. *The Bluest Eye.* 1970. New York: Plume-Penguin, 1993.

Nicholson, Linda, ed. *Feminism/Postmodernism*. New York: Routledge, 1990.
Nobili, Rev. Peter, ed. *A Legacy*. Precious Blood Fathers, Atlantic Vicariate, 1982.
Novak, Michael. *The Rise of the Unmeltable Ethnics*. New York: Macmillan, 1972.
Oliver, Lawrence J. "The Re-Visioning of New York's Little Italies: From Howells to Puzo." *MELUS*. 14:3–4 (1987): 5–22.
Olson, James. *Catholic Immigrants in America*. Chicago: Nelson-Hall, 1987.
Ong, Walter. *Orality and Literacy: The Technologizing of the Word*. New York: Methuen, 1982.
———. "Literacy and Orality in Our Times." *Journal of Communication* 30-1 (1980): 197–204.
Paulson, Wiliam R. *The Noise of Culture: Literary Texts in a World of Information*. Ithaca: Cornell UP, 1988.
Peragallo, Olga. *Italian American Authors and Their Contributions to American Literature*. New York: S.F. Vanni, 1949.
Pratt, Annis. *Archetypal Patterns in Women's Fiction*. Bloomington: Indiana UP, 1981.
Probyn, Elspeth. "Travels in the Postmodern: Making Sense of the Local." Nicholson 176–189.
Puzo, Mario. *The Godfather*. New York: Putnam, 1969.
———. *The Fortunate Pilgrim*. New York: Lancer Books, 1964.
Ranke-Heineman, Uta. *Eunuchs for the Kingdom of Heaven: Women, Sexuality, and the Catholic Church*. New York: Penguin, 1990.
Riis, Jacob. *How the Other Half Lives: Studies Among the Tenements of New York*. 1890. Cambridge, MA: Belknap-Harvard UP, 1970.
Rolle, Andrew. *The Italian Americans: Troubled Roots*. New York: Macmillan, 1980.
Ruddy, Anna C. *The Heart of the Stranger: A Story of Little Italy*. 1908. New York: Arno, 1975.
Ruffolo, Lisa. Telephone interview. 22 February 1996.
———. "My Grandfather's Suit." Tamburri et al. 75–81.
———. *Holidays*. St. Paul, MN: New Rivers P, 1987.
Savarese, Julia. *Final Proof*. New York: Norton, 1971.
———. *The Weak and the Strong*. New York: Putnam, 1952.
Schaub, Thomas Hill. *American Fiction in the Cold War*. Madison: U of Wisconsin P, 1991.
Showalter, Elaine, ed. *The New Feminist Criticism*. New York: Pantheon, 1985.
———. "Towards a Feminist Poetics." Showalter 125–143.
———. "Feminist Criticism in the Wilderness." Showalter 243–270.
Skaggs, Peggy. "Kate Chopin." *The Heath Anthology of American Literature*, Vol 2. Ed. Paul Lauter et al. Lexington, MA: D.C. Heath, 1990: 626–628.
Smith, Sidonie. *A Poetics of Women's Autobiography*. Bloomington: Indiana UP, 1987.
Sollors, Werner, ed. *The Invention of Ethnicity*. New York: Oxford UP, 1989.
———. *Beyond Ethnicity: Consent and Descent in American Culture*. New York:

Oxford UP, 1986.
Steiner, Rudolf. *Essential Steiner*. Ed. and Introduction Robert A. McDermott. San Francisco: Harper & Row, 1984.
Stimpson, Catherine R. "Zero Degree Deviancy: The Lesbian Novel in English." Warhol and Herndl 301–315.
Sullivan, Patrick J. *U.S. Catholic Institutions and Labor Unions 1960–1980*. New York: UP of America, 1985.
Talese, Gay. "Where Are the Italian-American Novelists?" *The New York Times Book Review*. 14 March 1993: 1+.
Tamburri, Anthony Julian et al., eds. *From the Margin: Writings in Italian Americana*. West Lafayette, IN: Purdue UP, 1991.
———. "*Umbertina*: The Italian/American Woman's Experience." Tamburri et al. 357–373.
Terkel, Studs. Preface. *Christ in Concrete*. By Pietro di Donato. 1939. New York: Penguin, 1993: vii.
Titon, Jeff Todd. "The Life Story." *Journal of American Folklore*. July/September (1980): 276–292.
Tomasi, Mari. *Like Lesser Gods*. Milwaukee: Bruce Publishing, 1949.
———. *Deep Grow the Roots*. Philadelphia: Lippincott, 1940.
Tong, Rosemarie. *Feminist Thought*. Boulder: Westview P, 1989.
Torgovnick, Mariana DeMarco. *Crossing Ocean Parkway: Readings by an Italian American Daughter*. Chicago: U of Chicago P, 1994.
Trapp, J.B.. ed. *Medieval English Literature*. New York: Oxford UP, 1973.
Tu Smith, Bonnie. *All My Relatives: Community in Contemporary Ethnic American Literature*. Ann Arbor: Michigan UP, 1993.
Viscusi, Robert. "A Literature Considering Itself: The Allegory of Italian America." Tamburri et al. 265–281.
von Huene Greenberg, Dorothee. "A *MELUS* Interview: Helen Barolini." *MELUS* 18-2 (1993): 91–108.
Waldo, Octavia. *A Cup of the Sun*. New York: Harcourt, 1961.
Walker, Alice. *In Search of Our Mothers' Gardens: Womanist Prose*. New York: Harcourt, 1983.
Warhol, Robyn R. and Diane Price Herndl, eds. *Feminisms: An Anthology of Literary Theory and Criticism*. New Brunswick, NJ: Rutgers UP, 1991.
Washington, Booker T. *Up From Slavery*. New York, Doubleday, 1901.
Weber, Max. *The Protestant Ethic and the Spirit of Capitalism*. New York: Scribner's, 1958.
Woolf, Virginia. *Three Guineas*. 1938. New York: Harvest-Harcourt, 1966.
Yezierska, Anzia. *Bread Givers*. 1925. New York: Persea, 1975.

Glossary

braccianti—Propertyless day laborers, from the Italian word for "arm"; the term literally means "a pair of arms." These men would hang about the center of the village, hoping to be hired for a day's wages (also called *giornalier*).

campanilismo—Spirit of village/regional identity.

contadini—The landed peasantry; they leased land from the much wealthier landowners and worked it. Especially in the south of Italy, the land was usually very barren and rocky, and yielded little profit for the *contadini*.

destino—Destiny.

festa—Feast day celebration, usually in honor of the Madonna or of a village or regional patron saint.

forestieri — "Stranger"or "foreigner"; someone from another village (also called *stranieri*).

italianità— Sense of one's "italianess," one's link to Italian culture, language, etc.

maestro—Master or teacher.

mala femmina—Literally, "bad woman"; also refers to a woman who fails to behave in traditionally feminine ways.

malocchio—The evil eye; also known as the "overlook."

Mezzogiorno—Term used to refer to the region of Italy south and east of Rome.

misèria—Literally, "misery"; term used to incorporate the terrible economic, political, and social conditions of the Mezzogiorno.

omertà—Silence, in the sense of deeply held cultural imperative that it is wrong and even dangerous to speak out. Also refers to oath to never to apply to legal bodies for justice, or to aid in crime investigations.

l'ordine della familglia—Code of family rule.

osteria—Pub.

padrone—Literally, "boss" or "overseer"; for immigrants, these men offered access to work, lodging, etc., but frequently took advantage of the newcomers' ignorance and fear.

paese — Village or region.

paesani—Literally, "villagers," but also used in reference to those from the same region of Italy.

puttana—whore.

serietà—Seriousness.

l'uomo di pazienza—"Man of patience"; code of ideal masculine behavior.

(la) via vecchia—"the old way"; the traditional set of values and manner of living in Italian culture.

Notes

Introduction

1. Bonnie Tu Smith's *All My Relatives: Community in Contemporary Ethnic American Literature* examines the emphasis on communal identity in the literature of African Americans, Asian Americans, Chicanos/as, and Native Americans. Though Tu Smith challenges claims for "white" ethnicity, such as those made by Michael Novak, as a "blatant play for the brass ring of power and status" (5–6), her discussion of the conflict between communal and individual identities in American literature has far-reaching implications for Italian-American writers.
2. The confirmation hearings of Supreme Court Justice Clarence Thomas, more than any other incident, perhaps, brought before the American public the complex interaction between gender and ethnic/racial ties. In response to questions about why she chose at this point to come forward with her allegations of sexual harassment against Thomas, Hill said, "[While] [i]t would have been more comfortable to remain *silent*. . . . I could not keep silent" (qtd. in Morrison vii) (my emphasis). Kimberlé Crenshaw notes, "That black people across a political and class spectrum were willing to condemn Anita Hill for breaking ranks is a telling testament to how deep gender conflicts are tightly contained by the expectation of racial solidarity" (433).
3. In contrast is Sandra Gilbert, whose best known feminist critical work, *The Madwoman in the Attic* (1979), is a fundamental source of feminist re-visionary scholarship. However, she writes poetry under her maiden name, Mortola; she reflects, "I am really Sandra Mortola Gilbert . . . and my mother's name was Caruso, so I always feel oddly falsified with this Waspish-sounding American name, which I adopted as a twenty-year-old bride who had never considered the implications of her actions!" (qtd. in Barolini, *The Dream Book* 22).
4. The issue of language does not concern Italian-American women writers in the same way as it concerns, for example, Chicana and Native American writers, who have debated the merits of using, respectively, Spanish, or Native languages, such as Athabaskan, over writing exclusively in English. Most Italian immigrants willingly gave up their "mother tongue" as part of the bargain of assimilation and success. Nonetheless, the psychological consequences of losing one's language are frequently documented in Italian-American literature; while, as Toni Morrison says, "Voluntary entrance into another culture . . . has certain satisfactions to mitigate the problems that may ensue," it is also true that "being rescued into an adversarial culture can carry a huge debt. . . . And if the language of one's culture is lost or surrendered, one may be forced to describe that culture in the language of the rescuing one"—a language that may result in "the reinforcement of cliché, the erasure of difference . . . the denial of history . . . [and] the inscription of hegemony" (xxvii–xxviii).

Chapter One

1. See Helen Barolini, *The Dream Book* (New York: Schocken, 1985) for an extensive discussion of these barriers (18–49).
2. For an overview of autobiography criticism, see Sidonie Smith, *A Poetics of Women's Autobiography* (3–15).
3. Heilbrun also reminds us of her earlier identification of 1970 as a turning point in women's biography, when Nancy Milford's *Zelda* was published. Heilbrun's insistence on this work's importance is based on "the way it revealed F. Scott Fitzgerald's assumption that he had the right to the life of his wife, Zelda, as an artistic property.... Only in 1970 were we ready to read not that Zelda had destroyed Fitzgerald, but Fitzgerald her: he had usurped her narrative" (12).
4. Bonnie TuSmith's *All My Relatives* argues against sociologist Robert Bellah's assertion that "Americans have lost the language for expressing communal values" (16). Tu Smith instead argues that ethnic American literature is rooted in the language of community: "[W]e can no longer take it for granted that the Bellah research group's 'first language of American individualism' adequately characterizes the 'American Way' in either life or art.... In various critical studies ... scholars have remarked on the collectivist or communal orientation of ethnic American literature" (21).
5. In important ways, Mamma Lena anticipates the central character of Helen Barolini's *Umbertina* (1979), a strong female whose intelligence, independence, and business sense ensure the family's social and economic success in America. The narrator says of Umbertina, "If there was one thing she was learning about American life, it was the need to be her own boss" (65).
6. The question of identity is a minor, but significant, motif throughout Rosa's narrative. At birth, she tells us, she was given the name Inez Ignazius, by which she is known until Mamma Lena takes her in and she becomes "Rosa." When her birth mother insists on calling her Inez, Rosa objects and refuses to answer to that name. Later, of course, we follow her name changes from her adoptive mother's (Cortesi) to her second husband's (she leaves her first husband's surname out of the story altogether). Ets informs us in the introduction that all place and personal names, including Rosa's, have been changed, though whether at Rosa's insistence or Ets's own respect for Rosa's privacy is not clear. Additionally, Rosa refuses to reveal her birth mother's true name even to Ets, "for she said everyone in the world would know that name" (7).

Chapter Two

1. As many scholars have noted, even authors who are today considered canonical, mainstream American writers were similarly dismissed during this period;

for example, Peggy Skaggs notes that "For many years, twentieth-century critics ignored *The Awakening*, anthologized a few short stories like 'Desiree's Baby' and 'The Benitou's Slave,' and called [Kate] Chopin a local color writer" (627).

2. Similarly, Tomasi wrote "The Italian Story in Vermont" under the aegis of the Vermont Historical Society, in which she also glosses over references to immigrant labor activity in that state.

3. One of the central tensions of Pietro di Donato's *Christ in Concrete* is between the sense of Geremio and the other brickworkers of themselves as artists, and the pervasiveness of Job, di Donato's term for the capitalistic system that renders the workers powerless, emasculated, and insignificant.

4. In *Theories of Labor Management*, Simeon Larsen and Bruce Nissen explain the traditional Catholic position on the labor movement, dating from 1891, when Leo XIII's social encyclical *Rerum Novarum* was published. While critical of the unjust conditions that created misery for the working class, this encyclical unequivocally rejected socialist solutions as being "*against natural justice*": "The abolition of private property, declared the pope, violates the natural rights of man. Thus it is not capitalism as a system which is responsible for the economic problems of the masses but a handful of the very rich who are misled by greed. . . . Individuals rather than classes are the root cause of the problem" (252).

5. This interest in documenting a "vanishing" way of life is one shared by many so-called "local color" or regional writers, such as Sarah Orne Jewett.

6. Mary Jo Bona, in *Claiming a Tradition*, argues that the mutilation of Denny's hand at the quarry represents a leveling of Denny with Petra, much as the blinding and maiming of Rochester in *Jane Eyre* equalizes the power between Jane and Rochester.

7. Like Tomasi, Benasutti makes a very brief acknowledgement of the labor activities of Italian immigrants during this period. Unlike Tomasi, however, her depiction of the violence that often accompanied labor unrest is much more explicit. Rosemary recounts the incident that impelled the family to move from the coal mines of western Pennsylvania to Philadelphia: a bloody battle between miners and "company men" that finds its way into their home, and results in the shooting death of one of the miners.

8. Mamma's determination is echoed by Barbardian immigrant Silla Boyce's resolve to "buy house" in Paule Marshall's *Brown Girl, Brownstones* (1981).

9. Feminist theorists such as Zillah R. Eisenstein have frequently noted the interdependence of the patriarchal model of the family and capitalism. In *The Radical Future of Liberal Feminism* (1981), Eisenstein argues that patriarchy, "a political structure that privileges men" (8), and capitalism are mutually interdependent: "Capitalism needs the system of social patriarchy and therefore must try to find supports for the patriarchal ordering of society" (204). Additionally, in *Rerum Novarum*, Pope Leo XIII asserts: "For it is a most

sacred law of nature that a father must provide food and all necessaries for those whom he has begotten . . . a man's children . . . should be provided by him with all that is needful . . . to keep themselves from want and misery. . . . Now, in no other way can a *father* effect this except by the ownership of profitable property, which he can transmit to his children by inheritance" (my emphasis) (Larsen and Nissen 259).

10. Similarly, after Geremio's death in Pietro di Donato's *Christ in Concrete*, his wife Anunziata lapses into a state of helplessness and passivity, while twelve-year-old Paul takes over as the "man" (that is, the breadwinner) of the family. In contrast, however, Puzo's first novel, *The Fortunate Pilgrim* (1964), depicts the active resolve of Fortunata to support her children after her husband's unexpected death.

11. Clearly, the alliteration of Lassiter, Lancelot, and Larry Lacey, as figures of romantic love, is deliberate, though Larry is obviously meant to be a "flesh and blood" corrective to Rosemary's distorted notions of love and sexual relationships.

12. I want to thank Lisa Hogeland for pointing to the parallel between this novel and the "passing" novel of African American literary tradition, such as Frances Watkins Harper's *Iola Leroy* (1892), Jessie Redmond Fauset's *Plum Bun* (1929), and Nella Larsen's *Passing* (1929), in their use of the theme of assimilation and return.

Chapter Three

1. An abbreviated form of the outline of this process includes 1. the "cell" discussion group, which explores both impediments to consciousness raising, such as romantic fantasies and self-blame, and developing theories and activities to overcome them; 2. consciousness-raising action; 3. organizing, meetings, and conferences (Morgan xxvi–xvii).
2. I want to thank Amy Elder for noting that this strategy is also employed in slave narrative and autobiographies, such as Booker T. Washington's *Up from Slavery* (1901).
3. Interestingly, other connections have also been made between the Italian and so-called "Okie" immigrant/literary experiences. The critical receptions and publication histories of *Christ in Concrete* and *The Grapes of Wrath* illustrate some of the external barriers faced by Italian-American writers (male and female). In his preface to the 1993 reprint of Pietro di Donato's *Christ in Concrete*, Studs Terkel notes the coincidence of the publication in 1939 of di Donato's powerful novel about an Italian immigrant's search for a better life, and of John Steinbeck's *The Grapes of Wrath*. Ironically, Fred Gardaphé notes in his introduction to the novel that di Donato's work "was chosen over . . . *The Grapes of Wrath* as a main selection of the 1939 Book-of-the-Month Club" (x), only to go out of print after its first and only reprinting in 1976.

4. I want to thank Lisa Hogeland for pointing out to me that disease metaphors are commonly found in discourses about feminism as well. Mary Jo Bona, in *Claiming a Tradition: Italian American Women Writers* (1989) and in "Broken Images, Broken Lives: Carmolina's Journey in Tina DeRosa's *Paper Fish*" explores "the topic of illness both as a realistic comment on the prevalence of sickness in underprivileged communities and as a metaphor for the immigrant experience of living in a world that does not readily welcome outsiders" ("Broken Images" 94). Bona sees this strategy/metaphor as common to many Italian-American women writers.

5. The depiction of writing as rebellion is, of course, common to feminist criticism and to feminist fiction. One important example is the nameless female narrator of Charlotte Perkins Gilman's "The Yellow Wallpaper" (1892), who persists in writing secretly against the orders of her physician/husband.

6. Michael Novak's *The Rise of the Unmeltable Ethnics* (1973) focuses on what he refers to as PIGS (Poles, Italians, Greeks, and Slavs), whom he calls the "forgotten ethnics" of melting pot America. However, even novels by and about other ethnicities frequently did not generate much interest; *Ella Price's Journal* sold well and was widely reviewed when it was published, while Toni Morrison's *The Bluest Eye*, published in 1971, went out of print almost immediately and was not revived until the early 1980s.

Chapter Four

1. Unlike the other three major female characters, Carla does not get her own section; her story is actually incorporated into the last part of Umbertina's. This decision in constructing the novel was based on Barolini's conviction that the "second generation is not as interesting . . . because they were so into Americanizing. And they have a *less* interesting life because they have no struggle. They simply are materially well off. Where is the drama. . . . Where is the tension?" (von Huene Greenberg 95).

2. In a 1993 MELUS interview, Barolini explains the genesis of this novel: "It really began with 'The Circular Journey,' a memoir in the *Texas Quarterly*. . . . *Umbertina* was written as a story about great-grandmother Umbertina and her namesake. . . . I had finished the novel and incorporated into this novel the other finished novel, *The Last Abstraction*. . . . [My] publisher . . . said 'I think that [The Last Abstraction] is the missing middle of *Umbertina* because it all takes place in Italy. It's the natural bridge'. . . . So it became 'Marguerite' " (von Huene Greenberg 100).

3. Rita Felski, in *Beyond Feminist Aesthetics: Feminist Literature and Social Change* (1989), observes that "it can be noted that the focus upon gender as the primary marker of a subjectivity which is conceived as a source of opposition to a patriarchal society can result in a somewhat schematic distinction between the false roles imposed upon the heroine and the true self which

comes to light during the course of the narrative.... It is as if the affirmation of female identity is felt to require at least a temporary bracketing of the multiple determinants of subjectivity that might threaten the claim to authenticity through which the narrative seeks to legitimate itself" (132). Barolini departs from this description by her emphasis on Marguerite's ethnicity as well as her gender, even as she insists on the novel being read as feminist rather than ethnic.

4. Barolini herself felt at school that "something was wrong, something was not right with me, and that was very clear to me . . ." (von Huene Greenberg 107).

5. Likewise, in *The Madwoman in the Attic*, Sandra Gilbert and Susan Gubar note the popularity of representations of Milton dictating his poetry to his daughters from the late eighteenth to the nineteenth centuries. They write, "Representing virtuous young ladies angelically ministering to their powerful father would seem to hold a mirror up to one of Western culture's fondest fantasies. At the same time, however, from a female point of view . . . the image of the Miltonic father *being ministered to* hints that his powers are not quite absolute, that in fact he has been reduced to a state of dependence upon his female descendants" (215).

6. It is significant, too, that the language of the WLM and of consciousness-raising groups is in terms of "mothers" and "sisters," even where true blood relations do not exist.

7. This is not to suggest, however, that Barolini views Tina's character as perfect, or that she disavows completely her allegiance to feminism; she acknowledges Tina's flaws, including her need to be dominant over Weezy and her somewhat antifeminist stance: "Feminism . . . is a very democratizing thing, and Tina has a bit of elitism" (von Huene Greenberg 99).

8. Rita Felski also notes that in these novels of self-discovery that "the violation of the natural world is perceived to reflect the oppression of women, the refusal of the values of an industrialized and urbanized modernity . . . (132). While the desolation of southern Italy is not the result of industrialization, it is the result of the oppressive behavior and greed exacted for centuries.

9. Likewise, Lawrence J. Oliver points to William Dean Howells's complaint "that Italian-American immigrants had lost their Old World charm and had become materialistic, 'surly,' and 'fierce for their full share of the political pottage' . . ." (9).

10. Similarly, Edvige Giunta notes of Donna, the female protagonist in Nancy Savoca's domestic comedy film *True Love* (1989) that "Donna's name emblematizes a social role she strives to fulfill, mistaking it for her opportunity to achieve self-realization. . . . she is *Donna* as *Woman*" ("The Quest for True Love" 17).

11. The theme of self-hatred, symbolized by rejection of outward signs of one's ethnicity, is a common one in Italian-American literature (and, indeed, in much ethnic literature). In a memoir entitled "South Brooklyn, 1947," writer

"I HAVE FOUND MY VOICE"   185

Fran Claro tells of her mother's rejection of her *italianità*: "Maria Louisa was her given name. It was a beautiful name.... Instead, she chose to call herself *Mary*—good old American *Mary*.... As she grew into adulthood, her childhood dreams of American respectability grew into a determination to separate her children from a culture she had learned to despise" (77–78).

12. Edvige Giunta reports being pleased to learn that a large bookstore carried Barolini's work, only to be "steered [away from the literature section and] ... toward another part of the bookstore ... 'Cooking.' Even bookstores ... have managed to keep Italian women in the kitchen" ("Blending 'Literary' Discourses" 1).

Chapter Five

1. Maso's definition of her work as "experimental" is one that applies both to her work and to Caponegro's. She says, "I think my work is viewed that way because my influences are other than fictive, and most people are working from a conventional literary tradition.... My father when I was young was a jazz musician and he exposed us to all kinds of music.... I had art lessons ... ballet lessons, piano lessons. These things seem to really inform my work. And film. I'm a film addict.... All these things inform the work in a way that make it appear experimental to people who are just grounded in the strict literary tradition" (Cooley 33).
2. Ruffolo dedicates the collection, simply, "To My Family."
3. According to Caponegro, these stories originated as part of her thesis; her director instructed her to "write some Chinese stories"—without studying Asian literary tradition or examples of the genre (Telephone interview).
4. Elizabeth Bowen's "The Demon Lover" (1945) and Joyce Carol Oates' "Where Are You Going, Where Have You Been?" (1970) are two contemporary instances of this convention.
5. This passage clearly echoes a passage in *Jane Eyre*; Jane reports a dream in which "I still carried the unknown little child: I might not lay it down anywhere, however tired were my arms—however much its weight impeded my progress, I must retain it" (310).
6. Hence the novel's title. The Ghost Dance and its messianic religion is essentially a Christian phenomenon, although its method of expression—ecstatic dancing, chanting, and singing—was seen as a tremendous threat by the whites who witnessed it, as evidenced by the slaughter at Wounded Knee in 1890. For a more detailed discussion of the Ghost Dance religion see James Mooney, *The Ghost Dance Religion and Sioux Outbreak of 1890*. Fourteenth Annual Report of the Bureau of American Ethnology, Pt. 2. Washington: GPO, 1893.
7. This reference recalls the salad-making scene in *Like Lesser Gods*. Toni Morrison uses the dandelion in a similar fashion in *The Bluest Eye* (1971).

Pecola Breedlove, the novel's protagonist, wonders "Why . . . people call them weeds? She thought they were pretty" (47). But, the narrator reflects, "Nobody loves the head of a dandelion. Maybe because they are so many, strong, and soon" (47).
8. As pointed out to me by Lisa Hogeland, this aspect of the novel also partakes of the lesbian grotesque tradition, quite apart from the utopian lesbian tradition, which includes novels such as Djuna Barnes's *Nightwood* (1937).
9. Felski's description of this sub-genre of women's fiction is quite similar to the feminist consciousness-raising novel discussed in Chapter Four.

Conclusion

1. However, as Mary Jo Bona notes, while "DeRosa's *Paper Fish*, although modernist in form and therefore partial to the theme of alienation, also promotes the values of group affiliation and family cohesion. Carmolina's coming-of-age is in fact dramatized within the confines of the parental home to reinforce and assure an identity derived from affiliation with the family" (*Claiming a Tradition* 339).

Index

A

abortion 82, 111, 112
Alvarez Saar, Doreen 5
Americanness 5
anima 139, 140
animus 139, 140
Anzaldùa, Gloria 67, 129, 130, 155
Aquinas, Thomas 5
autobiography 18, 19, 23, 37

B

Barolini, Helen 2, 3, 4, 5, 6, 9, 11, 23, 24, 48, 49, 75, 97, 122, 125, 133, 154, 158, 167, 169
Barthes, Roland 17, 138
Basile Green, Rose
   8, 13, 38, 70, 102, 169
Baym, Nina 165, 166, 167
Benasutti, Marion
   8, 9, 13, 37, 53, 66, 84, 144, 166, 168
Black Elk 19, 20
Blau DuPlessis, Rachel 95, 156
Bodenheimer, Rosemarie 43
Boelhower, William 8, 125
Bona, Mary Jo 47, 55, 64, 93, 98, 114, 121, 126, 163, 167, 169, 170
Bonomo Ahearn, Carol 70, 136
Boyce Davies, Carol 21, 23
Bryant, Dorothy 9, 95, 97, 137, 166, 168

C

Campbell, Jeremy 142, 146
Caponegro, Mary 10, 125, 126, 136, 148, 157
Capozzoli, Mary Jane 5
Cassatteri, Rosa 17, 165
Catholic Church 4
Chiavola Birnbaum, Lucia 11

Chodorow, Nancy 22
Chomsky, Noam 142
consciousness-raising 9
consciousness-raising novel
   69, 70, 83, 97, 104, 105
Coward, Rosalind 97, 122
creative ethnicity 84, 97

D

Daly, Mary 111
de Lauretis, Teresa 148
Dearborn, Mary 1
DeConde, Alexander 6
DeRosa, Tina
   8, 108, 163, 167, 168, 170
destino 44, 45, 100, 133, 135
di Donato, Pietro 13, 41, 119, 170
Dinnerstein, Dorothy 22
double-voiced discourse 82

E

education
   5, 76, 77, 79, 82, 86, 87, 88, 98, 145
Eisenstein, Zillah 56
epistemology 137, 156
ethnicity 1, 11, 125
Ets, Marie 20

F

family
   3, 43, 105, 107, 149, 153, 161, 168
female sexuality
   72, 78, 79, 146, 158
feminism 98
feminist 137
Ferraro, Thomas
   37, 56, 63, 69, 97, 105
festa 28, 117

Fiedler, Leslie 39
Flax, Jane 22
Fraser, Nancy 151
Freud, Sigmund 141
Friedan, Betty 70
Fuller, Margaret 8

G

Gallo, Patrick 7
Gambino, Richard 71
Gardaphé, Fred L.
   10, 108, 165, 169, 170
Garibaldi 5, 8
Gates, Jr., Henry Louis 11, 168
Giunta, Edvige
   8, 35, 106, 108, 123, 169, 170
Grosz, Elizabeth 141

H

Hall Ets, Marie 13
Heilbrun, Carolyn G. 22
heterosexuality 156, 159
Hogeland, Lisa Maria 9, 68, 75, 77
Holly, Carol T. 18, 19, 22
Howe, Irving 39

I

Iorizzo and Mondillo 6, 7
Irigaray, Luce 140, 141
Irigaray, Lucy 140
italianità 4

K

Kaplan, Amy 39, 40
Kristeva, Julia 11
Krupat, Arnold 18

L

La Sorte, Michael 57
la via vecchia 71, 85
Lacan, Jacques 141, 142

Leites, Edmund 117
lesbian sexuality 158, 159, 160
life story 17, 19
locale 153, 161
l'ordine della famiglia 23, 71
l'uomo di pazienza 85

M

Madonna 3, 4, 24, 25, 154
mala femmina 81
Mangione, Jerre 6, 38
mask 155, 156
Maso, Carole
   9, 10, 11, 126, 163, 168
Mazziotti, Gillan 6
mirror stage 141
Morreale, Ben 6
Mortola Gilbert, Sandra 97
mother 150, 153, 154, 155
motherhood 72

N

Neapolitans 7
Neihardt, John G. 18
Nicholson, Linda 151, 153, 157
northern Italians 6, 7, 58, 100
northern Italy 6

O

omertà 2, 158
Ong, Walter 20, 165
orality 20, 165
orature 165

P

passing 117
postmodern 150
postmodernism 11, 151
postmodernist 126, 137
Pratt, Annis 73, 139
Probyn, Elsbeth 153

psychiatry 81, 106
puttana 81, 154
Puzo, Mario 56, 105, 169

R

radical feminism 110
Ranke-Heineman, Uta 5
realism 39
Ribiero, Ana 9
Riis, Jacob 8
Ruddy, Anna C. 8
Ruffolo, Lisa 3, 10, 125, 126, 136

S

Sacco and Vanzetti 42
Sarachild, Kathie 69
Savarese, Julia 8
sexuality
 79, 137, 140, 141, 142, 145, 147, 156
Showalter, Elaine 82, 170
silence 2, 157, 158, 160
Smith, Sidonie 19, 22
Sollors, Werner
 120, 125, 135, 150, 152
southern Italians 5, 7
southern Italy 6
Stanford Friedman, Susan 23
Steiner, Rudolf 139
stiletto a 7
subjectivity 11
symbolic order 142

T

Talese, Gay 2, 169
Tamburri, Anthony 106
Titon, Jeff Todd 17, 19, 20, 21
Tomasi 41, 42
Tomasi, Mari
 8, 13, 37, 38, 39, 44, 66, 73, 154, 168
Trilling, Lionel 39, 42, 166

V

Vecoli, Rudolph J. 34
Virgin Mary 24, 29
Virginia Woolf 128
Viscusi, Robert 169

W

Waldo, Octavia 8
Weber, Max 5, 57, 117
Wittig, Monique 156
Women's Liberation Movement
 107, 111
work 5

Currents in Comparative Romance Languages and Literatures

This series was founded in 1987, and actively solicits book-length manuscripts (approximately 200–400 pages) which treat aspects of Romance Languages and Literatures. Originally established for works dealing with two or more Romance literatures, the series has broadened its horizons and now includes studies on themes within a single literature or between different literatures, civilizations, art, music, film and social movements, as well as comparative linguistics. Studies on individual writers with an influence on other literatures/civilizations are also welcome. We entertain a variety of approaches and formats, provided the scholarship and methodology are appropriate.

For additional information about the series or for the submission of manuscripts, please contact:

Tamara Alvarez-Detrell and Michael G. Paulson
c/o Dr. Heidi Burns
Peter Lang Publishing, Inc.
516 N. Charles St., 2nd Floor
Baltimore, MD 21201

To order other books in this series, please contact our Customer Service Department at:

800-770-LANG (within the U.S.)
(212) 647-7706 (outside the U.S.)
(212) 647-7707 FAX
or browse online by series at:
www.peterlang.com